The Smartphone Paradox

Alan J. Reid

The Smartphone Paradox

Our Ruinous Dependency in the Device Age

palgrave
macmillan

Alan J. Reid
Department of English
Coastal Carolina University
Conway, SC, USA

ISBN 978-3-319-94318-3 ISBN 978-3-319-94319-0 (eBook)
https://doi.org/10.1007/978-3-319-94319-0

Library of Congress Control Number: 2018950470

Cover credit: sodafish/DigitalVision Vectors/Getty Images
Cover design by Aki Nakayama

This Palgrave Macmillan imprint is published by the registered company Springer Nature Switzerland AG
The registered company address is: Gewerbestrasse 11, 6330 Cham, Switzerland

Contents

List of Images

CHAPTER 1

Introduction

"As much as I dislike to admit it, my smartphone plays quite a large role in my daily life. Whatever is going on, on my phone, that becomes the priority subconsciously. I feel that I am expected to quickly respond to texts, social media notifications, and phone calls, and as a result, I frequently check my phone to make sure that I am not missing anything or disappointing anyone. I'll be looking at my phone and think to myself, why am I on it right now?" These are the words of Sarah V., a 20-year-old college undergraduate, who embodies the characteristics of a typical smartphone user on campus. She was responding to my interview question: "Can you describe the degree to which your smartphone plays a role in your life?" In this particular study, I was investigating the relationship between smartphone usage and the psychological traits of narcissism and exhibitionism. What I uncovered was far more peculiar. I found that many smartphone users are critically self-aware of their technological habits, and yet they grapple internally with what can be described as the *smartphone paradox*: that this mobile device is simultaneously liberating yet controlling, unifying yet polarizing. It is that phrase, "Smartphone Paradox," that was chosen for the title of this book because it accurately captures how our smartphones function in ways that are incongruous with our beliefs. We perceive our devices to foster communication (when they likely alienate us socially), boost our knowledge (when they likely substitute knowledge for information), and increase our efficiency and productivity (when they likely distract and impede). Sarah's response to my question, which is

A. J. Reid, *The Smartphone Paradox*,
https://doi.org/10.1007/978-3-319-94319-0_1

representative of so many others, recognizes the many communicative affordances of her smartphone, but she does so with a slight disdain for it. Many of us can relate to her sentiment. Our smartphones enhance us by providing connection to others and access to information, but at the same time, they tether us to unrealistic digital expectations.

We often check our phones unwittingly in hopes of being gratified instead of making deliberate choices to use our smartphones to satisfy a specific need. Researchers often analogize this behavior to that of pulling a lever on a slot machine. To some degree, the dopamine rush that is triggered by checking our smartphones is not unlike that seen in gambling or heavy drug use, where immediate reinforcement perpetuates behavior through a reward-based learning process. In his book, *The Craving Mind*, Judson Brewer summarizes this habit loop as "*Trigger. Behavior. Reward.*"[1] Our smartphone might *trigger* us with a notification sound or a vibration, which preempts our *behavior* to check the phone, and we are subsequently *rewarded* either positively or negatively, further strengthening this cycle each time. We often turn to our devices for a gratification payoff that augments our indulgences. Henry David Thoreau aptly surmised this paradoxical condition in *Walden*, first published in 1854: "Men have become tools of their tools."[2] More than 160 years later, there is a cognitive dissonance that persists between us and our mobile devices, in which we possess both an awareness of our smartphone dependence and an inability, or perhaps an unwillingness, to regulate our desire to obtain technological gratifications. Our love affair with smartphones has catapulted us towards a technological crescendo—not unlike Gutenberg's printing press—where humanity is collectively transformed in both positive and negative ways.

Admittedly, this book presents a highly critical perspective of technology. I recognize that I emphasize the negative consequences of smartphone use and discount its positivity. And perhaps this one-sidedness explains why critics of technology often are dismissed as out-of-touch fogies who are resistant to change. Certainly, for every disruptive technology, there are alarmists. Sometimes, though, these cynics turn out to be right. I believe this to be one of those times. The price tag of digital technology is that it consequently deprives us of important thought processes. Famed media theorist Marshall McLuhan writes about this as being an

[1] Brewer, Judson. 2017. *The Craving Mind: From Cigarettes to Smartphones to Love—Why We Get Hooked and How We Can Break Bad Habits.* New Haven, CT: Yale University Press.

[2] Bode, C. (Ed.). 1974. *The Portable Thoreau.* New York: The Viking Press, Inc.

amputation of technology; while advancements in technology can extend our ability in one sense, it does so by compromising another. In other words, technology giveth and taketh away. This book underscores that which is taketh away.

Readers of this book will have very different relationships with their smartphones, ranging from the indifferent and casual smartphone user to the transfixed and addicted. Although to varying degrees, it is undeniable that the smartphone has had indelible effects on the ways that we act, think, and feel. I suspect that you might already agree with this statement in some capacity, and so in that regard, this book might only reaffirm what you already believe. But if you are skeptical that the smartphone has fundamentally shifted our personal and societal behaviors, I hope that this book will convince you otherwise. In full disclosure, this is not a self-help book. I do offer some actionable solutions for technological rehabilitation, but it is not an exhaustive list. There is a plethora of media (books, websites, videos, podcasts, etc.) aimed at helping you improve your technological self, and you should consult those resources for mindfulness strategies that work best for you. Instead, this book will give a brief history of the smartphone (Chap. 2), deconstruct why we use smartphones in the ways that we do (Chaps. 3 and 4), identify the ruinous effects that occur as a result of our smartphone dependency (Chaps. 5 and 6), and examine the ways in which we are combating invasive technology moving forward (Chaps. 7 and 8).

Writing a book about technology can be dangerously modish. Books are a permanent medium, and technology is fleeting. Like architecture, fashion, and music, technology is always evolving, and so writing about a particular device or technology is ephemeral. (I doubt you would be reading this book if it were titled *The Flip-Phone Paradox.*) That is why I ask that you read this book through the lens of smartphones but grant that this is a broader metaphorical framework applicable to all personal and mobile technologies, even if they have not yet been conceptualized or developed. This is a book about dependence on and gratification by our digital tools. Smartphones happen to be the vehicle for this book, but as we embark on wearable and implantable technology, screen-free devices, and neuromedia, the thesis remains the same: that which we invest of ourselves in technology is that which is lost.

A Plea for Awareness

I should stress that although this book is critical of technology, it is not anti-technology. My Ph.D. is in Instructional Design and Technology, and I am an Assistant Professor of First-Year Writing and Instructional Technologies at Coastal Carolina University, where I teach a variety of undergraduate and graduate courses in English, New Media, Education, and Liberal Studies. As adjunct faculty at Old Dominion University, I teach courses in cognition, gaming, and computer-based multimedia design in the Instructional Design and Technology doctoral program. In addition, I am an Evaluation Analyst at Johns Hopkins University, where I typically review and evaluate educational technologies developed by private companies for public school districts. I am far from being a Luddite; technology informs nearly all aspects of my life. As a father of four, I contribute my fair share of photos and videos to the social media du jour so that I might keep friends and family up to date on our lives. And I was born in late 1981, which, by most demographers' standards, is the demarcation year separating Generation X from the Millennial Generation.[3] No, it is not the intention of this book to shame younger generations for their digital habits or to sweepingly diagnose all technology users as addicts; rather, this book investigates the byproducts of insatiable gratification that accompanies all of our increasingly digital lives, morphing our mobile devices into habit machines that feed our on-demand impulses. This book is not an indictment of technology but an advocate for self-awareness and self-regulation instead.

I will confess here that I am not a model smartphone user. In fact, I am not sure that such a model even exists. Like many others, I sleep with my smartphone on my bedside table, and it is the first thing I check in the morning. I lose track of time while scrolling through my Twitter and Instagram feeds. I am guilty of texting and driving. I fidget with my device when I am trapped in uncomfortable or unfamiliar situations, and I check email and text messages while having a conversation with someone else. I catch myself checking my phone for no particular reason. My smartphone is omnipresent, and it has mutated into an extension of myself. This is precisely why I wrote this book.

[3] Dimock, Michael. 2018. Defining generations: Where Millennials end and post-Millennials begin. *Pew Research Center*. http://www.pewresearch.org/fact-tank/2018/03/01/defining-generations-where-millennials-end-and-post-millennials-begin/. Accessed 12 May 2018.

Recognizing this as unhealthy dependence, I have made concerted efforts to curtail my smartphone usage. I installed an app on my phone, Moment, to monitor my usage more closely and set limits on the length of time I can use my phone each day, forcing me to ration my usage. I also have tried completely separating myself from my device for extended periods of time. I would leave it in my car when I got home from work and at the house when running errands around town. But without my phone, I felt naked and vulnerable. What would I do if there was an emergency, or if I had missed something important that required an urgent response? (This did actually happen to me once; a co-worker sent out an email to the entire university saying she had been cleaning out her attic and had a box full of original vinyl records of *The Beatles*. She would give them all to the first person to reply to her email. I was the second to reply, and I have regretted it ever since.) I tried quitting my smartphone cold turkey, but it was not effective for me. I would only subsidize my device-free time by spending excessively more time on it later. Much like a nicotine fiend trying to quit smoking, I would often justify my relapses ("I'm expecting an important email" or "I need to see today's news"), and then overindulge in a smartphone binge. A sort of smartphone chain-smoker. Through my many conversations with others, I have found that this paradox is systemic; many of us cling to our devices yet secretly crave disconnection. And it is very likely that you either identify with one or more of these statements or know of someone who would.

The implication here is that we have normalized our techno-lives. We have come to accept that smartphones lurk in the background of every conversation and interaction, and we rarely expect full attentiveness from one another. We excuse our smartphone habits as important and necessary, constantly making justifications for their presence. But to others around us, the smartphone signals distractedness and unavailability, whether or not it is being used in productive ways. For me, this became painfully clear when my nine-year-old daughter, Stella, wrote an unsolicited letter to me and my wife, pleading for us to put down our phones and be more present at home.

In the one-page letter, Stella asked, "Why? Why do grownups do stuff on their phones so much, when they have kids they can play with?" She also suggested that my wife and I try to go two full days without using our phones. As an English professor, I beamed with pride that she clearly articulated her argument through a written petition and that she did so mostly with grammatically correct diction. (Though I definitely need to have a conversation with her about the overuse of exclamation points.) She even closed the letter with a call to action. But her message cut deep. Stella was expressing her feelings of neglect, and she was justified. Somewhere along the line, it had become commonplace for me and my wife to gaze longingly into our smartphones while at the park with our kids, during family meals, and while sitting in their beds at night waiting for them to fall asleep. It was customary that even during family movie nights, the kids would be engrossed in the movie while my wife and I sat next to each other on the couch, cradling our phones, sometimes being productive but sometimes just being entertained. Present, but not really.

Stella's letter came as a shock. Not because she was making a plea for attention, but because this letter marked a moment of realization that she had been aware of our problem this whole time and that she had found it severe enough to demand change. I am sure that this sentiment is relatable for many adolescents, yet it usually goes unspoken (at least penned in letter form). Stella is approaching a formative age where she is beginning to recognize the affordances of the smartphone. At night, she asks me to do flyovers of Paris with her in Google Earth. She asks Siri questions about France and the Eiffel Tower. For now, she is content being transported digitally to the places she hopes to visit one day, but soon, she will feel compelled to join social media and begin sculpting her online identity. Stella attends an affluent private school at which a recent survey revealed that the majority of its students receive their first smartphone by the third grade. Results from the survey also showed that most of the students prefer the smartphone to all other devices, outranking tablets, eReaders, desktop and laptop computers, and gaming consoles. One can't help but wonder how these students' technological preferences have been shaped by years of astutely observing their parents.

For me, raising children has further augmented my bubbling curiosity about the effects of smartphones on our behaviors. I first became interested in researching digital habits roughly ten years ago, when I began teaching. In 2007, I was fresh out of graduate school and found myself in my first teaching position as an instructor of Developmental English at a community college in a rural coastal town in North Carolina. Because smartphone technology was still in its infancy at that time (the first-generation iPhone would not be released until later that year) and the student population at this college typically came from lower socioeconomic backgrounds, smartphones in the classroom were uncommon in a landscape dominated by other screens such as laptops, iPod Touches, and eReaders like the Amazon Kindle and the Barnes & Noble Nook. Still, when I walked into the classroom as a teacher, I immediately recognized the distractibility these devices introduced into the learning environment. I looked to other faculty members for advice on how to deal with digital distraction, but everyone responded differently. Some banned devices in their classroom altogether while others simply looked the other way as students on devices disengaged from class. Much like our children do at home, today's students often hear conflicting messages from faculty about the worth (or lack thereof) of these personal devices. Children are told to put down the iPad by an adult holding a smartphone. Students are taught that digital literacy is important while sitting in classes that forbid mobile devices. Technology can function dually as a valuable tool in one instant and as an enemy in the next. Confusing indeed.

My teaching philosophy was forged out of a blend of the two extremes; I recognized the potential for a connected learner but acknowledged the need for boundaries. In fall of 2009, I entered my doctoral program with an interest in mobile learning and situated cognition; I wanted to design instruction that was inclusive of mobile devices and that exploited their potential for learning. Soon, wireless providers phased out cell phones in favor of data plans, and smartphone ownership increased substantially. In 2014, I accepted an assistant professorship at Coastal Carolina University in South Carolina, and by now, smartphones had become nearly ubiquitous. Today, I require that students bring a mobile device (smartphone, tablet, or laptop) to each class meeting. This is a far cry from my early days teaching in the community college, which comparatively, seemed barren of technology. Although some days I regret this pedagogical decision, the rationale was twofold: first, a mobile device expands the possibilities for in-class activities and peer-to-peer interaction, and second, I was fighting a losing battle in trying to deter student use of smartphones during class. In other words, if you can't beat 'em, join 'em. But the decision to embrace mobile devices in the classroom was more strategic than defeatism.

There is a flourishing body of research that vilifies smartphone usage in class, citing the dangers of multitasking, distraction, and decreased attention, and anecdotally, I have no doubt that these are all genuine concerns. Consequently, a growing number of professors are banning technology from their classrooms. In *The New York Times* piece titled "Laptops Are Great. But Not During a Lecture or a Meeting," Professor Susan Dynarski justifies her decision to make her classes technology-free on the basis of two ideas. First, research has shown that because typing is faster than handwriting, students who take notes on laptops are less likely to remember the information because they are not processing it as deeply when they type. Handwriting forces us to translate the information through careful stenography, and this leads to deeper understanding. Second, laptops can act as "visual pollution"[4] for students sitting in the vicinity of the technology, creating a residue of distraction for innocent bystanders. These are legitimate points, yet I find myself hesitant to believe that the answer is to exclude technology altogether. Many studies observe an underperformance of students who use smartphones or laptops in class, but often, these studies fail to account for the strategic design for use of technology to accomplish instructional objectives. Plus, banning smartphones from class creates an inauthentic environment that deprives students of the ability to develop the necessary skill of self-regulation that they will need later in the workforce, where there is no syllabus that outlines policy on technology. Jenae Cohn, a researcher at Stanford University, notes that the conflicting messages on the use of technology in academia have created "a generation of students being simultaneously rewarded and chastised for digital technology use."[5] Technological behaviors prohibited in one class might be lauded in another. Therefore, students must decipher class policies on personal technology and bend their own learning preferences and practices to the specification of the professor. Perhaps we should embrace the exciting and innovative ways to take advantage of mobile devices in the classroom rather than try to legislate them out of existence.

The English and New Media classes that I teach are a hybridity of the digital and the analog: at times requiring smartphones for activities such as discovery-based and peer-to-peer learning, and at other times, requiring a complete disengagement from technology in class, such as for reading longer texts. In 2016, my graduate teaching assistant, Chelsea Thomas, and I had begun to notice how the presence of smartphones welcomed inattentiveness for some students in class, but not for others. Some would try to disguise their smartphone activity by holding it in their laps, but the blue light emanating from under the table was a dead giveaway. Others would brazenly fidget with their devices in plain view. Was the temptation

[4] Dynarski, Susan. 2017. Laptops are great. But not during a lecture or a meeting. *The New York Times*, November 22, https://www.nytimes.com/2017/11/22/business/laptops-not-during-lecture-or-meeting.html?smid=tw-share. Accessed 12 Jan 2018.

[5] Cohn, Jenae. 2016. 'Devilish smartphones' and the 'stone-cold' internet: Implications of the technology addiction trope in college student digital literacy narratives. *Computers and Composition* 42: 80–94.

of smartphones too great, and would we have been better off banning devices from class altogether? Certainly, we had invited digital distraction into the classroom. Yet it was apparent that some students were better at regulating their usage during class, but why was this the case?

After class, Chelsea and I would casually hypothesize what sorts of factors influenced smartphone usage and how we could better control for them in our classroom. One possible explanation, we figured, was that individual personalities seemed to play a role in whether or not the student was able to easily toggle back and forth between digital and analog moments in class. We surmised that the same qualities that influenced a student's behavior in class, such as choosing to sit in the front row instead of the back or choosing to engage with a smartphone instead of paying attention in class, might be explained by the individual's psychological traits. A cursory review of research showed a correlation between smartphone usage and psychological traits like social interaction anxiety, neuroticism, and extraversion, but we decided to investigate smartphone usage through a different lens: narcissism. Besides the obvious sign of disrespect that it communicated to the professor and the rest of the class, making the deliberate choice to engage with the smartphone during lectures or class discussions seemed to signal self-absorption. In short, what the smartphone could offer was far more enticing and important than what the professor or the rest of the class could. Chelsea and I figured that a student who buried her face in her phone was exhibiting narcissistic behaviors, immersing herself in her own virtual world in place of the immediate one. We conducted a formal study in search of the relationship between narcissism and smartphone usage, and what we uncovered was striking.

In 2017, we published the findings of our study in an article titled "A Case Study in Smartphone Usage and Gratification in the Age of Narcissism" in the *International Journal of Technology and Human Interaction*. We tracked the individual smartphone usage habits of 43 college undergraduates and compared this data to their scores on the Narcissistic Personality Inventory (NPI-40), a 40-item self-report survey developed by two researchers at UC Berkeley. The survey presents participants with paired statements, one of which demonstrates a narcissistic quality. For instance, the participant is asked to select one of the two following statements:

A. The thought of ruling the world frightens the hell out of me.
B. If I ruled the world, it would be a better place.

The participant who selects B would receive one point since this is the more narcissistic thought. At the end of the survey, the points are tallied to determine one's relative level of narcissism. The scale is further divided into seven subscales: vanity, authoritativeness, self-sufficiency, superiority, exploitativeness, exhibitionism, and entitlement, and each subscale corresponds to a group of questions within the 40-item survey. The example question used above belongs to the entitlement subscale. Researchers who use the instrument caution that it is important to understand which traits of narcissism are dominant; someone registering high scores on the subscales of vanity, entitlement, exploitativeness, and exhibitionism is more worrisome than someone who identifies more with the authority, self-sufficiency, and superiority scales.

In our study, narcissism was shown to be inversely related to smartphone usage, which we measured as (1) total time spent on the device and (2) the number of times the device was checked throughout each day (checking habits). So, as smartphone usage increased, narcissism decreased. By contrast, those who scored highest on the NPI-40 showed the least amount of smartphone interaction. It turned out that our assumption was wrong; having a narcissistic personality might instead be beneficial in the classroom, at least in terms of distractibility. The most narcissistic students were not preoccupied with their social networks or connecting with others on their phones; they cherished the classroom interaction instead. The data in our study also revealed differences in genders; females reported significantly higher amounts of smartphone usage, and males registered significantly higher levels of narcissism. Females primarily used their devices for social or communicative purposes, whereas males skewed towards information-seeking. We also uncovered an inverse relationship between smartphone usage and GPA. As smartphone usage increased, overall GPA decreased.

In terms of dominant traits, we discovered a relationship between a student's checking habits and exhibitionism. Students who checked their phones most frequently registered higher scores on the exhibitionism subscale. Previous studies have identified "status"[6] as one of the types of gratifications obtained from checking a smartphone in public. In other words,

[6] Leung, Louis and Ran Wei. 1998. The gratifications of pager use: Sociability, information seeking, entertainment, utility, and fashion and status. *Telematics and Informatics* 15: 253–264.

brandishing a smartphone can communicate to others importance or fashionability. From the quantitative data and open-ended survey responses, we concluded that:

> With regards to usage, it is evident that smartphones play an integral role in today's society, especially in the lives of undergraduates, for a variety of reasons. Participants averaged roughly three and a half hours spent on the smartphone each day. If this figure is extrapolated to one month, the average time spent using the smartphone was 103 hours, or the equivalent to two and a half 40-hour work weeks, nearly three times the finding from the 2014 Nielsen Report (37 hours). Participants also exhibited frequent checking habits, averaging approximately one hundred checks per day. Oulasvirta et al. (2012, p. 107) explain that checking habits are "an important part of the behavior driving smartphone use" because the device affords quick access to "informational rewards," resulting in instant gratification. Interestingly, this case study also found a significant correlation between smartphone checking habits and the narcissistic trait of exhibitionism. One explanation for this may be that undergraduates often use their smartphones as a "social prop" (Lee, 2002) that, in turn, satiates a gratification of "fashion/status" (Leung and Wei 1998). Checking a smartphone in public may have more public than personal utility for some; the brand, model, and even smartphone accessories may function as a type of cultural currency and communicate socioeconomic status to others.[7]

In my research on smartphone behaviors, I have interviewed hundreds of people. Generally speaking, I have found that most people are aware of the ways in which they use their smartphones, but not necessarily the degree to which they depend on their devices. A common question that I ask interviewees is: "To what extent does your smartphone play a role in your life?" Many respondents take this opportunity to explain to me that they use their phones for communicating with loved ones, or for reading the news, or for using general productivity tools like email, calendar, alarm clock, and the calculator. But the essence of my question is not to understand *how* the smartphone is used, or for what purpose, it is to understand its meaningfulness to each person. I have found that most people are not comfortable discussing this on an intimate level, and many immediately take a defensive posture. Still, I am always surprised at the number of

[7] Reid, Alan J. and Chelsea N. Thomas. 2017. A case study in smartphone usage and gratification in the age of narcissism. *International Journal of Technology and Human Interaction* 13: 40–56.

respondents who begrudgingly acknowledge their tumultuous relationships with their devices yet continue the same behaviors. Consider these quotes from my most recent survey:

> *My smart phone comes everywhere with me, it is a major part of my daily life.* (Kristin, age 18)
>
> *It is at the level of necessity of a vital organ.* (Devon, age 18)
>
> *It's my lifeline, without it I feel lost.* (Shondra, age 22)
>
> *I use my phone as a distraction from the challenges of everyday life.* (Tobi, age 34)
>
> *I feel as though my smart phone is a part of me. I take it everywhere I go, and worry when I do not have it. I check it all the time even when I do not need to, and catch myself doing this and thinking, "what am I doing?" I know it is unhealthy and try to reduce my time on my smartphone, but usually I just fall back into my routine of usage.* (Jonathan, age 18)
>
> *It is my connection to others from whom I feel I need immediate responses, and I often wonder how I used to work without one.* (Barbara, age 41)
>
> *It has a ring on the back so that I can literally wear it as an extension of myself. I take it everywhere. I don't go an hour without looking at it. However, I'm young, and everyone else around me is doing the same!* (Danielle, age 30)

Each of these quotes identifies the smartphone as a necessity for one reason or another; this is a common narrative in most of the survey responses that I read. But what is different about these quotes, and many others, is that respondents often recognize an overdependence on their devices yet dismiss it as a reasonable trade-off for being connected. Tobi accepts that her smartphone is a "distraction from the challenges of everyday life." Danielle views hers as "an extension" of herself but justifies this because "everyone else…is doing the same." Shondra admits that she feels lost without her device. This is just a small sample of the types of responses I come across in my research, but the theme remains consistent: we acknowledge that our smartphones are integral to our lives, but we either ignore our level of our attachment or write it off as a cost of our digital lives. We negotiate with our technology.

Obviously, not everyone has an abusive relationship with their smartphone. Moderate smartphone use is vital to our twenty-first-century existence. But chances are that you might know someone who depends on his or her smartphone to an excessive degree, incapacitating other facets of their lives. As Michael Patrick Lynch laments in his book, *The Internet of Us: Knowing More and Understanding Less in the Age of Big Data*, overdependence on technologies is threatening because "we can overrely on them, overvalue them, and forget that their use has serious consequences."[8] These effects can range from the psychological to the corporal and can corrode our mental and physical health. Throughout this book, I lean heavily on an eclecticism of primary and secondary sources to make the argument that our relationship with smartphones must be reevaluated. By providing a self-examining lens through which we can think about our smartphone behaviors, this book presents an argument that our technological impulsivities are eroding our thinking ability and our relationships. This book proposes a compromise of responsibilities: that we expect more from developers of smartphone technology by way of ethical design, and that we develop a more conscious self-regulation of personal devices so that we might rescue back control over our technology and, ultimately, ourselves.

There are many reasons why you might be reading this book. Perhaps you suspect that your smartphone habits have started to have an effect on your daily life. Maybe you have noticed how smartphones have begun to interfere with your personal relationships and social interactions with others (this is called *phubbing*, and I address it in Chap. 6). Or, maybe you are struggling with whether or not to give in to your child's pleas for a smartphone. Or, just maybe, someone has assigned this book as a required reading for a course of some type. Regardless of the reason, I'm willing to bet your own smartphone is not too far away as you read this. And that is another reason why I wrote this book: not to reproach you, not to insist that you change your habits, but to promote a technological self-awareness that leads to a more calibrated relationship with our devices. I hope that as you read this book, you take time to meditate and reflect on your smartphone habits. For starters, how do you perceive your own relationship with your smartphone? How do you suppose others perceive this relationship?

You Are Your Phone

In many ways, we are our phones. The smartphone you carry is a physical, technological embodiment that communicates to the rest of us information cues such as your preferred brand (Are you an iOS or an Android

[8] Lynch, Michael P. 2016. *The Internet of Us: Knowing More and Understanding Less in the Age of Big Data*. New York: Liveright Publishing Corporation.

person?), your aversion to risk (Is your phone protected with a case? A plastic screen protector? Or is it naked?), your caretaking ability (Is your phone's screen broken?), even your propensity for technology adoption (Are you an early adopter? A laggard?). It takes only a split-second to make these assessments and use them to render our assumptions. In fact, it is an evolutionary remnant of primal survivalism that we constantly profile our surrounding environment and those within it. We involuntarily and unwittingly evaluate each other based on the visual information that we can gather; your clothing, your hygiene, the car you drive, the way you speak, all are observable clues that others use to shape their views of you. And your phone is no exception. It signifies a kind of tribal membership. You belong to the Apple tribe. Or the Samsung tribe. Or some other tribe. In fact, it is this tribal mentality that Steve Jobs masterfully exploited to turn Apple customers into the strongest smartphone brand loyalists.[9] iOS (iPhone) and Android users now account for over 90% of the world's smartphone owner population,[10] and the type of smartphone that you carry might be a predictor of your personality. According to one study, iOS owners tend to be younger, more extraverted, and more likely to view their smartphones as status objects. Android users, on the other hand, tend to be older and less interested in wealth or status.[11] Your phone, the condition it is in, and accessories you choose to furnish it say a lot about you.

We have an affinity for our devices, much more so than we have for other technologies like the television or computer. Perhaps our emotional connection is intensified with our smartphone because we carry them with us everywhere we go. Consequently, smartphones have become our digital companions; we treat our phones more like pets than communication devices. We have a visceral relationship with our smartphones that eclipses their actual utility. Take, for instance, the much-maligned notch design of the iPhone X. Never mind that this 0.5″ × 1.4″ black bar at the top of the screen disguises "one of the most amazing technological advancements in

[9] Kumar, Santhosh and Rahul P. Menon. 2017. Brand loyalty of customers in smartphone brands. *Indian Journal of Marketing* 47: 8–15.

[10] Shaw, Heather, David A. Ellis, Libby Rae Kendrick, Fenja Ziegler and Richard Wiseman. 2016. Predicting smartphone operating system from personality and individual differences. *Cyberpsychology, Behavior, and Social Networking* 19: 727–732.

[11] Lancaster University. 2016. What your choice of smartphone says about you. *ScienceDaily*. www.sciencedaily.com/releases/2016/11/161121144206.htm. Accessed 30 Nov 2017.

years,"[12] enabling facial recognition, a dot projector, infrared technology, and proximity sensors. iPhone users have voiced their discontent with the perceived design flaw as if it were an affront on their tech sensibilities. A discussion forum on MacRumors asks subscribers: "How are you adapting to the most controversial iPhone X design decision?"[13] Competitors such as Samsung have seized this opportunity to try and convert Apple customers, with one commercial depicting a fanboy who is waiting in line for the new iPhone sporting a ridiculous black bar spanning the front of his hairline. The commercial's personification of the iPhone is a master class in trolling.

If your phone is a window into your identity, then it becomes a subtle interface with others around you. Aside from the brand, model, and condition of your smartphone, the way you use it conveys to others your social status and your social connectedness.[14] We assume that the texting businessman is closing some sort of merger deal or reviewing important documents on his smartphone, yet we doubt that the teenage girl could be doing anything remotely productive with hers. We bury our faces in our screens when we wish to appear important or when we wish not to be bothered. We have a tacit understanding that someone wearing earbuds is off limits for conversation, residing behind a high-tech "privacy screen."[15] Indeed, most of us have been guilty of wearing earbuds but not actually listening to anything with them. Out of our smartphone behaviors, we have forged an implicit social contract that transcends language and culture—an unwritten and passive-aggressive smartphone constitution. We use the presence of our smartphones to send passive-aggressive messaging to those around us.

But beyond this interpersonal signaling, companies are beginning to interpret your smartphone habits as predictors of risk. *The Wall Street Journal* reports that some lending startup businesses ask customers to

[12] Meyer, Evi. 2017. iPhone X—Top 'notch'. *Medium*, September 25. https://medium.com/the-mission/iphone-x-top-notch-204e9284f54a. Accessed 2 Nov 2017.

[13] Clover, Juli. 2017. Embracing the notch: How are you adapting to the most controversial iPhone X design decision? *MacRumors*, November 14. https://www.macrumors.com/2017/11/14/iphone-x-embracing-the-notch/. Accessed 10 Dec 2017.

[14] Wei, Ran and Ven-Hwei Lo. 2006. Staying connected while on the move: Cell phone use and social connectedness. *New Media & Society* 8: 53–72.

[15] Mannering, Lindsay. 2015. Now playing in your headphones: Nothing. *The New York Times*, December 22. https://www.nytimes.com/2015/12/24/fashion/headphones-now-playing-nothing.html. Accessed 1 Dec 2017.

install a smartphone app so that they can view their smartphone habits, and ultimately, assess the user's creditworthiness. Individual factors such as the ratio of text messages sent to received, the number of contacts (even whether the contacts are saved with the last name), how frequently the smartphone's battery is charged, and how much travel occurs, all contribute to a larger mosaic of your financial risk. The ideal borrower receives more texts than sends, fills out all of their contacts' information, and preserves their smartphone's battery for longer periods of time.[16] In the eyes of companies, your financial risk can be explained by the data you generate from using your smartphone. Whether you like it or not, your smartphone reveals a lot about who you are—sometimes more than what you'd like.

Many of us are unaware of the extent to which we are glued to our smartphones. Studies consistently show that heavy smartphone users routinely underestimate their usage time[17] as well as the number of times they touch their phones throughout the day.[18] Additionally, smartphone users often report a sense of "time distortion" while engrossed in their screens, opening their phones for an intentional task but then being derailed into an unintentional activity. Perhaps you can recall a time that you have unlocked your phone to check an email or a text message (the intentional task), and then minutes later realize that you have somehow slid into YouTube or your Twitter feed (the unintentional activity). Losing track of time that we spend on our devices can help explain our delusional smartphone use. One study hypothesizes that we spend unplanned amounts of time on our devices because of the phenomenon known as "flow experience."[19] Researcher Mihaly Csikszentmihalyi describes flow in the following way:

[16] Dwoskin, Elizabeth. 2015. Lending startups look at borrowers' phone usage to assess creditworthiness. *Wall Street Journal*, November 30. https://www.wsj.com/articles/lending-startups-look-at-borrowers-phone-usage-to-assess-creditworthiness-1448933308. Accessed 14 Jan 2017.

[17] Lee, Heyoung, Heejune Ahn, Trung Giang Nguyen, Sam-Wook Choi and Dae Jin Kim. 2017. Comparing the self-report and measured smartphone usage of college students: A pilot study. *Psychiatry Investigation* 14: 198–204.

[18] Winnick, Michael. 2016. Putting a finger on our phone obsession. *dscout*. https://blog.dscout.com/mobile-touches. Accessed 4 May 2017.

[19] Thatcher, Andrew, Gisela Wretschko and Peter Fridjhon. 2008. Online flow experiences, problematic Internet use and Internet procrastination. *Computers in Human Behavior* 24: 2236–2254.

> Flow is a subjective state that people report when they are completely involved in something to the point of forgetting time, fatigue, and everything else but the activity itself. It is what we feel when we read a well-crafted novel or play a good game of squash, or take part in a stimulating conversation. The defining feature of flow is intense experiential involvement in moment-to-moment activity. Attention is fully invested in the task at hand, and the person functions at his or her fullest capacity.[20]

Perhaps you have experienced flow before. Many athletes and educators chase the flow experience for its ability to block out distraction and focus on the task at hand. But what if flow experiences on the smartphone *are* the distraction from the task at hand? While flow is a desirable state for a golfer or for a student, it leaves us with a distorted sense of time spent on the smartphone. Research indicates that smartphone users are especially susceptible to flow experiences because of the various applications, and this can easily lead to compulsive or even addictive behaviors.[21] Checking our phones for the wrong reasons, whether it be for social gratification or for escapism from our moods and surroundings, leads to flow experiences that exacerbate our thirst for interaction and stimulation, creating an automaticity in our unplanned smartphone behaviors. But this is an easy trap to fall into when our devices are always present and inescapable.

Emerging research suggests that our devices may be influencing us even when we are not using them. To date, many studies have examined the effects of the "mere presence" of smartphones, and their findings illustrate the degree to which we are affected by our devices. One view, sometimes referred to the "brain drain" hypothesis, suggests that having a smartphone within immediate proximity of its user diminishes brain power. In the paper titled "Brain Drain: The Mere Presence of One's Own Smartphone Reduces Available Cognitive Capacity,"[22] researchers manipulated the degree of smartphone presence by having participants store their devices in one of three conditions: on their desks (high salience),

[20] Csikszentmihalyi, Mihaly. 2014. *Flow and the Foundations of Positive Psychology: The Collected Works of Mihaly Csikszentmihalyi*. New York: Springer.

[21] Chen, Chongyang, Kem Z.K. Zheng, Xiang Gong, Sesia Zhao, Matthew K.O. Lee and Liang Liang. 2017. Understanding compulsive smartphone use: An empirical test of a flow-based model. *International Journal of Information Management* 37: 438–454.

[22] Ward, Adrian F., Kristen Duke, Ayelet Gneezy and Maarten W. Bos. 2017. Brain drain: The mere presence of one's own smartphone reduces available cognitive capacity. *Journal of the Association for Consumer Research* 2: 140–154.

close by but out of sight (medium salience), or in another room (low salience). The conclusion of their experiments was that the mere presence of smartphones negatively impacted available working memory and cognitive capacity. Another study conducted by researchers at the University of Southern Maine found that the presence of a smartphone impacted participants' attentional and cognitive demands, especially on complex tasks. Their explanation: "[I]f the mere presence of the cell phone has the potential to be distracting, then it may necessitate more of an 'out of sight, out of mind' requirement in some instances."[23] However, other research has indicated that the complete separation from users and their devices is also problematic. One study found that:

> [S]tudents are so dependent on their WMDs [wireless mobile devices] that anxiety increases when the device is absent—even when they are aware the device will be back in their possession shortly—and those who use the device more frequently become significantly more anxious as time passes than those who use it less frequently.[24]

Of course, the authors of each of these studies point out that results such as these are highly dependent on the user as well as the conditions under which smartphones are present (or are not present). These cognitive consequences are exaggerated in heavy smartphone users while only faint traces of these effects are found in those with little or no smartphone dependency. What is most significant, though, is that our smartphone is so baked into our identities that it can exert its gravitational pull on us even when it is not local. As technology progresses, devices become smaller, thinner, more discreet, eventually making this dependency harder to realize.

Often, advancements in technology mean a loss of physicality with our tools. DSLR cameras ousted manual film photography, email deposed handwritten letters, digital text squashed the physical book.[25] Although

[23] Thornton, Bill, Alyson Faires, Maija Robbins and Eric Rollins. 2014. The mere presence of a cell phone may be distracting: Implications for attention and task performance. *Social Psychology* 45: 479–488.

[24] Cheever, Nancy, Larry D. Rosen, L. Mark Carrier and Amber Chavez. 2014. Out of sight is not out of mind: The impact of restricting wireless mobile device use on anxiety levels among low, moderate and high users. *Computers in Human Behavior* 37: 290–297.

[25] It is no doubt that digital books have had an effect on print book sales, though not nearly to the extent that it has been predicted over the years. Surveys consistently find that

film cameras, books, and letters still exist (and likely always will), they have become quaint antiquities—often used ironically by hipsters and defiantly by artists. When the first-generation iPhone arrived with a touch screen, smartphone users bemoaned the loss of clickable keys. (This same criticism, by the way, could be heard when the word processer usurped the typewriter.) For many, replacing the mechanical with the digital represents the loss of an era, and partly, a loss of self. We develop nostalgia for our technology because it is so ingrained in our memories, our experiences, our being. The ways in which we perceive ourselves through the lens of technology is described as ***technological embodiment***.

Lisa Meloncon's book *Rhetorical Accessability* includes a chapter titled "Toward a Theory of Technological Embodiment," which explains how embodiment has emerged out of a philosophical view and into a technology-human interaction perspective. The chasm between humans and technology, once as wide as the ocean, has become narrowed to that of a babbling brook, one in which we playfully splash. As the line between human and technology becomes blurrier, we must reevaluate the ways in which we are changed. Seemingly, the next frontier in technology will seek to eliminate the space between our bodies and our devices as we pivot towards wearable and implantable technology. But, as we continue to explore this symbiosis of humans and technology, Meloncon ponders the point at which we become more technological than human. She asks, "When does our body not belong to us?" Presumably, we are approaching a watershed moment as we begin to view technology not for its "thingness" but as a critical part of our existence. Meloncon extends this point:

> Our society has evolved to the point that few users are outside the reach of technologies and the impact of those technologies on their everyday lives. We can no longer ask the basic question; how will the user interact with thing X? Rather, the question needs to be, how does this technologically embodied user imagine thing X as part of himself or herself and what does it mean to all of us?[26]

there is a general preference for paper-based text over the digital, and that students routinely choose print over digital textbooks, despite the cost difference. In short, digital text has not replaced the print book entirely, but it does pose an observable threat. Chapter 5 addresses this in more depth.

[26] Meloncon, Lisa. 2014. *Rhetorical Accessability*. New York: Routledge.

The author explains technological embodiment as *how* we are affected by our devices, not *what* we use them for. Thinking back to many of the responses from my students about the extent to which their smartphones play a role in their lives, many superficially consider *what* affordances the device provides them, but not *how* this embodiment shapes their lives on a deeper level. Our embodiment of technology differs in degree and type for each individual; one might not have a heavily dependent relationship with his smartphone, but instead might embody another technology such as his gun or a luxury car. From this human-technology interaction perspective, embodiment is simply how we see ourselves through our own technologies.

Shonte C. is a 19-year-old undergraduate college student. In response to one of my surveys regarding smartphone usage, Shonte indicated to me that she feels strongly that her smartphone is not only an extension of herself but that it is directly related to her self-image. I wanted to know more about this, so I sat down with Shonte and interviewed her at length in order to better understand her viewpoints on smartphones and technological embodiment. She began by emphatically describing what she calls "phone culture"—an implicit conditioning experienced by smartphone users, particularly in social settings. Shonte admitted that:

> People will judge you on the type of phone you have. There's a sort of status that comes with Apple or other high-end products. The quality of phone that you have is perceived as who you are as a person. If you have a lower-quality phone, people will dog you for it. It's not that it is anything malicious, but it's a sort of classism of our age. If you can afford newer stuff, you must have a higher status, you know. People want to connect with you more. If you want to be part of the in-crowd, you have to have the right device. I didn't use Snapchat when I had my Android phone because [the app] lends itself to Apple.

Shonte went on to describe the differences between the interfaces and usability of her Android and iOS phones, but she concluded by saying the brand switch was mostly due to how others perceived her through her device, not the design of the device itself. The 19-year-old explained that she was hesitant to participate on social media, particularly Snapchat, where it was evident which type of smartphone you own. Instead, she waited until her contract ended with her carrier and switched to an Apple iPhone. Now, she posts freely to social media, and proudly retains the default signature at the bottom of email messages that reads "Sent from my iPhone." Shonte's device dictated her online behaviors because it is more than a smartphone; it is a surrogate for her identity.

Shonte, a student of Digital Culture and Design, is familiar with a common assertion in New Media Studies that technology simultaneously gives us something and takes something else away. I asked Shonte if she felt that her phone cost her anything—emotionally, physically, cognitively, socially, or otherwise. She paused a moment and replied, "Of course it does." For Shonte, and I suspect for many others in her generation and younger, technology comes with an inherent and nonnegotiable price tag. It is so engrained in our daily lives, relationships, and workflows, that there is simply no turning back. Or, as Shonte put it:

> I view my phone as an extension of myself just because I use it for so much. I keep my notes in it, I set reminders for myself, I use it in my free time, I use it to avoid people, I use it to listen to music or just, to like, occupy my thoughts. But, it's just a tool. It's convenient. Honestly, though, without it, I'd probably have a better memory. I'd definitely have more focus. I'll watch YouTube videos and be on my phone at the same time because if I'm just watching the video, I'll get bored. I don't know if that's a bad thing, though. I don't get the same amount of stimulation from a show as I used to. I used to be able to just watch things, but now, if I don't have my phone with me, I think, "I could be doing something else, too." I have to make the most out of my time. I'm busy.

What Shonte is describing is known as *media multitasking*: a common practice where two or more forms of media are used concurrently. In general, media multitasking has been shown to obstruct cognitive control,[27] impact socio-emotional ability,[28] and impact sleep patterns.[29] In Shonte's case, she is multitasking to stave off boredom and to keep feeding a

[27] Alzahabi, Reem, Mark W. Becker and David Z. Hambrick. 2017. Investigating the relationship between media multitasking and processes involved in task-switching. *Journal of Experimental Psychology: Human Perception and Performance* 43: 1872–1894.

[28] Loh, Kep Kee and Ryota Kanai. 2014. Higher media multi-tasking activity is associated with smaller gray-matter density in the anterior cingulate cortex. *PLoS One* 9. https://doi.org/10.1371/journal.pone.0106698.

[29] van der Schuur, Winneke A., Susanne E. Baumgartner, Sindy R. Sumter and Patti M. Valkenburg. 2018. Media multitasking and sleep problems: A longitudinal study among adolescents. *Computers in Human Behavior* 81: 316–324. https://doi.org/10.1016/j.chb.2017.12.024.

voracious need for content. The mind craves content like a steam locomotive in constant need of coal shoveled into its boiler to maintain its speed. As I sat with Shonte, it became evident that she was displeased with the truth in her response. She laughed nervously and said, "Sorry. I'm talking too much." She then took a long pause, as if to build up a justification for her argument, then continued:

> You know, you have to lose something to progress. But I wouldn't say that our shift away from analog activities like note-taking and print reading is necessarily a bad thing. I'm sure people got a lot weaker when they stopped having to till farms with menial tools instead of mechanical ones. It's not worse; it's just different. The brain has just evolved to meet the times. I mean, you have the whole world at your fingertips. That's good right?

Shonte's response that "it's not worse; it's just different" is a common viewpoint. To be sure, she is not wrong. History has shown repeatedly that we adapt to our technologies, and we are not always worse off because of it. Just as we embraced agricultural machinery, it won't be long until we concede to self-driving cars. But as we pour more of ourselves into our technologies, the question is not how the technology makes our lives different, but how it makes *us* different. Whether we view our smartphone habits as productive, meaningless, or somewhere in between the two, it is worth reconsidering whether our smartphones leave us with a net gain or a net loss. In some cases, "different" assuredly can mean "worse." Therefore, it might be appropriate to ask whether or not the properties of a technology are inherently good or bad.

Kranzberg's First Law of Technology

In July 1986, Melvin Kranzberg, a Professor of History at Georgia Institute of Technology, delivered a visionary lecture in which he outlined what would later become known as Kranzberg's Laws of Technology. He represented these ideas as a "series of truisms [regarding] the study of the development of technology and its interactions with sociocultural change."[30] The first of Kranzberg's Six Laws argues that technology is a memetic force with far-reaching implications in various personal, social,

[30] Kranzberg, Melvin. 1986. Technology and history: Kranzberg's laws. *Technology and Culture* 27: 544–560.

and cultural arenas. Specifically, the law states that "Technology is neither good, nor bad; nor is it neutral." I have spent a good deal of time contemplating this seemingly contradictory statement while teaching it to my undergraduate and graduate students in new media and design. Admittedly, most are perplexed by it at first; how could technology, an inanimate product of human creation, be inherently good or bad? Consider the following exchange, paraphrased and cobbled together from the many conversations I have had regarding the non-neutrality of guns:

Me: Can technology be inherently good or bad?

Student: Depends on the technology.

Me: Ok. A gun. Is a gun a good or bad technology?

Student: Again, it depends on who is using the gun, and for what purpose. A gun is good technology in the hands of law enforcement, but bad technology in the hands of a criminal.

Me: So, a gun is a neutral technology that is dependent on the user?

Student: I guess so.

Me: Kranzberg says technology cannot be neutral. Suppose someone hears an intruder in the middle of the night. They reach for a gun and shoot him.

Student: Then it is a good use of the gun. It is a good technology.

Me: And if the intruder was not a criminal, but the person's son returning home from college unannounced? Does that change your opinion of the technology?

Student: Well, yes.

Me: So the gun is dependent on the user and on the context in which it is being used. But in all cases, the gun is *intended* to do harm, whether it is harmful to a good guy or a bad guy. It is non-discriminatory. Despite the reason for its use, the gun cannot be used to improve the condition of the targeted person or animal. Only hurt. Doesn't that render the gun non-neutral, regardless of the circumstances?

This type of debate can go on and on, and indeed it does; we are confronted with the neutrality-of-guns argument every time a mass shooting occurs, and its complexity might explain why the debate always ends in a legislative stalemate. Technology is ambiguous. The effects of technology are often unintentional and unpredictable. We tend to view new technologies only through the lens of our experiences with old technologies, a concept known as rearview-mirrorism. Marshall McLuhan once wrote, "When faced with a totally new situation, we tend always to attach ourselves to the objects, to the flavor of the most recent past. We look at the present through a rear-view mirror. We march backwards into the future."[31] We only know of technology what we have already experienced. The significance of Kranzberg's law is that it is a singular idea that can be applied to all technology: we cannot ascribe good or bad qualities to technology, yet we cannot dismiss their predisposed affordances. But it is holding these two thoughts in our heads simultaneously that gives us so much difficulty.

Let's first examine this law from a grammatical perspective. A cursory Google search will yield different (and mostly incorrect) iterations of the law—many of which roughly paraphrase Kranzberg's idea but have slight variations from the original language published in the article. I believe syntax and grammar are especially important here, as Kranzberg deliberately uses two independent clauses to underscore two distinct, but related points: (1) "Technology is neither good, nor bad" and (2) "nor is it neutral." Why not combine them to say more succinctly, "Technology is neither, good, nor bad, nor neutral"? Simply put, the latter point is dependent on the former. The first independent clause insists that technology cannot be defined as wholly good or bad. The second independent clause is there lest you should think that a technology, then by default, can be neutral. Instead, technology possesses underlying affordances that, when acted upon, can render that specific technology in either a positive or a negative way. These inert affordances render the technology as charged and non-neutral.

It was Martin Heidegger who argued for a clearer understanding for the essence of technology, and not just for the technology itself. The difference, according to his 1977 essay *The Question Concerning Technology*, is that the *essence of technology* is a larger means to an end, whereas *technology* refers to the device itself. Until we see our technologies through ourselves, we continue to be blinded by them. Heidegger says, "Technology is a way of revealing." Our devices, our instruments, are interpreters of our truths, but until we also recognize them as actors in the greater landscape of technology's influences, we remain enslaved by them:

[31] McLuhan, Marshall and Quentin Fiore. 1967. *The Medium is the Massage: An Inventory of Effects*. New York; London; Toronto: Bantam Books.

> Everywhere we remain unfree and chained to technology, whether we passionately affirm or deny it. But we are delivered over to it in the worst possible way when we regard it as something neutral...[32]

Heidegger corroborates Kranzberg's view of the non-neutrality of technology, and he further insists that "So long as we represent technology as an instrument, we remain held fast in the will to master it." The view that technology is a neutral, autonomous, and unstoppable force majeure dangerously insinuates that, by default, we become prisoners of our own technologies, lacking any ability to intervene in their dominion over us.

Determinism is a philosophical view that certain events are predisposed based on an existing condition, and that a singular outcome is inevitable. For instance, linguistic determinism supposes that our world view is shaped by the languages we speak. Because we are born into a language, this linguistic choice is predetermined for us by our parents and based on a variety of mitigating factors including time, geography, and socioeconomics. Similarly, theological determinism assumes the existence of God, that s/he is all-knowing, and therefore predetermines our future. This example conjures debate over free will and fate—ostensibly, we can ask the question, "Do we have governance over the actions we choose to execute, or are they pre-ordained for us?" This essential question of determinism might also be applied to technology. According to Raymond Williams, *technological determinism* is a "view of the nature of social change" in which "new technologies are discovered...which then sets the conditions for social change and progress."[33] A technological determinist believes that technology is neutral and that it develops autonomously and independent of society's influence. However, this philosophical outlook is flawed. It is pretty easy to find examples of technologies that did not flourish because they were rejected by mass society: Google Glass, Microsoft Zune, Vine. What separates natural social change and technologically-driven social change is the "intention of the process of research and development." Because technologies are deliberately conceptualized, designed, prototyped, and evaluated, the view of technological determinism remains questionable.

[32] Heidegger, Martin. 1977. *The Question Concerning Technology and Other Essays.* New York: Harper & Row.

[33] Williams, Raymond. 1974. *Television: Technology and Cultural Form.* New York: Schocken.

There are degrees of deterministic thought. For instance, hard and soft (or strong and weak) technological determinism differ quite substantially. McLuhan is considered a hard determinist because of his rigid view that technology is supreme. A more extreme of a hard determinist is Ted Kaczynski, or as he was known to the FBI, the Unabomber. Kaczynski was a domestic terrorist in the United States between the years 1978 and 1995, when he was finally captured and sentenced to eight life terms in prison. The Harvard-educated, ex-professor feared the consequences of technology; his 33-page manifesto, titled *Industrial Society and Its Future*, begins with:

> The Industrial Revolution and its consequences have been a disaster for the human race. They have greatly increased the life-expectancy of those of us who live in "advanced" countries, but they have destabilized society, have made life unfulfilling, have subjected human beings to indignities, have led to widespread psychological suffering (in the Third World to physical suffering as well) and have inflicted severe damage on the natural world. The continued development of technology will worsen the situation.[34]

The hard determinist is anti-technology, whereas the soft determinist concedes that technology drives social change, but there are other variables that inform that change. According to Ruth Finnegan, soft determinism is "the presence of a particular communication technology is an *enabling* or *facilitating* factor leading to *potential opportunities* which may or may not be taken up in particular societies or periods."[35] An example of a soft determinist view of technology comes from Lynn White Jr., Professor of Medieval History at Stanford, who wrote in his 1962 text, *Medieval Technology and Social Change*, "As our understanding of the history of technology increases, it becomes clear that a new device merely opens a door; it does not compel one to enter." Soft determinism attributes social change *primarily* to the technology—hard determinism *exclusively* to the technology.

Perhaps the farthest away from the view of technological determinism is that of *instrumentalism*. According to Nicholas Carr, author of *The Shallows: What the Internet is Doing to Our Brains*, instrumentalists:

[34] Kaczynski, Ted. 1995. *Industrial Society and Its Future*. http://editions-hache.com/essais/pdf/kaczynski2.pdf. Accessed 2 Jan 2018.

[35] Finnegan, Ruth. 1988. *Literacy and Orality: Studies in the Technology of Communication*. Oxford: Basil Blackwell.

> downplay the power of technology, believing tools to be neutral artifacts, entirely subservient to the conscious wishes of their users. Our instruments are the means we use to achieve our ends; they have no ends of their own. Instrumentalism is the most widely held view of technology, not least because it's the view we would prefer to be true.[36]

In this approach, technology does not guide us, we use technology to guide ourselves. But if we are to align our technological view with Kranzberg (as this book does), technology is not neutral, and it does carry with it positive and negative affordances.

Yet one more alternative theoretical view is called *social shaping of technology*, or SST. The underpinning of this approach is that the needs and desires of society dictate the path of technology. The theory lacks definition, as it contains a multitude of subtheories, including the social construction of technology, technological shaping of technology, and economic shaping of technology. In essence, the view of SST asserts that the development and adoption of technology hinges on social demand and is influenced by other cultural, political, and economic factors. As articulated by Mackay and Gillespie in *Social Studies of Science*, "Whilst not denying that technologies have social effects, the focus, rather, is on the social forces which give rise to particular technologies."[37] The SST view is concerned with effects of technology but also with the conditions out of which technology emerges. According to researchers at the University of Edinburgh, Robin Williams and David Edge:

> Central to SST is the concept that there are 'choices' (though not necessarily conscious choices) inherent in both the design of individual artefacts and systems, and in the direction or trajectory of innovation programmes. If technology does not emerge from the unfolding of a predetermined logic or a single determinant, then innovation is a 'garden of forking paths'. Different routes are available, potentially leading to different technological outcomes.[38]

[36] Carr, Nicholas G. 2011. *The Shallows: What the Internet is Doing to Our Brains*. New York: W.W. Norton & Company.

[37] Mackay, Hughie and Gareth Gillespie. 1992. Extending the social shaping of technology approach: Ideology and appropriation. *Social Studies of Science* 22: 685–716.

[38] Williams, Robin and David Edge. 1996. The social shaping of technology. *Research Policy* 25: 865–899.

The key differentiator between the vastly different technological outlooks of determinism and social shaping is *choice*.

Perhaps these theoretical stances might best be summed up by applying them to a common example—the smartphone—so that we are able to observe the differences in their outlooks. The hard determinist fears that the smartphone will eventually replace our brains by doing all our thinking for us, and there's nothing we can do to prevent it from happening. A soft determinist might recognize that smartphones have become a necessary tool in the twenty-first century but also acknowledge ways in which we might assuage their ramifications. An instrumentalist views the smartphone just as he would a calculator: an assistive tool with no other underlying properties. A social shaper would argue that the smartphone was not invented extraneously, but instead it was borne out of a sprawling population and its need to communicate and connect on-the-move. Image 1.1 provides a visual representation of this spectrum of theoretical frameworks.

This book most closely identifies with a social shaping outlook, which complements Kranzberg's view. That is, all technologies are fluid and derived from far-reaching social, cultural, political, and economic forces that carry simultaneously good and bad effects. Take, for instance, strip-mining for coal: a process that involves incrementally shaving off the tops of mountains in search of this valuable fossil fuel. And although many First World nations have emerged off of the backs of coal miners, there is a growing demand to abandon fossil fuels for cleaner energies such as solar, wind, and natural gas. A 1971 article in *The New York Times* describes strip-mining as the "rape of Appalachia."[39] Through the eyes of a developed and civilized nation, strip-mining for coal can hardly be viewed as a *good* technology because it is a process that levels natural landscapes, leaving them barren

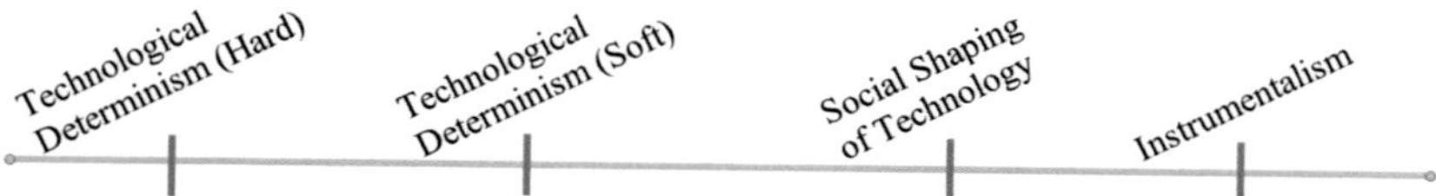

Image 1.1 The broad view of theoretical stances on technology. Source: Author

[39] Brabscome, James. 1971. Appalachia—Like the flayed back of a man. *The New York Times*, December 12. https://www.nytimes.com/1971/12/12/archives/appalachia-like-the-flayed-back-of-a-man-like-the-flayed-back-of-a.html. Accessed 22 Feb 2018.

and scarred in exchange for a fossil fuel that, when burned, poses serious environment and health concerns. Still, for developing Third World countries, coal remains a viable, affordable, and precious resource. So, we cannot say that the technological process of strip-mining for coal is necessarily good or bad; it just is. In his 1980 article, "Do Artifacts Have Politics," Langdon Winner underscores the importance of evaluating the invisible consequences of our technologies, stating, "If our moral and political language for evaluating technology includes only categories having to do with tools and users, if it does not include attention to the meaning of the designs and arrangements of our artifacts, then we will be blinded to much that is intellectually and practically crucial."[40] Technology always must be contextualized. With particular regard to the focus of this book, smartphones, it is important to assess not just how the tool is used and by whom, it is equally significant to ask why it is being used.

No technology is isolated. In his 1964 seminal book, *Understanding Media: Extensions of Man*, McLuhan describes technology as an extension of man; a car physically extends our legs, binoculars extend our vision, a microphone extends our voice. And just as technology extends, it also amputates. To elaborate on this point, McLuhan retells the Greek myth of Narcissus, who "mistook his own reflection in the water for another person" and, as a result, became numb to the rest of the world. McLuhan refers to this as being "a closed system":

> It is this continuous embrace of our own technology in daily use that puts us in the Narcissus role of subliminal awareness and numbness in relation to these images of ourselves. By continuously embracing technologies, we relate ourselves to them as servomechanisms. That is why we must, to use them at all, serve these objects, these extensions of ourselves, as gods or minor religions.[41]

Gods? Religions? Is this an exaggeration of our relationship with technology? Perhaps. Perhaps not. In the previous subchapter, I discussed how "you are your phone." In many ways, our smartphones are manifestations of ourselves, but not unlike Narcissus, we might also mistake our smart-

[40] Winner, Langdon. 1980. Do artifacts have politics? *Daedalus* 109: 121–136. http://innovate.ucsb.edu/wp-content/uploads/2010/02/Winner-Do-Artifacts-Have-Politics-1980.pdf. Accessed 26 June 2017.

[41] McLuhan, Marshall. 1964. *Understanding Media: Extensions of Man*. New York: McGraw-Hill.

phones for genuine social interaction with others when it is only a reflection of ourselves, all the while becoming numb to the rest of the world around us. McLuhan points out that, over time, we have come to understand the myth of Narcissus as a lesson in self-absorption—a story about a young man falling in love with himself. But this is inaccurate; Narcissus assumed the reflection to be another person, not himself. He was duped by his own reflection. Are the "meaningful" relationships we have by proxy of our devices truly authentic, or are we staring at a thin sheet of Gorilla Glass, unable to recognize our own reflection?

Like every technology, smartphones extend and amputate. By granting us on-demand access to the Internet, smartphones extend our access to information while simultaneously weakening our capacities to remember that information. Smartphones give us the world's library at our fingertips, yet digital reading has altered the ways in which we read, discouraging deep reading. Smartphones have changed the way we communicate, the way we consume news and information, and the way that we store knowledge in our own heads. It is neither a good nor a bad technology, and it is both a good and bad technology. And still, this does not render smartphones neutral.

A piece of technology, a disembodied object, can be negatively charged. In an article in *The Atlantic* titled "The Philosophy of the Technology of the Gun," Evan Selinger carefully refutes the popular argument that "Guns don't kill people. People kill people," citing the non-neutrality of guns. But applying this instrumentalist mantra to guns is oversimplified. As Selinger asserts, "since a gun's mechanisms were built for the purpose of releasing deadly projectiles outwards, it is difficult to imagine how one could realistically find utility in using a gun to pursue ends that do not require shooting bullets."[42] A gun is born to harm. Further, Selinger argues that the "gun design itself embodies *behavior-shaping values* [emphasis added]; its material composition indicates the preferred ends to which it 'should' be used." In other words, a gun is a means to an end, but it guides the action. The gun becomes an actor. It is no wonder, then, that in countries such as Britain and New Zealand, where the majority of police officers do not carry guns, there are significantly fewer shooting deaths

[42] Selinger, Evan. 2012. The philosophy of the technology of the gun. *The Atlantic*, July 23. https://www.theatlantic.com/technology/archive/2012/07/the-philosophy-of-the-technology-of-the-gun/260220/. Accessed 22 Jan 2018.

involving law enforcement.[43] Possessing a weapon or a tool increases the likelihood that it will be used. Likewise, smartphones are a guiding force in our behaviors. Many smartphone users cite "convenience" as a typical reason for engaging with their devices. It's just there, so I'll use it. If technology is indeed an extension of ourselves, then it is important to understand that a gun is more than a hunk of dormant metal when it is not in use, and a smartphone is more than specially organized computer chips and electrical components. For that matter, the smartphone is more than a phone; it is a beckoning call to action.

References

Alzahabi, Reem, Mark W. Becker, and David Z. Hambrick. 2017. Investigating the relationship between media multitasking and processes involved in task-switching. *Journal of Experimental Psychology: Human Perception and Performance* 43: 1872–1894.

Bode, C., ed. 1974. *The Portable Thoreau*. New York: The Viking Press, Inc.

Brabscome, James. 1971. Appalachia—Like the flayed back of a man. *The New York Times*, December 12. Accessed February 22, 2018. https://www.nytimes.com/1971/12/12/archives/appalachia-like-the-flayed-back-of-a-man-like-the-flayed-back-of-a.html.

Brewer, Judson. 2017. *The Craving Mind: From Cigarettes to Smartphones to Love—Why We Get Hooked and How We Can Break Bad Habits*. New Haven, CT: Yale University Press.

Carr, Nicholas G. 2011. *The Shallows: What the Internet is Doing to Our Brains*. New York: W.W. Norton & Company.

Cheever, Nancy, Larry D. Rosen, L. Mark Carrier, and Amber Chavez. 2014. Out of sight is not out of mind: The impact of restricting wireless mobile device use on anxiety levels among low, moderate and high users. *Computers in Human Behavior* 37: 290–297.

Chen, Chongyang, Kem Z.K. Zheng, Xiang Gong, Sesia Zhao, Matthew K.O. Lee, and Liang Liang. 2017. Understanding compulsive smartphone use: An empirical test of a flow-based model. *International Journal of Information Management* 37: 438–454.

Clover, Juli. 2017. Embracing the notch: How are you adapting to the most controversial iPhone X design decision? *MacRumors*, November 14. Accessed December 10, 2017. https://www.macrumors.com/2017/11/14/iphone-x-embracing-the-notch/.

[43] Smith, Alexander. 2017. The vast majority of UK police don't carry guns. Here's why. *NBC News*, September 15. https://www.nbcnews.com/news/world/why-london-won-t-arm-all-police-despite-severe-terror-n737551. Accessed 1 Nov 2017.

Cohn, Jenae. 2016. 'Devilish smartphones' and the 'stone-cold' internet: Implications of the technology addiction trope in college student digital literacy narratives. *Computers and Composition* 42: 80–94.

Csikszentmihalyi, Mihaly. 2014. *Flow and the Foundations of Positive Psychology: The Collected Works of Mihaly Csikszentmihalyi*. New York: Springer.

Dimock, Michael. 2018. Defining generations: Where Millennials end and post-Millennials begin. *Pew Research Center*. Accessed May 12, 2018. http://www.pewresearch.org/fact-tank/2018/03/01/defining-generations-where-millennials-end-and-post-millennials-begin/.

Dwoskin, Elizabeth. 2015. Lending startups look at borrowers' phone usage to assess creditworthiness. *Wall Street Journal*, November 30. Accessed January 14, 2017. https://www.wsj.com/articles/lending-startups-look-at-borrowers-phone-usage-to-assess-creditworthiness-1448933308.

Dynarski, Susan. 2017. Laptops are great. But not during a lecture or a meeting. *The New York Times*, November 22. https://www.nytimes.com/2017/11/22/business/laptops-not-during-lecture-or-meeting.html?smid=tw-share. Accessed January 12, 2018.

Finnegan, Ruth. 1988. *Literacy and Orality: Studies in the Technology of Communication*. Oxford: Basil Blackwell.

Heidegger, Martin. 1977. *The Question Concerning Technology and Other Essays*. New York: Harper & Row.

Kaczynski, Ted. 1995. *Industrial Society and Its Future*. Accessed January 2, 2018. http://editions-hache.com/essais/pdf/kaczynski2.pdf.

Kranzberg, Melvin. 1986. Technology and history: Kranzberg's laws. *Technology and Culture* 27: 544–560.

Kumar, Santhosh, and Rahul P. Menon. 2017. Brand loyalty of customers in smartphone brands. *Indian Journal of Marketing* 47: 8–15.

Lancaster University. 2016. What your choice of smartphone says about you. *ScienceDaily*. Accessed November 30, 2017. www.sciencedaily.com/releases/2016/11/161121144206.htm.

Lee, J. 2002. Tailoring cell phones for teenagers. *The New York Times*. http://www.nytimes.com/2002/05/30/technology/circuits/30TEEN.html?pagewanted=all.

Lee, Heyoung, Heejune Ahn, Trung Giang Nguyen, Sam-Wook Choi, and Dae Jin Kim. 2017. Comparing the self-report and measured smartphone usage of college students: A pilot study. *Psychiatry Investigation* 14: 198–204.

Leung, Louis, and Ran Wei. 1998. The gratifications of pager use: Sociability, information seeking, entertainment, utility, and fashion and status. *Telematics and Informatics* 15: 253–264.

Loh, Kep Kee, and Ryota Kanai. 2014. Higher media multi-tasking activity is associated with smaller gray-matter density in the anterior cingulate cortex. *PLoS One* 9. https://doi.org/10.1371/journal.pone.0106698.

Lynch, Michael P. 2016. *The Internet of Us: Knowing More and Understanding Less in the Age of Big Data*. New York: Liveright Publishing Corporation.

Mackay, Hughie, and Gareth Gillespie. 1992. Extending the social shaping of technology approach: Ideology and appropriation. *Social Studies of Science* 22: 685–716.

Mannering, Lindsay. 2015. Now playing in your headphones: Nothing. *The New York Times*, December 22. Accessed December 1, 2017. https://www.nytimes.com/2015/12/24/fashion/headphones-now-playing-nothing.html.

McLuhan, Marshall. 1964. *Understanding Media: Extensions of Man*. New York: McGraw-Hill.

McLuhan, Marshall, and Quentin Fiore. 1967. *The Medium is the Massage: An Inventory of Effects*. New York; London; Toronto: Bantam Books.

Meloncon, Lisa. 2014. *Rhetorical Accessability*. New York: Routledge.

Meyer, Evi. 2017. iPhone X—Top 'notch'. *Medium*, September 25. Accessed November 2, 2017. https://medium.com/the-mission/iphone-x-top-notch-204e9284f54a.

Oulasvirta, A., T. Rattenbury, L. Ma, and E. Raita. 2012. Habits make smartphone use more pervasive. *Personal and Ubiquitous Computing* 16 (1): 105–114.

Reid, Alan J., and Chelsea N. Thomas. 2017. A case study in smartphone usage and gratification in the age of narcissism. *International Journal of Technology and Human Interaction* 13: 40–56.

Selinger, Evan. 2012. The philosophy of the technology of the gun. *The Atlantic*, July 23. Accessed January 22, 2018. https://www.theatlantic.com/technology/archive/2012/07/the-philosophy-of-the-technology-of-the-gun/260220/.

Shaw, Heather, David A. Ellis, Libby Rae Kendrick, Fenja Ziegler, and Richard Wiseman. 2016. Predicting smartphone operating system from personality and individual differences. *Cyberpsychology, Behavior, and Social Networking* 19: 727–732.

Smith, Alexander. 2017. The vast majority of UK police don't carry guns. Here's why. *NBC News*, September 15. Accessed November 1, 2017. https://www.nbcnews.com/news/world/why-london-won-t-arm-all-police-despite-severe-terror-n737551.

Thatcher, Andrew, Gisela Wretschko, and Peter Fridjhon. 2008. Online flow experiences, problematic Internet use and Internet procrastination. *Computers in Human Behavior* 24: 2236–2254.

Thornton, Bill, Alyson Faires, Maija Robbins, and Eric Rollins. 2014. The mere presence of a cell phone may be distracting: Implications for attention and task performance. *Social Psychology* 45: 479–488.

van der Schuur, Winneke A., Susanne E. Baumgartner, Sindy R. Sumter, and Patti M. Valkenburg. 2018. Media multitasking and sleep problems: A longitudinal study among adolescents. *Computers in Human Behavior* 81: 316–324. https://doi.org/10.1016/j.chb.2017.12.024.

Ward, Adrian F., Kristen Duke, Ayelet Gneezy, and Maarten W. Bos. 2017. Brain drain: The mere presence of one's own smartphone reduces available cognitive capacity. *Journal of the Association for Consumer Research* 2: 140–154.

Wei, Ran, and Ven-Hwei Lo. 2006. Staying connected while on the move: Cell phone use and social connectedness. *New Media & Society* 8: 53–72.

Williams, Raymond. 1974. *Television: Technology and Cultural Form*. New York: Schocken.

Williams, Robin, and David Edge. 1996. The social shaping of technology. *Research Policy* 25: 865–899.

Winner, Langdon. 1980. Do artifacts have politics? *Daedalus* 109: 121–136. Accessed June 26, 2017. http://innovate.ucsb.edu/wp-content/uploads/2010/02/Winner-Do-Artifacts-Have-Politics-1980.pdf.

Winnick, Michael. 2016. Putting a finger on our phone obsession. *dscout*. Accessed May 4, 2017. https://blog.dscout.com/mobile-touches.

CHAPTER 2

A Brief History of the Smartphone

"We shape our tools and thereafter they shape us." This quote is often attributed on the Internet to Marshall McLuhan, although this never actually appears in any of his writings or speeches. Instead, the quote comes from Father John M. Culkin of Fordham University in a 1967 article in *The Saturday Review*, titled "A Schoolman's Guide to Marshall McLuhan."[1] Fifty years later, it is not quite that significant who is credited with this line, especially since its author, Father Culkin, essentially was paraphrasing McLuhan's views when he penned it. Culkin and McLuhan were contemporaries, and this perspective was referring broadly to communication technologies of the era—radio, television, and landline phones—not smartphones. More recently, Nicholas Carr has softened the determinist view by saying, "Sometimes our tools do what we tell them to. Other times, we adapt ourselves to our tools' requirements."[2] Here, Carr is referring to our dependence on the Internet, specifically, but his thesis rings true for all technologies. Whether it is Culkin, McLuhan, or Carr, the message remains the same, and it could not be more germane to this book. Technology reshapes the ways in which we interact with others and the ways that we see ourselves. Like the printing press, the steam engine, and the Internet, smartphones represent much more than the next step in

[1] Culkin, John M. 1967. A schoolman's guide to Marshall McLuhan. *The Saturday Review*, March 18, 51–53 and 70–72.

[2] Carr, Nicholas G. 2011. *The Shallows: What the Internet is Doing to Our Brains*. New York: W.W. Norton & Company.

A. J. Reid, *The Smartphone Paradox*,
https://doi.org/10.1007/978-3-319-94319-0_2

a long line of technological development; they are giant leaps of blind faith. Our total investment in the smartphone represents a hope that they will transform our lives in mostly positive ways and an optimism that overshadows any trepidation we might have. But cosigning ourselves to technology often leaves us with more questions than answers, as the novelty begins to wear off and we peel back the curtain to reveal our true relationship with our devices. If you are your phone, then it may be worthwhile to consider your ancestral roots.

It has been a decade since the launch of the first-generation iPhone, which is widely believed to be the most important innovation in smartphones. In his 2007 keynote address at the MacWorld expo (which you can view on YouTube), Apple's CEO Steve Jobs publicly demonstrated the groundbreaking technology for the first time. He showcased many of the features and affordances that would be considered baseline for today's smartphones, and the audience marveled. The original press release from Apple described the iPhone as "a revolutionary mobile phone, a widescreen iPod with touch controls, and a breakthrough Internet communications device."[3] Ten years ago, the smartphone arrived at a perfect confluence of our societal wants and needs: to be able to communicate freely, to be networked, to be informed, to be entertained, to be mobile. In his closing remarks of the keynote address, Jobs emphatically stated that the iPhone is "a revolution of the first order." And he was right—to an extent.

Certainly, the debut of the iPhone marks an important technological landmark, but a slightly deeper investigation into the annals of history will show that the first-generation iPhone was an amalgamation of the visions, ideas, and conquests of the many who came before Steve Jobs. As Brian Merchant writes in his definitive book on the iPhone, *The One Device: The Secret History of the iPhone*, although the success of the first-generation iPhone was unprecedented, the template for the smartphone definitely was not. Opinions vary on when we can pinpoint the development of the first smartphone, as it was a slow evolution of design. As Merchant recounts in his book, the first device to be marketed and packaged explicitly as a "smartphone" was launched seven

[3] Apple. 2007. Apple Reinvents the Phone with iPhone. January 9. https://www.apple.com/newsroom/2007/01/09Apple-Reinvents-the-Phone-with-iPhone/. Accessed 4 Nov 2017.

years before Jobs's iPhone. The Ericsson R380 was a flip phone that ran a primitive operating system, Symbian OS, and its clunky touch-screen consisted of only 120 × 360 pixels and required the use of a stylus. Although these technical specifications seem archaic to us now, this is the first example of the word "smartphone" used to market a communications device. There are several more examples of smart-phones that preceded Apple, but because the iPhone was such a vast improvement on these devices, we often associate it with the arrival of the modern smartphone. Still, Merchant reminds us that:

> The smartphone, like every other breakthrough technology, is built on the sweat, ideas, and inspiration of countless people. Technological progress is incremental, collective, and deeply rhizomatic, not spontaneous…The technologies that shape our lives rarely emerge suddenly and out of nowhere; they are part of an incomprehensibly lengthy, tangled, and fluid process brought about by contributors who are mostly invisible to us.[4]

History likely will credit Steve Jobs as the mastermind behind the iPhone. He introduced it to the world in 2007 and continued to deliver annual keynote addresses for the next four years—each time revealing new developments and feature upgrades. His closeness with the device paired with his masterful salesmanship eclipsed those engineers, designers, and technicians in the audience who were actually more responsible for bringing the iPhone to life. Jobs was a charming figurehead who had very little to do with the physical development of the smartphone. Instead, as Malcolm Gladwell describes in an article written for *The New Yorker*, Jobs resembled more of a "tweaker" than an inventor. He says, "The visionary starts with a clean sheet of paper and re-imagines the world. The tweaker inherits things as they are and has to push and pull them toward some more nearly perfect solution." And Jobs, according to Gladwell, was the "greatest tweaker of his generation."[5] Still, our selective memories likely will nominate Steve Jobs as the inventor of the first smartphone, despite the decades of legwork that made the iPhone possible. Already, technology articles

[4] Merchant, Brian. 2017. *The One Device: The Secret History of the iPhone*. New York: Hachette Book Group.

[5] Gladwell, Malcolm. 2011. The tweaker. The real genius of Steve Jobs. *The New Yorker*, November 14. https://www.newyorker.com/magazine/2011/11/14/the-tweaker. Accessed 8 Dec 2017.

published in both *The Guardian*[6] and *The Atlantic*[7] have traced the history of smartphones, and they begin with Jobs's keynote address in 2007.

The first-generation iPhone unarguably ushered in the smartphone era. Since its inception, there have been more than 24,000 different types of Android smartphones alone.[8] (Comparatively, only 18 different models of the iPhone have been produced to date.) But we cannot forget about another iconic device: BlackBerry. In *Losing the Signal: The Untold Story Behind the Extraordinary Rise and Spectacular Fall of BlackBerry*, authors Jacquie McNish and Sean Silcoff chronicle the short-lived success of the smartphone made popular by businessmen and businesswomen. The BlackBerry, developed by the Canadian company Research in Motion Limited (RIM), first was conceptualized in 1999 as a two-way pager (the BlackBerry 850), but the web-enabled device that boasted productivity tools such as email, notes, faxing, and text messaging emerged later, in 2002.

BlackBerry was a pioneer in the exploitation of mobile phone users' dependence on their devices. Perhaps most notably, the BlackBerry was one of the first mobile devices to implement "push" email—flipping the traditional model of retrieving emails manually to being automatically notified when new emails arrive. Today, this "push" notification system contributes to an incessant checking of our devices, but early focus group research with push email functionality indicated that users were not supportive of the feature. McNish and Silcoff quote one focus group participant who had grown frustrated after a trial period with his BlackBerry: "If this thing buzzes every time I get an e-mail, you'd better ship it with a hammer." Indeed, it was a common tactic for RIM salespeople to use what co-CEO Jim Balsillie dubbed the "puppy dog pitch," where potential BlackBerry users could take the device home with them for a one-month trial. Balsillie and his salespeople almost certainly were betting that the addictive properties of the mobile device would prevail; and they were right. Only two years later, the Urban Dictionary had an entry for the term "CrackBerry": "A nickname for the popular RIM communication

[6] Arthur, Charles. 2012. The history of smartphones: Timeline. *The Guardian*, January 24. https://www.theguardian.com/technology/2012/jan/24/smartphones-timeline. Accessed 1 Dec 2017.

[7] Estes, Adam C. 2012. The history of the smartphone begins with Steve Jobs. *The Atlantic*, January 24. https://www.theatlantic.com/technology/archive/2012/01/history-smartphone-begins-steve-jobs/332723/. Accessed 2 Dec 2017.

[8] Open Signal. 2017. Android fragmentation (August 2015). http://opensignal.com/reports/2015/08/android-fragmentation/. Accessed 9 July 2017.

device named Blackberry. The device, which is a phone, PDA, and e-mail appliance has gained outrageous popularity. Users/owners are typically addicted to checking e-mail and swapping short messages on the device. It appears as though they are addicted as a crackhead is to the pipe."[9]

BlackBerry reached its peak sales figures in mid-2011, and since then, the number of units sold has been declining rapidly. At one point in 2009, the device held 20% of the global smartphone market share, but as of 2017, that share has plummeted to 0.0481%.[10] Once considered a technological vanguard, the BlackBerry is now in the throes of its collapse. But this is the fate of all technology. Or, as McNish and Silcoff conclude: "If the rise and fall of BlackBerry teaches us anything it is that the race for innovation has no finish line, and that winners and losers can change places in an instant."[11]

In addition, the coming and going of mobile technologies throughout the years has left us in a semantic fog. We lazily interchange the terms *smartphone*, *cell phone*, and *mobile phone*, but the truth is that the first two terms are vastly different, technically, and both belong to the order of "mobile," and so this is extremely broad, or at least hierarchically unequal, to refer to either as a *mobile phone*. Instead, this book primarily uses the modern term *smartphone*, which at its core, is a cellular telephone with advanced computing affordances. Occasionally, I swap the word *smartphone* for the more generic and all-encompassing term *device* so as to avoid repetitious phrasing. This is the story of the smartphone.

Hello, World

On March 10, 1876, Alexander Graham Bell spoke into his prototypical telephone, "Mr. Watson, come here—I want to see you."[12] Watson then appeared, and Bell asked him to repeat the words back to him, which he did successfully. Not exactly the cleverest inaugural sentence spoken over the

[9] Urban Dictionary. 2017. Crackberry. https://www.urbandictionary.com/define.php?term=Crackberry. Accessed 7 July 2017.

[10] Gartner. 2017. Gartner says worldwide sales of smartphones grew 7 percent in the fourth quarter of 2016. February 15, https://www.gartner.com/newsroom/id/3609817. Accessed 7 July 2017.

[11] McNish, Jacquie and Sean Silcoff. 2016. *Losing the Signal: The Untold Story Behind the Extraordinary Rise and Spectacular Fall of BlackBerry*. New York: Flatiron Books.

[12] *Alexander Graham Bell—Lab Notebook*. n.d. http://lcweb2.loc.gov/cgi-bin/ampage?collId=am-reas&fileName=trr002page.db&recNum=21&itemLink=http%3A%2F%2Fwww.loc.gov%2Fexhibits%2Ftreasures%2Ftrr002.html&linkText=9. Accessed 9 Aug 2017.

telephone. The first email was equally as forgettable; Ray Tomlinson self-delivered a message in 1971, but he doesn't recall its content. According to an interview with Tomlinson, the messages "were often just gibberish—strings of characters of a few phrases from the Gettysburg Address."[13] Neil Papworth is credited with having sent the first text message on December 3, 1992, which read: "Merry Christmas." Jack Dorsey, Twitter co-founder, posted the first tweet on March 21, 2006, at 3:50 pm: "just setting up my twttr." These are hardly noteworthy messages, yet the initial messages sent via telephone, email, text, and Twitter comprise some of the most significant milestones in recent technological history. The point here is that momentous advancements in technology often are unforeseen and self-unaware.

The phrase "hello, world" is a reference to the early days of programmable computing when programmers would test the configuration of a computer language by inputting code. If the syntax was configured properly, the output would read "hello, world" on the terminal screen. This made it possible to read and compare different computer languages. Today, novice programmers still use the phrase "hello, world" to test their understanding of computer programming. An example of the original script used for C Programming might look like this:

```
#include <stdio.h>

main( )
{
        printf("hello, world\n");
}
```

The phrase "hello, world" is a type of immediate feedback that informs the programmer whether or not the line of code is formatted correctly. But the phrase also has come to symbolize an arrival—I'm here. All technologies have their "hello-world" moments, but few turn out to be truly memorable.

[13] NPR. 2009. The man who made you put away your pen. November 15. https://www.npr.org/templates/story/story.php?storyId=120364591. Accessed 10 Aug 2017.

In 1973, Motorola's Martin Cooper publicly showcased his prototype, named the DynaTAC, by making the first documented cellular phone call—to his embittered competition and chief rival, Joel Engel at Bell Labs. Thirty-four years later, the first-generation iPhone (widely acknowledged as the first modern smartphone) materialized, equally aware of its self-importance. On January 9, 2007, Steve Jobs unveiled the iPhone, which, according to his co-inventor, was developed out of Jobs's disgust with Apple's main competitor, Microsoft. In his biography, Jobs says of Microsoft CEO, Bill Gates, "[He] is basically unimaginative and has never invented anything, which is why I think he's more comfortable now in philanthropy than technology."[14] During his keynote, Jobs demonstrated how to delete a contact from the iPhone by using a simple tap of the finger. The contact he chose was Tony Fadell, the chief designer behind the Apple iPod, who was reported to have had a tumultuous relationship with Jobs. The symbolic act of deleting Fadell on stage became reality when he departed Apple shortly thereafter. (Fadell would land on his feet, co-founding Nest Labs, Inc. Today, he is an outspoken critic of technology companies such as Google and Apple, citing their ethical malfeasance in their design of habit-making technologies.)

Cooper and Jobs shared something else besides their cutthroat proselytism: an arrogance that their devices would be revolutionary. In an interview, Cooper commented on the impact of the invention of the cellular phone, saying, "We joked that in the future, when you were born you would be assigned a telephone number and if you didn't answer the phone, you were dead."[15] As it turns out, he wasn't far off. A failure to sustain our digital lives may leave us dead, if only figuratively. Similarly, in his keynote address, Jobs said of the iPhone, "This will change everything." Both men were prophetic, indeed, and both had a flare for the dramatic.

The actual invention of the smartphone is hard to pinpoint as a single moment in time, as it has evolved incrementally from many other technological developments. In a nutshell, the landline-based telephone paved the way for the mobile phone, which facilitated the cellular phone, which then splintered into a variety of Internet-enabled phones and personal digital assistants (PDAs), all of which informed the first-generation iPhone.

[14] Isaacson, Walter. 2011. *Steve Jobs*. New York: Simon & Schuster.

[15] Teixeira, Tania. 2010. Meet Marty Cooper—The inventor of the mobile phone. *BBC News*, April 23. http://news.bbc.co.uk/2/hi/programmes/click_online/8639590.stm. Accessed 22 Feb 2017.

There are multiple criteria that can be used to define a smartphone: wireless connectivity, web browsing, touch screen, messaging, and monthly data plans are among the requirements. By this measure, the Simon Personal Communicator developed by Frank Canova Jr. at IBM might be considered the first smartphone. The Simon combined the voice-calling features of a cellular phone with the productivity tools of a PDA.[16] Its success was limited, selling only around 50,000 units, presumably because of its steep price tag and a skeletal cellular infrastructure network. Famously, Steve Jobs reviled one of the signature features of the Simon, the stylus, by saying, "God gave us 10 styluses. Let's not invent another."[17] The significance of Apple's flagship device was that it clearly redefined what we could expect from a smartphone. Consequently, most will point to the iPhone as the first authentic smartphone, despite its considerable remixing of design and even the reuse of the name "iPhone."

The table below is only a snapshot of the many important steps in the evolution of the modern smartphone. The timeline is punctuated by two events—the debut of Bell's speaking telephone and Apple's first-generation iPhone, respectively—because they mark the most memorable achievements in communication technologies. These two events, though technologically worlds apart, sparked irreversible change in the way we perceive communication and ourselves, and both men—Bell and Jobs—have since been galvanized as central figures in the history of modern communications.

1876	Alexander Graham Bell's "speaking telephone" is debuted at the Centennial Exhibition in Philadelphia.
1910	By now, in the United States, with a population of 92 million, there were seven million phones in operation.[18]
1917	Eric Tigerstedt of Finland receives a Danish patent for the first mobile handset, which he described as a "pocket-sized folding telephone with a very thin carbon microphone."[19] Sadly, there was no infrastructure to support his prototypical device in 1917.

[16]Tweedie, Steven. 2015. The world's first smartphone, Simon, was created 15 years before the iPhone. *Business Insider*, June 14. http://www.businessinsider.com/worlds-first-smartphone-simon-launched-before-iphone-2015-6. Accessed 12 Jun 2017.

[17]Isaacson, W. 2011. *Steve Jobs*. New York: Simon & Schuster.

[18]Merchant, Brian. 2017. *The One Device: The Secret History of the iPhone*. New York: Hachette Book Group.

[19]Sethi, Anand Kumar. 2016. Eric Magnus Campbell Tigerstedt. In *The European Edisons*. New York: Palgrave Macmillan.

1946 AT&T launched the first mobile phone service in St. Louis. The primitive car phone cost around $2000—more than the price of a new car. The lack of network infrastructure meant that service was spotty and calls often were dropped.[20]

1955 Europe establishes the first mobile phone company, Televerket, located in Sweden.

1968 The FCC agrees to allocate bandwidth frequencies specifically devoted to the cellular phone market in the United States. This request was previously denied in years 1947, 1949, and 1958 because the "FCC could not spare the frequencies."[21]

1973 Martin Cooper of Motorola makes the first cellular phone call—to his rival at AT&T's Bell Labs. The DynaTAC cost around $4000 and required 10 hours of charge time for 30 minutes of use.[22]

1978 The first trial cellular network in the United States was made available to residents in Chicago, IL, and Newark, NJ, with broadcast service radiuses of 8 miles and 1.4 miles, respectively.

1979 Japan opens the world's first commercially available cellular phone network, named Mobile Control Station (MCS).[23]

1983 The first American cellular phone network is launched. The first call is made to Alexander Graham Bell's grandson in Germany. Initial setup cost was roughly $3000 and required a monthly fee of $45. Additional airtime charges ranged from 24 to 40 cents per minute, depending on the time of day.

1992 Frank Canova Jr. of IBM patents the Simon Personal Communicator, often recognized as the first smartphone. It is displayed at the COMDEX computer industry trade show, and it retails for $895.

1996 In March, Hewlett-Packard launches the OmniGo 700LX, capable of running an early version of Windows.

1996 In August, Nokia releases a cellular PDA (personal digital assistant) called the Nokia 9000 Communicator. It boasted Internet connectivity and was the first to use a hinged "clamshell design," what would later become a standard of flip phones.

1998 A touch screen, Internet-enabled, mobile phone is released by a company called InfoGear Technology, later acquired by Cisco Systems. The name of the device: iPhone. It retails for $299. Users can choose from tiered data plans ranging from $4.95 to $24.95/month. A review posted on CNN reads: "Why pay a premium of $5 a month forever to the company that just sold you a $300 phone?"[24]

1999 In Japan, NTT DoCoMo (a phrase that translated to "anywhere"), introduces i-mode service, enabling Internet access on cellular phones.

(*Continued*)

[20] Klemens, Guy. 2010. *The Cellphone: The History and Technology of the Gadget That Changed the World*. Jefferson, NC: McFarland & Company.

[21] Klemens, Guy. 2010. *The Cellphone: The History and Technology of the Gadget That Changed the World*. Jefferson, NC: McFarland & Company.

[22] History Things. 2017. The history of the cell phone. http://historythings.com/the-history-of-the-cellphone/. Accessed 4 Jun 2017.

[23] Klemens, Guy. 2010. *The Cellphone: The History and Technology of the Gadget That Changed the World*. Jefferson, NC: McFarland & Company.

[24] Hogan, Mike. 1998. iPhone is a desktop telephone married to an Internet browser. Object: Internet cruising. *CNN*, November 2. http://edition.cnn.com/TECH/computing/9811/02/netphone.idg/. Accessed 5 Jun 2017.

(continued)

1999	The first BlackBerry device is introduced. The monochromatic screen featured email and limited web browsing. Americans would later jokingly refer to these phones as "CrackBerry" because of their addictive properties.
2007	The iPhone premieres. Apple is sued by Cisco Systems for trademark infringement on the use of the name "iPhone." It is later learned that Cisco failed to register a Declaration of Use when it acquired InfoGear Technology, and subsequently loses the lawsuit.

This particular timeline ends here, but ten years later, we are enthralled with our devices more than ever. Global smartphone demand in 2017 increased 1% from the year prior, to 1.46 billion units, totaling $479 billion.[25] North America, in particular, saw the greatest demand growth, selling 201.3 million units and raking in $28.5 billion. Perhaps one of the contributing reasons for the continued uptick in mobile phone sales is the shortening lifecycles of products and their designed obsolescence. Astra Taylor is a documentarian and an activist, and she describes the technological waste problem with which we are faced in her book *The People's Platform: Taking Back Power and Culture in the Digital Age*. She argues:

> Products "designed for the dump," as people in the business call them—made to break and engineered to be difficult or impossible to fix—ensure a steady revenue stream. Thus a company such as Apple, seeking to shorten the replacement cycle of their wares, makes it easier and more affordable for consumers to buy a new gadget than change the battery in an old one. We are deceived into thinking longevity is not an option.[26]

In 2016, Apple released an environmental report on its iPhone, detailing the company's dedication to "environmental management" of its products. But the report also admits that the intended lifespan of its iPhone is only three years, after which time it should be replaced.[27] One could argue here that a device with more longevity would have a smaller footprint on the environment. Technology companies are often accused of planned obsolescence of their products, but Apple already has acknowledged that

[25] GFK. 2018. Global smartphone average sales price sees record year-on-year growth in 4Q17. January 24. http://www.gfk.com/insights/press-release/global-smartphone-average-sales-price-sees-record-year-on-year-growth-in-4q17/. Accessed 5 Feb 2018.

[26] Taylor, Astra. 2014. *The People's Platform: Taking Back Power and Culture in the Digital Age*. New York: Metropolitan Books.

[27] Apple. 2017. iPhone 7: Environmental Report. https://images.apple.com/environment/pdf/products/iphone/iPhone_7_PER_sept2016.pdf. Accessed 8 July 2017.

older iPhone models are slowed deliberately by updating their software. At the time of this writing, the company continues to be under investigation in France, where planned obsolescence of consumer products is a federal crime that could result in prison sentencing or 5% of annual profits.

While planned obsolescence implies that a company is deliberately sabotaging its own products in order to force the buyer into a newer model, it might be more plausible that buyers simply cannot resist the newer smartphone models that are being produced annually by most technology companies. This year alone, there are 23 new models of smartphones scheduled to be released, including two new models from Apple. Last year's model, the iPhone X, was the first mainstream smartphone to come with a four-figure price tag ($1000)—more than the average cost of a Windows-based PC or laptop. It is rumored, however, that Apple will discontinue its production of the iPhone X, citing lackluster sales figures. But as an article in *Engadget* points out, "Regardless of whether it sold as fast or as well as Apple hoped it would, the iPhone X did its job. It showed people what the iPhone could be."[28] There will always be a market for high-end technology, and the iPhone X is not the most expensive smartphone on the market. Not by far.

The personalized luxury smartphone marketplace targets wealthy buyers with unlimited budgets for their devices. Even luxury car companies have joined the smartphone game; the Lamborghini 88 Tauri and the Signature Touch for Bentley cost $5250 and $9000, respectively. Or perhaps the threat of device hacking could entice celebrities to purchase these smartphones that specialize in encryption and security: the Solarin ($14,000) or the Diamond Crypto ($1.3 million). Of course, there is a robust marketplace for taking factory model smartphones and encrusting them with gold (Gresso Meridian Black, $9500), diamonds (VIPN Black Diamond, $300,000), and rare materials such as meteorites (Mobiado Grand Pioneer, $9798). And then there's the Black Diamond iPhone: a solid gold body outlined with 600 white diamonds, an Apple logo filled with 53 additional diamonds, and a 26-carat black diamond, totaling $15.3 million. But you needn't take out a loan to purchase your luxury smartphone; if you happen to have a first-generation iPhone still sealed in

[28] Velazco, Chris. 2018. Apple isn't really killing the iPhone X. *Engadget*, January 23. https://www.engadget.com/2018/01/23/apple-isnt-killing-the-iphone-x/. Accessed 1 Feb 2018.

its original factory packaging, it could fetch as much as $24,995, as this is the Buy It Now price currently listed by a seller on eBay.

It is highly unlikely that you will purchase one of these luxury smartphones, but it is quite feasible that you will pay more than $1000 for your next smartphone, if you haven't already done so. The initial cost of purchasing a smartphone can range in the hundreds of dollars to more than one thousand, depending on the type of device, service plan, and carrier you choose. In addition, smartphone users rack up monthly charges that can easily exceed that of a car payment. Currently, individual plans for unlimited data cost anywhere between $65 and $95 per month, depending on the carrier; a family of four might pay $120–$240 per month for a similar unlimited data plan. Estimating conservatively, an individual should budget around $1000 per year in phone service, and a family of four can expect to pay more than double that. Owning a smartphone is costly. It's not surprising, then, that a 2017 report from Pew Research Center suggests there is a widening gap in device ownership between lower-income and higher-income Americans. Roughly 30% of lower-income adults (making less than $30,000 per year) do not own a smartphone, yet "these devices are nearly ubiquitous among adults from households earning $100,000 or more a year."[29] The smartphone has become an accessory to our mobile lives, while slowly becoming a financial drain in service contracts and constant device upgrades, and further dividing the haves and the have-nots, the connected and the disconnected.

Since the inception of the first-generation iPhone, the gestalt of the smartphone has remained relatively unchanged; undoubtedly, someone from ten years ago would instantly recognize today's iPhone. It is the internal makeup of smartphones, however, that has improved significantly. A phenomenon known as Moore's Law might best explain how this is possible. Gordon Moore co-founded Intel, an American technology company that manufactures various technological hardware such as motherboards, integrated circuits, semiconductor chips, and microprocessors: ingredients that power small computing technologies such as laptops and smartphones. Moore's 1965 paper published in *Electronics*, explained that the number of transistors that could fit into an integrated circuit would double

[29] Anderson, Monica. 2017. Digital divide persists even as lower-income Americans make gains in tech adoption. *Pew Research Center*. http://www.pewresearch.org/fact-tank/2017/03/22/digital-divide-persists-even-as-lower-income-americans-make-gains-in-tech-adoption/. Accessed 1 Feb 2018.

every two years.[30] Essentially, more transistors equated to faster processing power, and the rapid miniaturization of these electrical components would occur exponentially. For more than 40 years, Moore's Law proved true. As integrated circuitry accommodated more transistors, devices became faster and smaller. But many viewed this more as a self-fulfilling prophecy than an observation of a natural law; after all, Intel was in the business of manufacturing the very components its co-founder had predicted would increase exponentially. Today, the number of transistors "vastly outnumbers all the leaves on the Earth's trees,"[31] but Moore's Law is not sustainable for much longer. A 2016 article in *MIT Technology Review* titled "Moore's Law is Dead. Now What?" suggests that shrinking transistors might only be able to account for faster processing for another five years. Moore himself has even said that "[S]omeday it has to stop. No exponential like this goes on forever."[32]

It is reasonable to conclude that smartphones are poised to undergo a radical transformation. In the near future, smartphone developers are focusing on more efficient battery technologies such as solar charging and motion charging. A 2016 article even describes textile-based technology that weaves fiber electrodes into clothing to harvest and store solar energy for charging smartphones.[33] Even further on the horizon are high-concept smartphone designs like foldable screens that use paper-thin organic light-emitting diode (OLED) material, 3D screens and built-in hologram technology, and advanced augmented reality capabilities.[34] The Taiwanese company Polytron Technologies has already developed a working prototype for a translucent smartphone, which uses a "smart glass… that starts off opaque, or cloudy, in its powered down state, but when electricity is applied, the liquid crystals inside the glass align in such a way where light

[30] Moore, Gordon E. 1965. Cramming more components onto integrated circuits. *Electronics* 38: 33–35.

[31] Cross, Tim. n.d. Technology quarterly: After Moore's Law. *Economist*. https://www.economist.com/technology-quarterly/2016-03-12/after-moores-law. Accessed 12 Dec 2017.

[32] Friedman, Thomas L. 2015. Moore's Law turns 50. *The New York Times*, May 13. https://www.nytimes.com/2015/05/13/opinion/thomas-friedman-moores-law-turns-50.html. Accessed 29 Dec 2017.

[33] Chai, Zhisheng, Nannan Zhang, Peng Sun, Yi Huang, Chuanxi Zhao, Hong Jin Fan, Xing Fan, and Wenji Mai. 2016. Tailorable and wearable textile devices for solar energy harvesting and simultaneous storage. *ACS Nano* 10: 9201–9207.

[34] Poh, Michael. n.d. 5 key features to expect in future smartphones. *Hongkiat*. https://www.hongkiat.com/blog/future-smartphone-features/. Accessed 12 Dec 2017.

can pass through the glass, thus making it transparent."[35] Soon, smartphones will be even more inconspicuous, allowing us to integrate them more deeply into our everyday lives.

Personal communications have metamorphosed in the 140 years since Bell's speaking telephone successfully transmitted his voice waves to his assistant in the other room. The famed inventor successfully predicted that one day we would be able to communicate wirelessly, and if he were around today, Bell might be astounded to learn of the advancements in telephony. But he also might be dumbfounded upon discovering that the voice-calling feature of the smartphone is actually the least used function on the device, not even breaking into the top ten of most common smartphone uses, as a recent survey found.[36] It turns out that we'd rather text than talk. For better or worse, the smartphone has single-handedly redefined the ways in which we interact with each other.

Ubiquitous Devices

I bought my first smartphone in 2008. The Motorola Q featured a BlackBerry-style QWERTY keyboard and a 2.4″ color screen display. It had already been on the market for two years, and I opted out of the data package from Verizon. This meant I could only really use it for rudimentary tasks like calling and texting. The 1.3-megapixel camera pales in comparison to today's 12-megapixel iPhone X or the 16-megapixel Samsung S6. Still, I had left my flip phone behind for the brave new world of smartphones. The standard single-line Verizon plan at the time cost \$29.^{99} per month and allotted 200 Anytime Minutes, 500 Night & Weekend Minutes, and charged \$1.^{99} per MB of sent and received data (this is roughly ten email messages).[37] As far as I can recall, my first smartphone was not the accessory that it has become now. I rarely used it for anything other than texting and calling, and even then, I had to carefully ration my minutes. During and immediately following my time in

[35] Plafke, James. 2013. Meet the future: This is Polytron's transparent smartphone prototype. *Geek.com*, February 8. https://www.geek.com/geek-pick/meet-the-future-this-is-polytrons-transparent-smartphone-prototype-1539121/. Accessed 14 Dec 2017.

[36] Express. 2017. Revealed: Top uses of our smartphones—And calling doesn't even make the list. https://www.express.co.uk/life-style/science-technology/778572/Smartphone-phone-common-reason-use-call. Accessed 2 Dec 2017.

[37] Verizon. 2018. Why choose Verizon Wireless? https://www.verizonwireless.com/pdfs/collateral/VZW_Customer_Brochure_1107.pdf?cmp=COMM_RELCON. Accessed 3 Feb 2018.

graduate school, my smartphone functioned mostly as a social media tool—posting to Facebook and Twitter, namely. This might be explained by the confluence of several life events—getting engaged, then married, then having children—that coincided with the atmospheric rise of Facebook and Twitter among family and friends. For me, the late 2000s was the heyday for social media. Now, my smartphone serves more of a productivity role: answering emails, keeping notes, and reading news stories, primarily. In fact, I drafted and proofread parts of this book from my smartphone.

As of January 2017, Pew Research Center reports that roughly 77% of Americans own a smartphone: a figure that has more than doubled since 2011.[38] Not surprisingly, the most pronounced rate of smartphone ownership is within the 18–29-year-old demographic, which is approaching 92%. But what is even more evidential of smartphone ubiquity is the adoption rate among older populations and lower-income individuals. Since 2015, the rate of smartphone ownership among Americans aged 50 and older has increased significantly, as has ownership among households earning less than $30,000 per year. These two groups typically are identified as "Laggards" and are associated with the last stage of the technology adoption life cycle (TALC). The TALC model, introduced by Geoffrey Moore in 1991, was adapted from the diffusion of innovations theory, first proposed by Everett Rogers in his 1962 book, *Diffusion of Innovations*. The theory asserts that new technologies experience a normal distribution of adoption rates. As shown in Image 2.1, the majority of people fall into either the Early or Late Majority categories—those consumers who typically are not the first or the last to adopt a product.

In many contexts, as is the case with smartphones, it is likely that the Late Majority and Laggard groups are dragged slowly into technology adoption. Major wireless retailers such as Verizon and AT&T offer its customers few mobile phone options outside of smartphones, and other retailers such as Walmart have capitalized on the older and lower-income segments of the population by offering low-cost, no-contract, and pay-as-you-go smartphone plans. This means that consumers are gently nudged towards owning a smartphone, having otherwise limited options. This slow immersion is typical of innovative technologies until they reach full ubiquity.

The phrase "market saturation" is used in business to mean the point at which "the volume of a product or service in a marketplace has been

[38] Smith, Aaron. 2017. Record shares of Americans now own smartphones, have home broadband. *Pew Research Center*. http://www.pewresearch.org/fact-tank/2017/01/12/evolution-of-technology/. Accessed 4 Jan 2018.

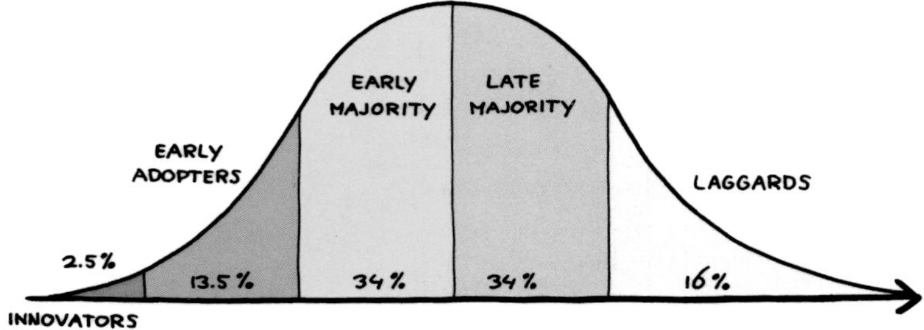

Image 2.1 The technology adoption life cycle. Source: Jurgen Appelo (Appelo, Jurgen. "Innovation adoption curve." Flickr. https://www.flickr.com/photos/jurgenappelo/5201275209. Accessed 4 Mar 2018)

maximized in its current state."[39] Indeed, few technological products ever reach complete saturation; television is generally considered a ubiquitous technology, despite Nielsen reports that approximately 96.5% of homes in the United States own a television.[40] Once a product reaches market saturation, it usually begins to enter its final stage: obsolescence. In fact, television ownership has been on the decline since 2001; the number of households without a television has doubled just in the last six years, according to the U.S. Energy Information Administration.[41] This can be largely attributed to the diverse array of screens on which consumers can now stream content.

Once thought to be fully ubiquitous, the landline telephone is another example of adoption fluidity. A 2016 report from the U.S. Department of Health shows that more than half of all Americans have severed their ties with the traditional landline phone in exchange for wireless service. Some (39%) maintain both a landline and wireless

[39] Investopedia. n.d. Market saturation. https://www.investopedia.com/terms/m/marketsaturation.asp. Accessed 31 Jan 2018.

[40] Nielsen. 2017. Nielsen estimates 119.6 million TV homes in the U.S. for the 2017–18 TV season. August 25. http://www.nielsen.com/us/en/insights/news/2017/nielsen-estimates-119-6-million-us-tv-homes-2017-2018-tv-season.html. Accessed 6 Sep 2017.

[41] U.S. Energy Information Administration. 2017. Average number of televisions in U.S. homes declining. February 28. https://www.eia.gov/todayinenergy/detail.php?id=30132. Accessed 4 Feb 2018.

service, but only 6% of Americans rely totally on a landline phone.[42] As for smartphones, it is not quite accurate to say that they have reached market saturation, though ownership numbers are still climbing. An article in the *MIT Technology Review* points out that the smartphone adoption rate has spread faster than any other technology in human history, citing that they have "also outpaced nearly any comparable technology in the leap to mainstream use."[43] While the landline phone took nearly half a century to penetrate half of American households, it has only taken the modern smartphone about four years.

In the United States, there are varying degrees of smartphone adoption according to age, gender, ethnicity, and socioeconomic status. Based on the data from a 2018 Pew Research Center survey, the most likely type of person to own a smartphone is an 18–29-year-old White or Hispanic male with a college degree, who identifies as living in an urban area, and who earns more than $75,000 annually.[44] The Center also reports that higher-income Americans also are more likely to own multiple Internet-enabled devices in addition to a smartphone, such as a tablet, laptop, or desktop computer. Perhaps the greatest predictor of smartphone ownership in the United States is income. According to the Pew Research Center, approximately 30% of lower-income Americans (those earning less than $30,000 per year) do not own a smartphone, and nearly 50% are not connected to a broadband service at home. Predictably, the vast majority of lower-income Americans do not own a tablet—a device that is nearly ubiquitous in higher-income American households (those earning more than $100,000 per year).[45]

[42] Blumberg, Stephen J. and Julian V. Luke. 2017. Wireless substitution: Early release of estimates from the national health interview survey, July–December 2016. *National Center for Health Statistics*. https://www.cdc.gov/nchs/data/nhis/earlyrelease/wireless201705.pdf. Accessed 23 Jan 2018.

[43] DeGusta, Michael. 2012. Are smartphones spreading faster than any technology in human history? *MIT Technology Review*, May 9. https://www.technologyreview.com/s/427787/are-smart-phones-spreading-faster-than-any-technology-in-human-history/. Accessed 9 Feb 2018.

[44] Pew Research Center. 2018. Mobile fact sheet. http://www.pewinternet.org/fact-sheet/mobile/. Accessed 8 Jan 2018.

[45] Anderson, Monica. 2017. Digital divide persists even as lower-income Americans make gains in tech adoption. *Pew Research Center*. http://www.pewresearch.org/fact-tank/2017/03/22/digital-divide-persists-even-as-lower-income-americans-make-gains-in-tech-adoption/. Accessed 8 May 2018.

This disparity between income level and device ownership is referred to as the *digital divide*, and it is not unique to the United States. The Pew Research Center found that, globally, "In every single country, younger people, those with more education and those with an income above the country median are more likely to own a smartphone compared with older, less educated and poorer members of their societies."[46] Smartphone ownership as a function of income disparity was worst in Greece and Italy, and this differential was lowest in Canada. Education level also fuels the digital divide. Again, Italy has the worst differential in device ownership between the lowest and highest educated, and this gap is the smallest in the Netherlands.[47]

Smartphone ownership is at an all-time high in the United States, and it continues to climb around the world. And although there are reliable predictors of smartphone ownership, there is no singular profile of a smartphone owner; they are diverse in age, gender, race, and wealth. As devices become cheaper to produce, they will reach full saturation, decreasing their prices and bridging the digital divide. Non-profit programs like Close the Gap and EveryoneOn.org vow to bring affordable Internet-enabled devices to those who remain unconnected in the United States. But just as swaths of the population are still trying to connect, many are choosing to disconnect. Indeed, the rise of the smartphone has networked a global village, but it also has amplified the voices of hyperbolic prediction-makers, alarmists, and doomsday prophets.

Smartphone Hysteria

Technology is polarizing. Pessimistic futurists hysterically warn about the demise of society's youth culture, while technological evangelicals extol a promising, new world. In reality, neither scenario is ever fully realized. Throughout history, the conversation about the consequential effects of

[46] Poushter, Jacob. 2017. Smartphones are common in advanced economies, but digital divides remain. *Pew Research Center*. http://www.pewresearch.org/fact-tank/2017/04/21/smartphones-are-common-in-advanced-economies-but-digital-divides-remain/. Accessed 6 Mar 2018.

[47] Poushter, Jacob. 2017. Smartphones are common in advanced economies, but digital divides remain. *Pew Research Center*. http://www.pewresearch.org/fact-tank/2017/04/21/smartphones-are-common-in-advanced-economies-but-digital-divides-remain/. Accessed 6 Mar 2018.

technology takes place virtually every time a new development becomes culturally widespread. Socrates argued that writing would yield forgetfulness, as an "elixir not of memory, but of reminding." Leaders in every major religion stalled the adoption of the printing press because of its ability to "spread heretical opinions."[48] Parents and teachers condemned SMS text messaging because of the fear that it would erode writing and communication skills.[49] The pattern here is not hard to decipher; new technologies challenge the status quo, and as a result, there is a natural inclination to resist their adoption and to warn of an ensuing deterioration of culture. But in his article, "It's Time For a Serious Talk About the Science of Tech 'Addiction'," Robbie Gonzalez argues that this time, it is different: "Of course we've been here before. Anxieties over technology's impact on society are as old as society itself; video games, television, radio, the telegraph, even the written word—they were all, at one time, scapegoats or harbingers of humanity's cognitive, creative, emotional, and cultural dissolution. But the apprehension over smartphones, apps, and seductive algorithms is different. So different, in fact, that our treatment of past technologies fails to be instructive."[50] Or, as Susan Greenfield, Professor of Synaptic Pharmacology at the University of Oxford, forewarned in 2011: "Human identity, the idea that defines each and every one of us, could be facing an unprecedented crisis."[51] The hysteria over smartphones is real.

Perhaps unarguably, the smartphone has disrupted the way we think and the way we interact, and it has radically altered the ways in which we see ourselves, others, and the world. But this is not unique to our existence. In her book, *Proust and the Squid: The Story and Science of the Reading Brain*, Maryanne Wolf juxtaposes our modern hysteria with ancient history:

[48] Nasr, Walid G. 2016. Print or not print: Is that still the question? *The Aga Khan University*. http://ecommons.aku.edu/uk_ismc_faculty_publications/2. Accessed 4 Dec 2017.

[49] Crystal, D. 2008. *Txtng: The Gr8 Db8*. Oxford: Oxford University Press.

[50] Gonzalez, R. 2018. It's time for a serious talk about the science of 'tech addiction.' *Wired*, February 1. https://www.wired.com/story/its-time-for-a-serious-talk-about-the-science-of-tech-addiction/. Accessed 1 Feb 2018.

[51] Greenfield, Susan. n.d. Modern technology is changing the way our brains work, says neuroscientist. *Daily Mail*. http://www.dailymail.co.uk/sciencetech/article-565207/Modern-technology-changing-way-brains-work-says-neuroscientist.html. Accessed 14 Mar 2018.

> And what of future generations? Are Socrates' concerns about unguided access to information more warranted today than they were in ancient Greece? Or will the demands of our new information technologies—to multitask, and to integrate and prioritize vast amounts of information—help to develop equally if not more valuable skills that will increase our human intellectual capacities, our quality of life, and our collective wisdom as a species?[52]

Remember the view of the technological determinist: resistance to technological progress is futile, as technology itself is autonomous and unstoppable. Perhaps a more reasonable position is to acknowledge that technological evolution is a motivation embedded deeply in the human condition and that we should practice some level of discretion in its adoption and implementation when it comes to the ways in which we use our smartphones.

Too often, we hear the capitalist's argument that technology simply provides us with more choice, but just as the railroad and automobile provided more choices for transportation, the Internet has provided us with more choices for information, communication, shopping, dating, entertainment, and many other things. And while this is true to some extent, we overlook the reciprocal choices that technology makes for us. Adopting the railroad and automobile has improved transportation but worsened the environment. Adopting the Internet has connected loved ones as well as hate groups, terrorist networks, and child pornographers. It is a reductionist argument to say that we benefit simply from having choices when these technological choices have irreversible consequences. It is indisputable that technological advancement impacts culture in both positive and negative ways and that its benefits and consequences are often unforeseen and unintended. Likewise, we must understand that technology, in this case smartphones, is not a neutral medium either.

While teaching a graduate course in Design & Cognition, I asked my students during a discussion: How do we know when we actually have a problem with a technology and when it is overblown hype? I was referencing the growing number of research studies that suggest we may be seeing a neurological adaptation to the way we think as a result of our Internet behaviors, and I was surprised to hear that every one of my students felt that it was overblown hype. "Technological progress is cyclical," one

[52] Wolf, Maryanne. 2007. *Proust and the Squid: The Story and Science of the Reading Brain*. New York: HarperCollins Publishers.

student said, "they probably said the same thing about cars when they first arrived on the scene, and we couldn't imagine living without them now. We'll probably be saying the same things about Internet technologies in five years." Another student likened our smartphones to gaming: "People said that video games would rot our brains. Now, we value them as educational tools." Point taken. Indeed, the major obstacle to the central argument in this book is that there is a strong track record of hysteria accompanying technological innovation.

But in the case of the Internet, and by extension, the mobile devices on which we primarily access the Internet, we have fundamentally shifted the ways in which we interact with each other and with information, as well as how that media makes us feel. Unlike traditional one-way media such as radio and television, where a passive consumer absorbed the content, our smartphones are two-way interaction devices that demand attention and never leave our sides. The smartphone has mobilized our media consumption habits that once were relegated to a living room or an office space. And we are still figuring out how to manage all of it. Like a scuba diver coming up too quickly from the depths of the ocean, we are experiencing a decompression sickness with our information processing technologies. The question is not whether or not technology will change us, but what it is that we sacrifice in the process.

There are many conflicting messages about how our technologies are (or are not) affecting us, and with all of the noise, it is difficult to tell what is cause for concern and what is empty hysteria. Today's news media is overly saturated with stories of tech addiction; television segments on shows like *60 Minutes* and *The Today Show* routinely report statistics and findings from headline-grabbing, pop science studies. This only fuels the smartphone hysteria, causing smartphone users to recoil instead of lean in. Seemingly, the general consensus in popular press is that teens and young children have a problem with technology simply because they are the first generation to have grown up with it. Here are some headlines from recent news stories on smartphones that I found on the web:

"Smartphones Are Making Today's Teens Unhappy, Psychologist Says"
"Yes, Smartphone Addiction Does Harm Your Teen's Mental Health"
"Our Smartphone Addiction Is Killing Us"
"Have Smartphones Destroyed A Generation?"
"Are Smartphones Ruining America's Youth?""The Risk of Teen Depression and Suicide Is Linked to Smartphone Use, Study Says"
"Are Teenagers Replacing Drugs with Smartphones?"

It's no wonder we have difficulty talking about the subject of smartphone habits in a reasonable way; the popular press has desensitized the subject in exchange for mouse clicks. Sadly, these titles come from reputable sources such as NPR, *The Atlantic*, and *The New York Times*, whose audience demographic skews older. The implication here, presumably, is that these articles are targeted at parents of teenagers and young children. Certainly, it is not helpful to begin a discourse about responsible smartphone behaviors by asking "Are Teenagers Replacing Drugs with Smartphones?" (The answer to that question, by the way, is no.) We should not be treating our relationships with smartphones in the same way that we do a drug crisis. First Lady Nancy Reagan's plea to 1980s youth to "Just Say No" to drugs arguably backfired, succeeding only in giving young teens a matriarchal figure to rebel against. Similarly, adults launching a war on smartphones would have the same tangled effects that it did for illicit drugs. For these reasons, the term *addiction* when used in the context of technology, and smartphones in particular, has become a dirty word, and it can shut down the conversation rather quickly.

Anecdotally, while preparing this book, I reached out to a number of public and private K-12 schools so that I might survey and interview students of all ages about their smartphone usage. Most schools declined my request, citing the negative perception that students and parents already have towards this subject, no doubt the result of a barrage of mischaracterizations by popular culture. Broaching this subject with youth is like walking on eggshells. In one of my email correspondences with a school counselor, she ultimately refused my request to hold a focus group with students at her school, saying:

> Sorry. Kids are just in a place where they think adults just don't understand and always think smartphones are bad. They HATE it when we (adults) imply they are addicted to screens. I have to be careful when and how I address technology concerns in order to avoid [the students] shutting down. The same thing happened when we started to address bullying several years back. They were so sick of hearing about it, that they shut us out.

I encountered responses like these frequently. Never mind the value of self-reflecting on smartphone habits, students were flat out sick and tired of being told they are addicted to technology and that it is their fault. Having a meaningful conversation about technology habits becomes difficult when the attempts are perceived as accusatory rather than inquisitive.

Right now, technology users (and especially adolescents and teenagers) are hearing a barrage of information that both demonizes and vindicates them for their digital habits. On one hand, younger generations are praised for digital literacies and for being tech savvy, and on the other hand, penalized for their attachment to the very same devices. In her book, *It's Complicated: The Social Lives of Networked Teens*, social researcher danah boyd acknowledges that struggles with impulse control are a clear and present danger when it comes to device usage, particularly for teenagers, but that "addiction rhetoric positions new technologies as devilish..." According to boyd:

> The problem with popular discussions about addiction is that it doesn't matter whether people are chemically or psychologically dependent on a substance or behavior. Anyone who engages in a practice in ways that society sees as putting more socially acceptable aspects of their lives in jeopardy are seen as addicted.[53]

Framing smartphone dependency as an addictive disorder positions the user as a vulnerable addict. In the article titled "'Devilish Smartphones' and the 'Stone-Cold' Internet: Implications of the Technology Addiction Trope in College Student Digital Literacy Narratives," Jenae Cohn argues that we can open up the conversation about technology dependency by helping users recognize "how virtual interactions and tools can not only detract, but also can augment and supplement embodied interactions" and encourage them to "become active participants, rather than passive decriers" of technology.[54] According to Cohn, the assumption that young adults live in a blended world of the virtual and the real, where they are unable to distinguish the two, is not necessarily the lived experience of youth, despite what is constantly projected in the media. Rather, connected teens and adolescents are very much aware of their dual worlds and have become quite adept at toggling between the two.

I interviewed Dr. Cohn so that she might elaborate on her perspective. She spoke at length about the smartphone as an extension of our minds

[53] boyd, danah. 2015. *It's Complicated: The Social Lives of Networked Teens.* New Haven, CT: Yale University Press.

[54] Cohn, Jenae. 2016. 'Devilish smartphones' and the 'stone-cold' internet: Implications of the technology addiction trope in college student digital literacy narratives. *Computers and Composition* 42: 80–94.

and bodies but pointed out that because we already exist as a hybridity of machine and man, the smartphone should not be pathologized. She says, “We have to get over the idea that technology itself is some intruder upon the natural.” Rather, according to Cohn, we should view smartphones as an organizational tool—a way to manage the unprecedented vast amount of information that is constantly requesting our attention. Cohn further questions the effects of the smartphone, likening it to medical technologies like contacts and hearing aids and noting that “we’re okay when we have a perception of control.” The counterargument, though, is that we become threatened by smartphones because they are intellectual technologies, by which Nicholas Carr means “tools that extend our mental rather than our physical capacities.”[55] Contact lenses and hearing aids enhance our physical ability, but smartphones redefine our intellect. Still, Cohn and I agree that change is necessary for the ways in which we engage with digital technology. Specifically, she believes that we should begin by observing our digital habits, mapping out our behaviors, and empowering ourselves by using our smartphones in more authentic ways.

When it comes to smartphones and what they are doing to us, there is no shortage of social critique. But we might consider this from a medical perspective, too. Aside from the general improprieties, have we developed addictive-like behaviors when it comes to checking our smartphones, our social media, our email? Might *this* warrant a label of addiction? To help answer this question, I spoke with Dr. Judson Brewer, the Director of Research at the Center for Mindfulness at UMass Medical School and a Research Affiliate in the Department of Brain and Cognitive Sciences at MIT. Brewer draws upon his successful clinical program for smoking cessation as the framework for his current work in mitigating technology addiction. I asked Dr. Brewer whether or not we should view our smartphone habit as a full-fledged addictive disorder. He responded, “This is not a technology problem; it is a neurology problem.” He elaborated further:

> We should just take a neutral standpoint. Look, is a knife good or bad? It’s helpful for surgery, not so helpful in a street fight. So, are they good or bad? Well, they’re just knives. It’s how we use them. A scalpel could kill somebody, or it could save somebody’s life. Really helping people understand

[55] Carr, Nicholas G. 2008. Is Google making us stupid? What the Internet is doing to our brains. *The Atlantic*. July/August. https://www.theatlantic.com/magazine/archive/2008/07/is-google-making-us-stupid/306868/. Accessed 11 Jan 2018.

> what technology does and where it can get caught by our own addictive habit loops is a good neutral way to approach the situation. It's neither good nor bad; it's understanding how our minds work.

Of course, taking the stance that technology is entirely neutral directly contradicts Kranzberg's First Law. Instead, as I proposed in this chapter, smartphones possess inert affordances that charge their use, similar to that of a gun. Nevertheless, Brewer's approach to curbing our digital indulgence is not to chastise, label, or demonize users, but to educate them. For him, the smartphone dilemma is not about rhetoric or semantics; it is simply neurological. And therefore, so is the solution. In my conversation with Dr. Brewer, I asked him whether or not we should refrain from using the word *addiction* in concert with technology, as critics such as boyd and Cohn have suggested. He said, "It doesn't matter. If you rub somebody's face in the shit enough, they're eventually going to smell it."

It dawns on me that the sentiment towards smartphone dependency has a strong parallel with other divisive topics. Sometimes, what seems to be scientifically ironclad remains a hotly contested and politicized view. For years now, climatologists have been warning about the potentially devastating effects of human behavior on our climate, yet only 42% of Americans believe global warming poses a serious threat.[56] A 2016 literature review of 11,944 research papers reveals that the overwhelming majority of climate scientists (97.2%) who publish studies on the subject are in consensus that human activity causes global warming.[57] Yet, even the current President of the United States and many members of his administration, including the head of the Environmental Protection Agency, have expressed skepticism or flat-out denial of climate change. Public deniability of scientific-based evidence for climate change and the subsequent views held by trained experts seems illogical, yet it is prevalent in nearly all arenas. The effects of smartphones on our behavior are similarly polarizing. People have been warned about the devastating effects of technology, but because most of

[56] Saad, Lydia. 2017. Global warming concern at three-decade high in US. *Gallup*. http://news.gallup.com/poll/206030/global-warming-concern-three-decade-high.aspx?g_source=Politics&g_medium=lead&g_campaign=tiles. Accessed 26 Jan 2018.

[57] Cook, John, Naomi Oreskes, Peter T. Doran, William R.L. Anderegg, Bart Verheggen, Ed W. Maibach, J. Stuart Carlton, Stephan Lewandowsky, Andrew G. Skuce, Sarah A. Green, Dana Nuccitelli, Peter Jacobs, Mark Richardson, Barbel Winkler, Rob Painting and Ken Rice. 2016. Consensus on consensus: A synthesis of consensus estimates on human-caused global warming. *Environmental Research Letters* 11.

the consequences are intangible, many defer to their personal beliefs and anecdotal evidence. When we have firsthand experience with something, whether it be with smartphones or the climate, we often mistake that experience for logic. But if we listen to the experts on digital distraction, some of whom are directly responsible for developing these technologies, they are sending a very loud and cohesive message.

Tony Fadell is a former Apple employee who was instrumental in the design of the iPod Touch (he is affectionately called the "Podfather"). He also played a formative role in designing and building the first-generation iPhone before leaving Apple to work on his own startup company, Nest Labs. Fadell, you will remember, was the one who Jobs suggestively deleted as a contact during the famous keynote address. Since his departure from Apple, Fadell has been an outspoken critic of the technology that he himself has helped to create, demanding that companies like Apple and Google bear responsibility in their design. Fadell recently unleashed a fury of tweets on digital habits, in which he concluded that "Device addiction is real." Fadell is not alone, either. In the book *The One Device: The Secret History of the iPhone*, Brian Merchant interviews numerous former and current designers and engineers at Apple. He recalls:

> I made it a point in my interviews to ask those who worked on the original iPhone project how they felt about the device they'd unleashed upon the world—and was surprised to find a near-universal ambivalence. Most were awed by the reach of the device, by the boom of apps it begot. Most also mentioned the downsides of its constant distraction, lamenting couples eating dinner together gazing silently into their devices.

In June 2017, during an open panel discussion at the IDEO design studio, former Apple employees Bas Ording, Brian Huppi, and Greg Christie described their own uneasiness towards the iPhone that they helped design and build. Christie, who directed the human interface team at Apple, said of the iPhone's influence, "In terms of whether it's net positive or net negative, I don't think we know yet… I don't feel good about the distraction. It's certainly an unintended consequence."[58] We are living out the plot of a bad sci-fi movie, and this is the part where the mad scientist inventors are powerless over the mutant smartphone that has been unleashed upon the rest of us.

[58] Statt, Nick. 2017. The creators of the iPhone are worried we're too addicted to technology. *The Verge*, June 29. https://www.theverge.com/2017/6/29/15893960/apple-iphone-creators-smartphone-addiction-ideo-interview. Accessed 9 Sep 2017.

Many are beginning to fight back, however. On January 6, 2018, a group of shareholders, who "collectively own approximately $2 billion in value of shares of Apple Inc.,"[59] published an open letter to Apple's Board of Directors. Their purpose was to demand that Apple address the epidemic of smartphone dependency that plagues youth, citing the overwhelming amount of research that finds "unintentional negative consequences" for frequent smartphone users. The shareholders place the blame squarely on the company, saying that "the potential long-term consequences of new technologies need to be factored in at the outset, and no company can outsource that responsibility to an app designer, or more accurately to hundreds of app designers, none of whom have critical mass." The company has a responsibility, the shareholders argue, to "[pay] special attention to the health and development of the next generation" because it is "both good business and the right thing to do." When investors are speaking out, pleading for more regulation, we ought to listen.

Within one week of the open letter from Apple shareholders, *The New York Times* ran an article titled "It's Time for Apple to Build a Less Addictive iPhone." The author, Farhad Manjoo, argues that Apple has "a moral responsibility to—and a business interest in—the well-being of its customers."[60] The problem, of course, is that economic incentive is stronger than a moral one, and Apple is entrenched in the attention economy. A technology giant like Apple urging you to put down your smartphone is as perplexing as Marlboro saying they want you to quit smoking.

As I carefully walk the tightrope that separates hysterical outrage from legitimate concern, I am reminded of a line in Douglas Adams's *The Salmon of Doubt*: "Anything that is in the world when you're born is normal and ordinary and is just a natural part of the way the world works. Anything that's invented between when you're fifteen and thirty-five is new and exciting and revolutionary and you can probably get a career in it. Anything invented after you're thirty-five is against the natural order of things."[61] I am 35 years old at the time of this writing, so I frequently ask

[59] Board of Directors, Apple, Inc. 2018. Open letter from JANA partners and CALSTRS to Apple Inc. https://thinkdifferentlyaboutkids.com/index.php?acc=1. Accessed 6 Jan 2018.

[60] Manjoo, Farhad. 2018. It's time for Apple to build a less addictive iPhone. *The New York Times*, January 7. https://www.nytimes.com/2018/01/17/technology/apple-addiction-iphone.html. Accessed 2 Feb 2018.

[61] Adams, Douglas. 2003. *The Salmon of Doubt: Hitchhiking the Galaxy One Last Time*. New York: Ballantine Books.

myself if I am being cynical or if there really is an overt danger posed by our smartphones. Are smartphones truly addictive? Or, is this yet another example of overreaction to a novel technology? The answer, as far as I can tell, is both. We are overreacting, *and* the consequences are real. To put Kranzberg's spin on it, smartphones are good *and* bad. That said, we cannot ignore the growing number of voices of technology experts, developers, and critics who are getting collectively louder.

References

Adams, Douglas. 2003. *The Salmon of Doubt: Hitchhiking the Galaxy One Last Time*. New York: Ballantine Books.

Alexander Graham Bell—Lab Notebook. n.d. Accessed August 9, 2017. http://lcweb2.loc.gov/cgi-bin/ampage?collId=am-reas&fileName=trr002page.db&recNum=21&itemLink=http%3A%2F%2Fwww.loc.gov%2Fexhibits%2Ftreasures%2Ftrr002.html&linkText=9.

Anderson, Monica. 2017. Digital divide persists even as lower-income Americans make gains in tech adoption. *Pew Research Center*. Accessed February 1, 2018. http://www.pewresearch.org/fact-tank/2017/03/22/digital-divide-persists-even-as-lower-income-americans-make-gains-in-tech-adoption/.

Appelo, Jurgen. 2018. Innovation adoption curve. *Flickr*. Accessed March 4, 2018. https://www.flickr.com/photos/jurgenappelo/5201275209.

Apple. 2007. Apple reinvents the phone with iPhone. January 9. Accessed November 4, 2017. https://www.apple.com/newsroom/2007/01/09Apple-Reinvents-the-Phone-with-iPhone/.

———. 2017. iPhone 7: Environmental Report. Accessed July 8, 2017. https://images.apple.com/environment/pdf/products/iphone/iPhone_7_PER_sept2016.pdf.

Arthur, Charles. 2012. The history of smartphones: Timeline. *The Guardian*, January 24. Accessed December 1, 2017. https://www.theguardian.com/technology/2012/jan/24/smartphones-timeline.

Blumberg, Stephen J., and Julian V. Luke. 2017. Wireless substitution: Early release of estimates from the national health interview survey, July–December 2016. *National Center for Health Statistics*. Accessed January 23, 2018. https://www.cdc.gov/nchs/data/nhis/earlyrelease/wireless201705.pdf.

Board of Directors, Apple, Inc. 2018. Open letter from JANA partners and CALSTRS to Apple Inc. Accessed January 6, 2018. https://thinkdifferentlyaboutkids.com/index.php?acc=1.

boyd, danah. 2015. *It's Complicated: The Social Lives of Networked Teens*. New Haven, CT: Yale University Press.

Carr, Nicholas G. 2008. Is Google making us stupid? What the Internet is doing to our brains. *The Atlantic*. July/August. Accessed January 11, 2018. https://www.theatlantic.com/magazine/archive/2008/07/is-google-making-us-stupid/306868/.

———. 2011. *The Shallows: What the Internet is Doing to Our Brains*. New York: W.W. Norton & Company.

Chai, Zhisheng, Nannan Zhang, Peng Sun, Yi Huang, Chuanxi Zhao, Hong Jin Fan, Xing Fan, and Wenji Mai. 2016. Tailorable and wearable textile devices for solar energy harvesting and simultaneous storage. *ACS Nano* 10: 9201–9207.

Cohn, Jenae. 2016. 'Devilish smartphones' and the 'stone-cold' internet: Implications of the technology addiction trope in college student digital literacy narratives. *Computers and Composition* 42: 80–94.

Cook, John, Naomi Oreskes, Peter T. Doran, William R.L. Anderegg, Bart Verheggen, Ed W. Maibach, J. Stuart Carlton, et al. 2016. Consensus on consensus: A synthesis of consensus estimates on human-caused global warming. *Environmental Research Letters* 11: 048002.

Cross, Tim. n.d. Technology quarterly: After Moore's Law. *Economist*. Accessed December 12, 2017. https://www.economist.com/technology-quarterly/2016-03-12/after-moores-law.

Crystal, D. 2008. *Txtng: The Gr8 Db8*. Oxford: Oxford University Press.

Culkin, John M. 1967, March 18. A schoolman's guide to Marshall McLuhan. *The Saturday Review*, 51–53 and 70–72.

DeGusta, Michael. 2012. Are smartphones spreading faster than any technology in human history? *MIT Technology Review*, May 9. Accessed February 9, 2018. https://www.technologyreview.com/s/427787/are-smart-phones-spreading-faster-than-any-technology-in-human-history/.

Estes, Adam C. 2012. The history of the smartphone begins with Steve Jobs. *The Atlantic*, January 24. Accessed December 2, 2017. https://www.theatlantic.com/technology/archive/2012/01/history-smartphone-begins-steve-jobs/332723/.

Express. 2017. Revealed: Top uses of our smartphones—And calling doesn't even make the list. Accessed December 2, 2017. https://www.express.co.uk/life-style/science-technology/778572/Smartphone-phone-common-reason-use-call.

Friedman, Thomas L. 2015. Moore's Law turns 50. *The New York Times*, May 13. Accessed December 29, 2017. https://www.nytimes.com/2015/05/13/opinion/thomas-friedman-moores-law-turns-50.html.

Gartner. 2017. Gartner says worldwide sales of smartphones grew 7 percent in the fourth quarter of 2016, February 15. Accessed July 7, 2017. https://www.gartner.com/newsroom/id/3609817.

GFK. 2018. Global smartphone average sales price sees record year-on-year growth in 4Q17, January 24. Accessed February 5, 2018. http://www.gfk.

com/insights/press-release/global-smartphone-average-sales-price-sees-record-year-on-year-growth-in-4q17/.

Gladwell, Malcolm. 2011. The tweaker. The real genius of Steve Jobs. *The New Yorker*, November 14. Accessed December 8, 2017. https://www.newyorker.com/magazine/2011/11/14/the-tweaker.

Gonzalez, R. 2018. It's time for a serious talk about the science of 'tech addiction.' *Wired*, February 1. Accessed February 1, 2018. https://www.wired.com/story/its-time-for-a-serious-talk-about-the-science-of-tech-addiction/.

Greenfield, Susan. n.d. Modern technology is changing the way our brains work, says neuroscientist. *Daily Mail*. Accessed March 14, 2018. http://www.dailymail.co.uk/sciencetech/article-565207/Modern-technology-changing-way-brains-work-says-neuroscientist.html.

History Things. 2017. The history of the cell phone. Accessed June 4, 2017. http://historythings.com/the-history-of-the-cellphone/.

Hogan, Mike. 1998. iPhone is a desktop telephone married to an Internet browser. Object: Internet cruising. *CNN*, November 2. Accessed June 5, 2017. http://edition.cnn.com/TECH/computing/9811/02/netphone.idg/.

Investopedia. n.d. Market saturation. Accessed January 31, 2018. https://www.investopedia.com/terms/m/marketsaturation.asp.

Isaacson, Walter. 2011. *Steve Jobs*. New York: Simon & Schuster.

Klemens, Guy. 2010. *The Cellphone: The History and Technology of the Gadget that Changed the World*. Jefferson, NC: McFarland & Company.

Manjoo, Farhad. 2018. It's time for Apple to build a less addictive iPhone. *The New York Times*, January 7. Accessed February 2, 2018. https://www.nytimes.com/2018/01/17/technology/apple-addiction-iphone.html.

McNish, Jacquie, and Sean Silcoff. 2016. *Losing the Signal: The Untold Story Behind the Extraordinary Rise and Spectacular Fall of BlackBerry*. New York: Flatiron Books.

Merchant, Brian. 2017. *The One Device: The Secret History of the iPhone*. New York: Hachette Book Group.

Moore, Gordon E. 1965. Cramming more components onto integrated circuits. *Electronics* 38: 33–35.

Nasr, Walid G. 2016. Print or not print: Is that still the question? *The Aga Khan University*. Accessed December 4, 2017. http://ecommons.aku.edu/uk_ismc_faculty_publications/2.

Nielsen. 2017. Nielsen estimates 119.6 million TV homes in the U.S. for the 2017–18 TV season, August 25. Accessed September 6, 2017. http://www.nielsen.com/us/en/insights/news/2017/nielsen-estimates-119-6-million-us-tv-homes-2017-2018-tv-season.html.

NPR. 2009. The man who made you put away your pen, November 15. Accessed August 10, 2017. https://www.npr.org/templates/story/story.php?storyId=120364591.

Open Signal. 2017. Android fragmentation (August 2015). Accessed July 9, 2017. http://opensignal.com/reports/2015/08/android-fragmentation/.

Pew Research Center. 2018. Mobile fact sheet. Accessed January 8, 2018. http://www.pewinternet.org/fact-sheet/mobile/.

Plafke, James. 2013. Meet the future: This is Polytron's transparent smartphone prototype. *Geek.com*, February 8. Accessed December 14, 2017. https://www.geek.com/geek-pick/meet-the-future-this-is-polytrons-transparent-smartphone-prototype-1539121/.

Poh, Michael. n.d. 5 key features to expect in future smartphones. *Hongkiat*. Accessed December 12, 2017. https://www.hongkiat.com/blog/future-smartphone-features/.

Poushter, Jacob. 2017. Smartphones are common in advanced economies, but digital divides remain. *Pew Research Center*. Accessed March 6, 2018. http://www.pewresearch.org/fact-tank/2017/04/21/smartphones-are-common-in-advanced-economies-but-digital-divides-remain/.

Saad, Lydia. 2017. Global warming concern at three-decade high in US. *Gallup*. Accessed January 26, 2018. http://news.gallup.com/poll/206030/global-warming-concern-three-decade-high.aspx?g_source=Politics&g_medium=lead&g_campaign=tiles.

Sethi, Anand Kumar. 2016. Eric Magnus Campbell Tigerstedt. In *The European Edisons*. New York: Palgrave Macmillan.

Smith, Aaron. 2017. Record shares of Americans now own smartphones, have home broadband. *Pew Research Center*. Accessed January 4, 2018. http://www.pewresearch.org/fact-tank/2017/01/12/evolution-of-technology/.

Statt, Nick. 2017. The creators of the iPhone are worried we're too addicted to technology. *The Verge*, June 29. Accessed September 9, 2017. https://www.theverge.com/2017/6/29/15893960/apple-iphone-creators-smartphone-addiction-ideo-interview.

Taylor, Astra. 2014. *The People's Platform: Taking Back Power and Culture in the Digital Age*. New York: Metropolitan Books.

Teixeira, Tania. 2010. Meet Marty Cooper—The inventor of the mobile phone. *BBC News*, April 23. Accessed February 22, 2017. http://news.bbc.co.uk/2/hi/programmes/click_online/8639590.stm.

Tweedie, Steven. 2015. The world's first smartphone, Simon, was created 15 years before the iPhone. *Business Insider*, June 14. Accessed June 12, 2017. http://www.businessinsider.com/worlds-first-smartphone-simon-launched-before-iphone-2015-6.

Urban Dictionary. 2017. Crackberry. Accessed July 7, 2017. https://www.urbandictionary.com/define.php?term=Crackberry.

U.S. Energy Information Administration. 2017. Average number of televisions in U.S. homes declining, February 28. Accessed February 4, 2018. https://www.eia.gov/todayinenergy/detail.php?id=30132.

Velazco, Chris. 2018. Apple isn't really killing the iPhone X. *Engadget*, January 23. Accessed February 1, 2018. https://www.engadget.com/2018/01/23/apple-isnt-killing-the-iphone-x/.

Verizon. 2018. Why choose Verizon Wireless? Accessed February 3, 2018. https://www.verizonwireless.com/pdfs/collateral/VZW_Customer_Brochure_1107.pdf?cmp=COMM_RELCON.

Wolf, Maryanne. 2007. *Proust and the Squid: The Story and Science of the Reading Brain*. New York: HarperCollins Publishers.

CHAPTER 3

Habit-Making Devices

In the process of writing this book, I surveyed hundreds of smartphone users, conducted numerous focus groups, and interviewed authors, academics, and medical experts. Over time, and throughout my years teaching, I have observed a general malaise with smartphone users when it comes to studying and characterizing their smartphone habits. We are guarded about our usage patterns and behaviors, just as we are with our religious and political views. We are sensitive to these things because they are intimately formative in shaping who we are. As I discussed in Chap. 1, a smartphone is more than a device; it is a revelatory window into our virtual selves. Though we are not wholly defined by this technology, it does offer an important clue into the embodied self, and sometimes, we don't like what we see. I was not surprised, then, that the interviews and focus groups I conducted for this book revealed many smartphone users who were reluctant to discuss their digital habits and who actually preferred to remain willfully ignorant of them instead. Some, I'm sure, would rather an audit of their taxes than of the contents of their phones. And it is perhaps not a coincidence that the users who were the most defensive about their smartphone usage tended to have the highest levels of dependency on their devices. Because of the hypersensitivity that surrounds our smartphone usage, it is with careful trepidation that I even refer to our dependencies on smartphones as an *addiction*. So, let's explore what we actually mean when we use the term addiction and how smartphones fit into the wider landscape of behavioral addiction.

A. J. Reid, *The Smartphone Paradox*,
https://doi.org/10.1007/978-3-319-94319-0_3

Addiction is a formal, diagnosable medical disorder, but for a simpler nonmedical definition, I turn once again to addiction expert, Judson Brewer. He describes addiction as "continued use, despite adverse consequences."[1] And there are shades of addiction; Brewer adds, "The degree to which our lives and those around us upside down helps determine the level of severity. In this way, we can view addictions along a spectrum calibrated as much on the degree to which our behaviors affect our lives as on the behaviors themselves." If we are to apply this definition to our own smartphone habits, the question then becomes, how do we distinguish *regular use* from *use with adverse consequences*? Like many behavioral addictions, the answer is unique to each of us. An adverse consequence can be as serious as causing a car accident as a result of texting and driving, but it also can be as subtle as the degradation of relationships with significant others due to the fragmented attention that occurs when our devices are present. Often, addiction affects both the user and others close to the user. The ways in which we measure personal consequence will inform our addictiveness.

The phrase *smartphone addiction* is a serious and loaded term, and its flippant use has turned it into more of a shameful social indictment than a medical affliction. Colloquially, smartphone addiction has come to refer simply to an overdependence on our devices, but a legitimate addictive disorder must first be recognized by the Diagnostic and Statistical Manual of Mental Disorders (DSM-5), the leading diagnosis handbook for the American Psychiatric Association (APA). According to the most recent version of the DSM-5, the term *addiction* is officially defined as:

> a complex condition, a brain disease that is manifested by compulsive substance use despite harmful consequence. People with addiction (severe substance use disorder) have an intense focus on using a certain substance(s), such as alcohol or drugs, to the point that it takes over their life.[2]

Addiction may be subdivided into *substance addiction* and *behavioral addiction*, where *substance* refers to alcohol and drugs, and *behavior* refers to our repeated actions. There is a growing movement that supports the inclusion of smartphone addiction in the DSM as a designated behavioral addiction. In recent years, researchers across universities in Taiwan recently have

[1] Brewer, Judson. 2017. *The Craving Mind: From Cigarettes to Smartphones to Love—Why We Get Hooked and How We Can Break Bad Habits*. New Haven, CT: Yale University Press.

[2] American Psychiatric Association. 2017. *What Is Addiction?* www.psychiatry.org/patients-families/addiction/what-is-addiction. Accessed 9 Dec 2017.

proposed a set of criteria for diagnosing smartphone addiction, but it has not yet been adopted by the APA.[3] The criteria set includes the identification of behavior patterns similar to Internet gaming disorder, gambling disorder, and Internet addiction, all of which differ from substance addiction disorders. But there is a resistance to include smartphone addiction as a diagnosable medical condition. At the time of this writing, the working draft of the World Health Organization's (WHO) 2018 International Classification of Diseases makes no mention of smartphone addiction but categorizes gambling and gaming under "Disorders due to addictive behaviours."[4] It is more likely that health organizations will recognize broader areas of behavioral addiction, such as *technology addiction*, before doing so with narrower terms like smartphone addiction. Internet addiction disorder (IAD) and Internet use disorder (IUD) are both associated with technology addiction, which is defined as "a type of behavior addiction that involves human-machine interaction and is non-chemical in nature."[5] Asian countries such as China, Japan, and South Korea have classified technology addiction as a public health crisis, but the United States continues to see a negligence of mental health treatment options and coverage, despite the Mental Health Parity and Addiction Equity Act, which was passed in 2008 and promised equitable access to mental health treatment.

There are other problems that prevent smartphone addiction from being acknowledged by the medical community. For starters, an addiction might be identified at a point where it "takes over" one's life or, using Brewer's definition, "use despite adverse consequences." By this standard, every student who has stealthily checked his or her phone in class is an addict; researchers at the University of Nebraska at Lincoln reported that despite most professors having a policy regarding the use of digital devices in class, students use their phones for non-class-related purposes an average of 11 times per class meeting, which resulted in 20% of compromised class time.[6] The argument could be made that this is use of the smart-

[3] Lin, Yu-Hsuan, Chih-Lin Chiang, Po-Hsien Lin, Li-Ren Chang, Chih-Hung Ko, Yang-Han Lee and Sheng-Hsuan Lin. 2016. Proposed diagnostic criteria for smartphone addiction. *PLoS One* 11. https://doi.org/10.1371/journal.pone.0163010.

[4] World Health Organization. 2018. https://icd.who.int/dev11/l-m/en#/http%3a%2f%2fid.who.int%2ficd%2fentity%2f1041487064. Accessed on 4 May 2018.

[5] Griffiths, Mark D. 1996. Gambling on the Internet: A brief note. *Journal of Gambling Studies* 12: 471–473.

[6] McCoy, Bernard R. 2016. Digital distractions in the classroom, Phase II: Student classroom use of digital devices for non-class related purposes. *Journal of Media Education* 7: 5–32.

phone despite adverse consequence, though this would label the lion's share of college students as smartphone addicts. Likewise, productivity in the workplace has decreased, and the majority of employers point to the smartphone as the culprit. Characterizing most of the student and working population as addicts is hardly meaningful.

Furthermore, smartphone dependency is wrongly compared to illicit drug usage. In his book, *The Tetris Effect*, Dan Ackerman[7] uses the example of Tetris, a game popular in the 1990s, to explain: "There's a reason why many compelling online experiences, be they games or social media mentions, are often compared to drugs… each of these experiences can be classified as having a pharmatronic quality. That key descriptor refers to a technology experience, typically software-driven, that exhibits the same addictive qualities as a drug." The term *pharmatronic* debuted in a 1994 article in *Wired* magazine, which posited that technology addiction originates with the technology rather than the user. Others disagree. A 2018 TechCrunch article titled "Stop Blaming Apple and Take Responsibility for Tech Addiction" argues that it is the user who ultimately chooses their relationship with technology. The author insists, "No one is forcing consumers to buy an iPhone, use Facebook, stare at Twitch, masturbate to porn, or any of the other millions of things you can do with technology. Everyone one of those actions is a choice we make…"[8] But this argument dismisses the inherently and powerfully addictive properties of technology. Just like an addictive drug, the non-neutrality of technology exacerbates the original choice we made to use that technology. Today, few are still playing Tetris, but the pharmatronic qualities of modern app-based games like Bejeweled and Candy Crush have improved masterfully, capitalizing on our most basic human instincts for gratification.

It is no doubt that using the term *addiction* to describe an overuse and overdependence on smartphones might be hyperbolic, and not to mention, medically inaccurate. But semantics aside, an overreliance on a substance or a behavior can be extremely detrimental to one's overall well-being, especially when it goes unnoticed.

[7] Ackerman, Dan. 2016. *The Tetris Effect: The Game that Hypnotized the World*. New York: PublicAffairs.

[8] Zichermann, Gabe. 2018. Stop blaming Apple and take responsibility for tech addiction. *TechCrunch*, February 4. https://techcrunch.com/2018/02/04/stop-blaming-apple-and-take-responsibility-for-tech-addiction/. Accessed 7 Feb 2018.

Habit, Compulsion, and Addiction

Smartphone behaviors can range from minimal, habitual interactions to an excessive addictive disorder. The APA delineates repeated behaviors into habits, compulsions, and addictions, though there is some overlap in these terms. Habits are at the least harmful end of the spectrum; a habit is routine sequencing that becomes automated. Whether it is a good habit (e.g. saying please and thank you) or bad habit (e.g. biting one's fingernails), the activity is involuntary but still capable of being regulated or stopped. Beyond this is compulsion. The APA defines a compulsive activity as the repetitive behaviors that are executed even if they "significantly interfere with a person's daily activities and social interactions," and compulsive behaviors are in reaction to anxiety or feared situations. For example, someone who locks the house doors at night and then checks them several times before going to bed is exhibiting compulsive behavior. The behavior is to certify that the doors are locked; the fear is that an intruder might break into the house. Similarly, compulsive behavior can be a response to an anxiety, such as the fear of missing something that we might perceive to be important on social media. As represented in Image 3.1, the most extreme genre of behavior is addiction. Whereas compulsive behaviors originate from anxiety or fear, addictive behaviors can be compulsive by nature, but they seek rewards. Often, the afflicted are able to perceive their addictive behaviors but are unable to stop them, just as heavy smartphone users can be aware of their digital behaviors, even if they become detrimental, but are unable to regulate them. Exhibiting Pavlovian-like responses to social media, text message, and email notification alerts might only register as habitual or compulsive behavior, but sometimes these behaviors become uncontrollable, even in the face of consequence. In addition, extreme reliance on smartphones only increases the desire for more usage, as addictive tendencies amplify perceived increases in enjoyment and usefulness.[9] Heavy smartphone usage begets more usage.

In preparing this book, I administered a 30-item survey that was adapted from the Smartphone Addiction Inventory (SPAI) originally created by Yu-Hsuan Lin, Li-Ren Cheng, Yang-Han Lee, Hsien-Wei Tseng,

[9] Bernroider, Edward W. N., Barbara Krumay and Sebastian Margiol. 2014. Not without my smartphone! Impacts of smartphone addiction on smartphone usage. *Semantic Scholar*. https://pdfs.semanticscholar.org/76df/ba5bbb987a46d2abc61d746f766695422bc4.pdf. Accessed 12 Jan 2018.

Image 3.1 A visualization for the hierarchy of behaviors. Source: Author

Terry B.J. Kuo, and Sue-Huei Chen.[10] I surveyed 202 individual smartphone users, ages 15 and older, with diverse backgrounds. The majority of respondents indicated that their smartphone usage has become increasingly more time-consuming. 59.9% agreed or strongly agreed with the statement, "I find that I have been using my smartphone for longer and longer periods of time." Similarly, 57.9% agreed or strongly agreed with the statement that "Over time, I have substantially increased my amount of smartphone usage." As we normalize the growing amounts of time that our devices demand from us, we foster an insatiable thirst for gratification from our devices.

Dr. David Greenfield is Assistant Clinical Professor of Psychiatry at the University of Connecticut School of Medicine and the founder of The Center for Internet and Technology Addiction (CITA), a treatment and rehabilitation center for technology addiction, dependency, and abuse. Dr. Greenfield has been writing on the addictive effects of technology since the late 1990s and is a renowned expert on Internet and technology addiction, under which smartphone addiction is categorized. He has appeared on CNN, *Good Morning America*, *The Today Show*, Fox News, NPR, along with many other media outlets to raise awareness for his cause. Greenfield was the first to coin the oft-used analogy of the smartphone as "the world's

[10] Lin, Yu-Hsuan, Li-Ren Chang, Yang-Han Lee, Hsien-Wei, Tseng, Terry B.J. Kuo and Sue-Huei Chen. 2014. Development and validation of the Smartphone Addiction Inventory (SPAI). *PLoS One* 9: e98312. https://doi.org/10.1371/journal.pone.0098312.

smallest slot machine."[11] I interviewed him for this book, specifically with regard to smartphone addiction. Greenfield acknowledges the problematic terminology surrounding the issue of smartphone dependency, which is rarely parsed into addiction, compulsion, or habit. Instead, we use the term *smartphone addiction* to describe anyone who exhibits frequent smartphone usage. He explains:

> We have nothing on the books, yet, that speak specifically to smartphone addiction. And part of the issue is that this technology has expanded so rapidly—far quicker than anything in the history of technological adoption, from the printing press on down—nothing has been adopted this fast. In 10 years, 90% of the U.S. population has a smartphone. Medicine moves much slower than that.

Being fully aware that smartphone addiction is yet to be officially recognized by professional medical associations, for the sole purpose of this book, I will use the term *smartphone dependency* to mean a level of unmanageable dependence on one's smartphone that is detrimental to one's professional and/or personal relationships. Greenfield speculates that "the vast majority of us are probably compulsive, impulsive, abusive, or overusing our technology at times," but this does not qualify as addiction. He adds that not all smartphone use is equivalent. Responding to an email is different from and arguably more productive than casual gaming or scrolling through social media. Therefore, to justify an addiction, there must be "some deleterious impact of overall functioning." Perhaps this is what makes pinpointing smartphone addiction so challenging. Many of us rely on our smartphones in habitual or even compulsive ways, but in reality, only a small number of us exhibit "unmanageable" smartphone usage (Greenfield estimates this to be only about 6% of the population). Diagnosis as a reflection of smartphone usage time, alone, is not sufficient.

Many researchers have used self-report survey instruments to determine addiction levels with smartphones, and there are numerous quizzes online that claim to diagnose your level of smartphone addiction. However, one major limitation of self-reported data is social desirability bias, which is when participants respond to surveys (such as smartphone addiction quizzes) not truthfully, but instead in a way that portrays themselves in a

[11] Greenfield, David. 2017. Are smartphones really so smart? *The Huffington Post*, March 24. https://www.huffingtonpost.com/dr-david-greenfield/are-smartphones-really-so-smart_b_9526956.html. Accessed 11 Nov 2017.

socially positive light. If a user strongly denies that he or she exhibits a smartphone dependency, then it is likely that his or her answers will reflect this perception and not the objective truth. For instance, in my survey, I asked 202 smartphone users if they have ever experienced close calls with physical danger as a result of smartphone use. 72% disagreed (50% strongly disagreed). When I followed up this question by asking more specifically if they have almost gotten into a car accident while texting and driving or have had a close call with another person or object while walking and texting, most changed their response. The semantics in a self-report survey are highly sensitive and can easily misrepresent data.

Another limitation of testing users' addictiveness through self-report is reference bias or comparing responses using different standards. For instance, a popular online survey developed by Dr. Greenfield often is used to help determine the degree to which people depend on their smartphones. The survey, which was published in *The New York Times*, asks respondents questions like "Do you feel your use of your phone decreases your productivity at times?" This question is a bit leading, directly insinuating that phone use decreases productivity. But in fact, if you are using your smartphone to respond to emails, pay bills, or get directions, it is a highly productive tool. Consider this question if it was reframed as "Does multitasking with your smartphone increase or decrease your productivity?" Now, the question is not leading (giving the respondent the choice of either increase or decrease, rather than presupposition). And, presumably, it gets to the essence of the question, which is determining how smartphone use interferes with tasks. Even still, this revised question is predicated on the assumption that the user, first, is *aware* of his or her productivity levels, and second, understands that a smartphone encourages multitasking, which likely inhibits productivity. The nature of this question remains problematic because as I have observed through my own research, smartphone users typically do not view their smartphone use as an explicit interruption of a task, nor do they view multitasking as a detriment to productivity; rather, it is viewed as a badge of efficiency despite the abundant evidence that multitasking is counterproductive. In fact, of the 202 people I surveyed, 78% disagreed that their smartphone has had a negative effect on school or job performance, and nearly half (49.6%) said that they can text on the phone and talk to others simultaneously. A major obstacle in the identification of smartphone dependency is that self-report surveys measure the participant's perception, not the objective reality, and can easily generate false or misleading data, that if left unpacked, distort the truth.

For perhaps the most accurate collection of self-report data on smartphone addiction, we might return to Dr. Judson Brewer who utilizes a brief diagnostic checklist adapted from the DSM. Because this checklist is substance-agnostic, it presents a more generalized approach to measuring our smartphone dependency, something that might help limit social desirability bias. In the 11-item survey (found below), respondents place a checkmark next to each statement that is true, where X is a placeholder for the activity or substance being measured for its addictiveness. In this context, the X represents smartphone usage.

- Using X for longer than you meant to.
- Wanting to cut down or stop using X but not managing to.
- Spending a lot of time using, or recovering from using, X.
- Cravings and urges to use X.
- Not managing to do what you should at work, home, or school because of X.
- Continuing to use X even when it causes problems in relationships.
- Giving up important social, occupational, or recreational activities because of X.
- Using X again and again, even when it puts you in danger.
- Continuing to use X even when you know you have a physical or psychological problem that could have been caused or made worse by it.
- Needing more of X to get the effect you want (tolerance).
- Developing withdrawal symptoms that can be relieved by using X more.

Tallying one point for each agreeable statement, you can determine the degree to which your smartphone usage registers as addictive behavior: mild (2–3 tallies), moderate (4–5 tallies), severe (6 or more tallies). Yet even with this survey iteration, respondents still must possess an accurate self-awareness of their habits and behaviors.

As part of my data collection for this book, I asked smartphone users whether they agreed or disagreed with the following statement: "I am probably addicted to my smartphone." This question was deliberately posed as the final question of a 30-item survey; by this point, participants had just marked their agreement or disagreement with 29 previous statements that likely increased their self-awareness of their personal smartphone habits and behaviors. Surprisingly, nearly half (46.5%) identified as a smartphone addict. Female participants were more likely to agree with the statement than males, and the self-identified "addicts" spanned ages 15–60. There did not seem to be a discernable trend, whether by age or gender, for those who saw themselves as addicts. And herein lies the problem; the 94 participants who agreed with the statement are likely not addicted to their smartphones. They almost certainly are habitual users and are likely exhibit compulsive behaviors, but addicts? Probably not. We face a complicated pathway for treatment if we cannot precisely assess our behaviors.

With substance addiction, the substance can easily be quantified. With a behavioral addiction, however, measurement becomes difficult and vague, especially if the behavior is an everyday action such as using technology or eating. Therefore, in the context of everyday behaviors, we must examine the reasons for engaging in the behavior, not just that the engagement occurs. Consequently, we cannot make a diagnosis based on observation alone. For instance, it would be wrong to assume that someone who is using his or her phone at inopportune moments, such as during dinner or class, is a smartphone addict. By doing so, we are stripping the term of its seriousness and desensitizing others to their own smartphone dependencies. A 2015 paper in the *Journal of Behavioral Addictions* questions whether we are overpathologizing everyday life. The authors maintain that excessive engagement in an activity or behavior does not necessarily constitute a disorder, but instead argue that it is a "constellation of factors" that are activity-specific that can explain the presence or nonpresence of a medical disorder. They continue:

> [A]ccording to the criteria commonly used to identify behavioral addictions, it is likely that the excessive involvement in any type of activity can be considered as a psychiatric disorder (see Mihordin, 2012, for a critical discussion and an illustration applied to model railroading). This phenomenon is not anecdotic and is susceptible to result in a severe overpathologization of everyday behaviors.[12]

Further complicating the diagnosis of a smartphone addiction is the lack of tangible consequences. An overeater might gain excessive weight; a shopaholic will eventually run out of money. But a smartphone depen-

[12] Billieux, Joel, Adriano Schimmenti, Yasser Khazaal, Pierre Maurage and Alexandre Heeren. 2013. Are we overpathologizing everyday life? A tenable blueprint for behavioral addiction research. *Journal of Behavioral Addictions* 4: 119–123.

dency might only manifest itself as observable behavior marked by time spent on the device, which is not sufficient for diagnosis. Here, the consequences of overuse are more abstract. Smartphone addiction can have different effects on its users, according to the type of usage. Someone who engages heavily in social media use might experience psychological effects such as depression, whereas a nomophobic (someone who fears being without his or her mobile device) might exhibit physiological effects such as an increased level of anxiety. Behavioral addictions are extremely nuanced, and effects are not always pronounced, making it difficult to diagnose the problem.

For a similar perspective, we might refer here to the skepticism that surrounds video game addiction—a behavioral addiction recognized as Internet Gaming Disorder (IGD) by the American Psychological Association.[13] Consider the WHO's beta draft of International Classification of Diseases, which defines gaming disorder in the following way:

> Gaming disorder is characterized by a pattern of persistent or recurrent gaming behaviour ('digital gaming' or 'video-gaming'), which may be online (i.e., over the internet) or offline, manifested by: 1) impaired control over gaming (e.g., onset, frequency, intensity, duration, termination, context); 2) increasing priority given to gaming to the extent that gaming takes precedence over other life interests and daily activities; and 3) continuation or escalation of gaming despite the occurrence of negative consequences. The behaviour pattern is of sufficient severity to result in significant impairment in personal, family, social, educational, occupational or other important areas of functioning.[14]

Substituting the phrase "gaming" for "smartphone use" also would accurately describe a smartphone disorder, but it is unlikely that this will be recognized by the APA any time soon.

Analogous to research on gaming, much of the academic literature on smartphone addiction is conflicting, which garbles the premise that an overreliance on the smartphone can have disastrous consequences on our mental health. No doubt, there are unique cases where the smartphone is responsible for psychological and even physiological ailment, but it remains

[13] American Psychiatric Association [APA]. 2013. *Diagnostic and Statistical Manual of Mental Disorders*. 5th ed. Arlington, VA: American Psychiatric Association.

[14] World Health Organization. 2018. https://icd.who.int/dev11/l-m/en#/http%3a%2f%2fid.who.int%2ficd%2fentity%2f1448597234. Accessed on 4 May 2018.

to be shown that this is indeed causation rather than correlation. Perhaps it is that smartphones are responsible for amplifying, rather than causing, underlying triggers for mental health problems or addictive predisposition, as suggested by the authors of a 2017 study that investigated excessive Internet use: "[D]ysfunctional coping significantly predicts excessive Internet and gaming use, providing support for a self-medication hypothesis of addictive disorders."[15] It's plausible that, for some, the smartphone has become a convenient coping mechanism.

Smartphones, much like video games, can bring extreme behaviors to the foreground. There is a longstanding argument that video games promote violent tendencies in players; aggressive video games can be found in nearly all mass shooters' background histories. Take, for example, the 1999 Columbine school shooting, in which 2 high school students shot and killed 12 students and 1 teacher before taking their own lives. At that time, the massacre was the deadliest mass school shooting in US history. It was later revealed that the gunmen, Eric Harris and Dylan Klebold, played Doom: an online first-person shooter game. This prompted a statement issued by the President of the American Psychological Association, Daniel B. Borenstein, M.D., that reads: "We are convinced that repeated exposure to entertainment violence in all its forms has significant public health implications."[16] In the wake of senseless tragedy, everyone was searching for answers, and video games seemingly provided the most obvious one.

In 2001, relatives of the victims filed a $5 billion lawsuit, naming 25 computer software companies who produce violent video games. According to the lawsuit: "Absent the combination of extremely violent video games and these boys' incredibly deep involvement, use of and addiction to these games and the boys' basic personalities, these murders and this massacre would not have occurred."[17] Yet research on the connection between gaming and violence has produced contradictory findings, and studies have been plagued with methodological problems.

[15] Kuss Daria, Thomas J. Dunn, Klaus Wölfling, Kai W. Müller, Marcin Hędzelek and Jerzy Marcinkowski. 2017. Excessive Internet use and psychopathology: The role of coping. *Clinical Neuropsychiatry* 14: 73–81.

[16] Psychiatric News. 2018. Media violence can harm children, Borenstein says. http://psychnews.org/pnews/00-10-06/media.html. Accessed 2 Feb 2018.

[17] Ward, Mark. 2001. Columbine families sue computer game makers. *BBC News*, May 1. http://news.bbc.co.uk/2/hi/science/nature/1295920.stm. Accessed 2 Feb 2018.

Paradoxically, it is argued that playing video games is both productive, as they provide an outlet for aggression, and harmful, as they simulate a training ground for real-world execution. But as more research is generated, it is becoming apparent that games are instead "situational variables" which heighten or intensify, rather than create, aggression structures in players. In essence, playing a violent video game for a prolonged amount of time can have an additive effect; "This means that those whom already are high in certain factors, mainly hostility, are much more at risk to become more aggressive due to influence by violent video games."[18] Conversely, playing violent video games has no effect on aggression levels of those rated low in hostility. An in-depth analysis of the Columbine school shooting was published in the *American Journal of Forensic Psychiatry*, and its author, Jerald Block, M.D., concluded that Harris and Klebold acted out their aggression not because the game had instilled it in them but because their gaming privileges were revoked by their parents in the year prior to the shooting.

> The problem is not the content but, rather, living one's life in an alternative place without real touch, real smells, or real accomplishment. Such a life may lead to an existential crisis. Who am I—the virtual persona or the real one? Is my life a fiction and, if so, which world is false? Where do I exist, in my body or somewhere on the Internet? Such questions might come to the forefront when one is abruptly severed from that virtual life, triggering a crisis.[19]

This existential line of questioning might also be applied to smartphone users who are co-dependent on their devices. A total investment of ourselves into our devices obscures the real and the virtual, and smartphones have become so engrained in our lives that some, undoubtedly, will argue that the virtual *is* the real. (This new existence has been described as the technoself, which I discuss further in Chap. 7.) If this is the case, we ought to treat technology as an integral part of the self rather than as a toy that can be seized as a form of punishment.

[18] Kooijmans, Thomas A. 2004. Effects of video games on aggressive thoughts and behaviors during development. *Personality Research*. http://www.personalityresearch.org/papers/kooijmans.html. Accessed 3 Feb 2018.

[19] Block, J.J. 2007. Lessons from Columbine: Virtual and real rage. *American Journal of Forensic Psychiatry 28*. http://murderpedia.org/male.H/images/harris-eric/lessons-from-columbine.pdf. Accessed 9 Feb 2018.

A 2017 article published in *The Telegraph* titled "What Will Happen If I Take My Child's Phone Away?" profiled the mother of a 13-year-old boy, who made the drastic decision to confiscate his smartphone for an entire year after it had become the flashpoint for so many arguments in the home. In this particular success story, the boy (ironically, also named Dylan) ultimately was grateful for his mother's extreme parenting intervention, despite many experts' recommendation that regulating smartphone use "does not have to be an all-or-nothing approach."[20] Here, this parenting maneuver paid off, but it is not inconceivable that barring the device from someone who is fraught with latent hostility and has an unhealthy attachment to his phone might only escalate the situation. Devorah Hunter, author of *Screenwise: Helping Kids Thrive (and Survive) in Their Digital World*, acknowledges the delicate position of parents of adolescents and teenagers who exhibit problematic smartphone use: "Honestly, many of us are sick, and I've seen it firsthand, but taking away your teen's phone and telling them it's to protect them is the perfect way to hurt your chances of discussing mental illness with them in the future."[21] Hunter echoes the same arguments made by danah boyd and Jenae Cohn, in which perpetuating the addiction narrative trope is counterproductive to the conversation on mental health, but we must find a way to reconcile the sensibilities of smartphone users with the actual repercussions of addiction.

In reality, the majority of us will not experience the pronounced effects of a behavioral addiction to our smartphones, and statistically speaking, you most likely are not a smartphone addict. But many of us might already feel as though we are "addicted." Whether we interpret this as a figurative or literal meaning of the term, perhaps it is our incessant phone-checking that contributes to this perception. An addiction does not simply emerge from nothing; it is the culmination of an increasing need to be satiated, gratified, or pleased by a substance or behavior. The seemingly innocuous action of checking our phones to see if we missed a call, a text, an email, or some other type of notification might actually be the underpinning of behavioral addiction.

[20] Carey, Tanith. 2017. What will happen if I take my child's phone away? *The Telegraph*, January 16. http://www.telegraph.co.uk/women/family/will-happen-take-childs-phone-away/. Accessed 29 Jan 2018.

[21] Guernsey, Lisa. 2017. Don't take you're your teen's phone. *Slate*, August 10. http://www.slate.com/articles/technology/future_tense/2017/08/smartphones_haven_t_destroyed_a_generation.html. Accessed 1 Sep 2017.

Checking Habits

Smartphones are our personal saviors; they rescue us from uncomfortable and unfamiliar situations, and they are the first line of defense against boredom. We regularly find ourselves habitually reaching for our devices, often without being prompted by a notification and without having a goal in mind. Researchers define this more specifically as a *checking habit*, or "automated behaviors where the device is quickly opened to check the standby screen or information content in a specific application,"[22] and it is arguably more insidious than our directed interactions with smartphones because it affords an instant gratification that is often unknowingly sought after. In every instance of phone-checking, there is potential for gratification; consulting our phone gives us an informational reward that is either obtained or it is not, much like pulling the lever of a slot machine. And we perform these rote machinations until we are rewarded with an interaction: an email, a text, a "like." Something. Anything. Over time, engaging in this gratification-seeking behavior further strengthens our desire to be digitally satiated, and this consequently weakens our ability to exist fully in the natural world, to exist in the now. We toggle endlessly between our digital and analog environments, straddling the two with one foot in the natural and the other in a digital construct.

Actual figures vary widely in terms of the average number of times Americans check their phones each day; the frequently cited 2013 report[23] from the venture capital firm Kleiner Perkins Caufield & Byers found that the average smartphone user checks his or her phone roughly 150 times per day, though more recent studies have shown lower figures. Developers at Apple reported an average of 80 screen unlocks per day in 2016[24]; a study from the same year found an average of 85 checks per day[25]; and my own research from 2017 reported an average of 97 checks per day.

[22] Oulasvirta, Antti, Tye Rattenbury, Lingyi Ma and Eeva Raita. 2012. Habits make smartphone use more pervasive. *Personal and Ubiquitous Computing* 16: 105–114.

[23] Stern, Joanna. 2013. Cellphone users check phones 150×/day and other internet fun facts. *ABC News*, May 29. https://abcnews.go.com/Technology/cellphone-users-check-phones-150xday-and-other-internet-fun-facts/blogEntry?id=19283674. Accessed 9 Jan 2018.

[24] Krstic, Ivan. 2016. How iOS security really works. *Apple, Inc.* http://devstreaming.apple.com/videos/wwdc/2016/705s57mrvm8so193i8c/705/705_how_ios_security_really_works.pdf. Accessed 2 Jan 2018.

[25] Andrews, Sally, David A. Ellis, Heather Shaw and Lukasz Piwek. 2015. Beyond self-report: Tools to compare estimated and real-world smartphone use. *PLoS One* 10. https://doi.org/10.1371/journal.pone.0139004.

It should be noted that determining checking habits on a smartphone is a difficult metric. When studies or analytic firms report "checks" as a measurement, they are essentially referring to the deliberate act of unlocking the phone completely, that is, by swiping open the lock screen or unlocking the phone with a passcode. But the actual number of checking habits is likely much higher, considering tapping the home button or glancing at the screen also should constitute a check. Each time we receive a notification on our home screen, and we peek at our phone, this is a gratification sought and a check that goes unregistered. Perhaps, then, we should consider a different analytic when measuring our propensity for checking our devices. The research firm dscout reports that the number of times we physically touch our smartphones each day is around 2617 times.[26] Though not every "touch" is necessarily a "check," we might assume that the actual number of checks per day lies somewhere between these numbers. Regardless, our checking behaviors beg the question: What is it that makes us reach for our devices so often?

Likening our smartphones to slot machines is a commonly used analogy. When we check our phone or engage in any rewards-based behavior, such as pulling the lever of a slot machine, we are experiencing one of the most basic tenets of behavioral psychology: operant conditioning. This concept, first introduced by B.F. Skinner,[27] suggests that it is through our actions that we experience either a positive or negative reinforcement, which then informs either our continuation or discontinuation of that action. Checking our smartphone for a notification, much like pulling the lever of a slot machine, provides us with either a reward or a punishment in that moment. In the context of smartphone-checking, seeing a notification on the home screen of the device positively reinforces (rewards) the checking behavior, whereas a check that results in seeing no notification negatively reinforces (punishes) the behavior. In essence, the more notifications we field on our devices, the more frequently we will check them. Conversely, if notifications are rare, this might further disengage us from our devices. Arguably, even seeing an undesirable notification, such as a missed call from a marketer or a dreaded email, still qualifies as a reward, as we are positively reinforced for our check, and our immediate need for interaction is satisfied. Part of the lure of checking our phones is that we

[26] Winnick, Michael. 2016. Putting a finger on our phone obsession. *dscout*. https://blog.dscout.com/mobile-touches. Accessed 4 May 2017.

[27] Skinner, B.F. 1938. *The Behavior of Organisms*. New York: Appleton-Century-Crofts.

do not always know whether or not there is a notification waiting for us. According to Dr. David Greenfield, "the variability and unpredictability of rewards are what makes the smartphone so particularly addictive."

There is another layer to this that might help explain our phone-checking behavior: classical conditioning. Russian physiologist Ivan Pavlov was among the first to document his experiments with stimuli-response conditioning. Pavlov observed a response from his dogs (specifically, their salivation) when he presented them with a stimulus (an audible sound) and then food. Both classical and operant conditioning would later become the foundations of the behaviorism movement—an educational approach that was popularized in the early twentieth century and that was concerned primarily with learning outcomes rather than processes. The difference between operant and classical conditioning is that in operant conditioning, our behaviors are shaped by the positive or negative reinforcers that we seek. Classical conditioning, however, maintains that the environment, rather than our actions, shapes behavior. In this sense, we might consider our reactions to actually seeing or hearing a notification come through on our devices. Each smartphone notification, whether it is audible or visual, is a stimulus that invokes a conditioned response. Not surprisingly, the average response time to text notifications is just 90 seconds.

Checking our phones seems like an inconsequential habit, but compulsive phone-checking often has unintended effects. For one, checking habits have been shown to disrupt sleep patterns. A 2016 study conducted by the consultancy firm Deloitte found that 50% of 18–24-year-olds check their smartphones in the middle of the night. The most frequently reported reasons for nocturnal smartphone usage are checking the time, followed by checking for instant messages, social media notifications, then personal emails.[28] It seems our smartphone has a magnetism that overpowers our subconscious. Our rogue smartphone use can lead to sleep disorder, which, if sustained, can have long-term mental and physical side effects.

In addition, our checking habits likely exacerbate our smartphone usage, as they are a gateway to other smartphone-related activities, often unplanned. Smartphone use, even when goal-directed, can become sidetracked easily. One study found that when a primary smartphone task is interrupted by a secondary unplanned task, the original task completion

[28] Deloitte. 2018. There's no place like phone. https://drive.google.com/file/d/0B5buBct5cGDZN1d2T1BWQXF3ck0/view. Accessed 4 Feb 2018.

time can be delayed up to 400%.[29] If smartphones are slot machines, then phone-checking is like walking into the casino; we could easily turn around and walk out, but it is much easier to entertain our impulse to stay and play. Yet according to Daniel Goleman, author of *Emotional Intelligence: Why It Can Matter More Than IQ*, "There is perhaps no psychological skill more fundamental than resisting impulse. It is the root of all emotional self-control, since all emotions, by their very nature, led to one or another impulse to act."[30] It is important to be aware of our own checking habits, as they are the barometer of our impulse control.

Of the 202 people I surveyed for this book, many reported having robust checking habits; 60.4% check their phones while eating a meal, and 65.9% consult their devices while watching television or a movie. 82.2% agreed with the statement, "I sometimes find myself checking my smartphone for no specific reason." More than one-third of respondents (37.1%) agreed that they feel the urge to start using their smartphone again, immediately after they stop using it. Moreover, the majority (63.8%) claimed that reaching for and checking their smartphone is the first thought they have each morning. Although to be fair, when I pose this question in a focus group setting, the respondents usually will defend their actions by adding that they use their phone as an alarm clock, and this explains why they reach for it first thing. But when pressed further, they also admit that they use this moment, first thing in the morning, to check the notifications on their locked screen or their social media feeds to see if they had missed anything overnight. In this sense, the "alarm clock excuse" is more of a disguise for usage—a justification for starting the day off digitally. Indeed, 82% of Millennials check their phone within an hour of waking up.[31] I suspect the smartphone on the bedside table certainly does afford a wake-up alarm and a digital output of the time, but it also acts like a tiny present waiting to be opened each morning.

Consulting our phone more than 100 times throughout the day means that the majority of our phone-checking results in nothing, but it is this intermittent reinforcement schedule that keeps us coming back for more.

[29] Leiva, Luis, Matthias Böhmer, Sven Gehring and Antonio Krüger. 2012. Back to the app: The costs of mobile application interruptions. In *Proceedings of the 14th International Conference on Human-Computer Interaction with Mobile Devices and Services–Mobile HCI* 12: 291–294.

[30] Goleman, Daniel. 2012. *Emotional Intelligence: Why It Can Matter More Than IQ*. Random House, LLC.

[31] Coupofy. 2017. Millennials & their smartphone habits. http://www.coupofy.com/millennials-smartphone-behavior-report-2016/#infographics-title. Accessed 11 Nov 2017.

A variable interval is a type of simple schedule of reinforcement, in which a behavior is reinforced after an *n* amount of time, but not always on that *n* amount.[32] Results are unpredictably looming, which heightens our curiosity and anxiety. For instance, pulling the lever of a slot machine might give us a payout after five minutes of playing the slot machine, or it might take several hours (or not at all). While slot machines are entirely luck-based, reinforcement schedules on our smartphones are not. The amount and type of notifications received will depend heavily on our individual profiles; the frequency at which you are receiving notifications will be informed by variables such as whether or not you are a heavy texter or emailer, receive news notifications from news apps, are active on social media, among other things. This smartphone profile also will likely impact your phone-checking expectations. Frequent texters or highly active social media users might anticipate more notifications because of the nature of their device usage. Of course, notifications can be configured in smartphone settings, which also will alter our reinforcement schedules.

This unpredictability of reinforcement is what makes smartphone-checking so tantalizing. Couple this with a "fear of missing out" on something important, or FOMO, and this largely explains our phone-checking habits. But there is also the biological view of addictive and compulsive behaviors, which indicates there is a chemically induced activation of the brain's neurological pathways that plays a role in this type of behavior reinforcement. Much of the literature on smartphone addiction talks specifically about dopamine, which has been described as the brain's "pleasure chemical." According to Dr. Greenfield, "all addictions whether it's drugs, alcohol, gambling, food, sex, share the activation of mesolimbic pathways that have to do with dopamine and other neurochemicals that are elevated from pleasurable responses." He has even referred to the smartphone as a "portable dopamine dump"[33] because of the relationship between dopamine and pleasure-seeking activities. Dopamine, it is argued, is released in the brain following an enjoyable act, thus using feedback signaling to encourage a continuation of that act. An article in *The Atlantic* titled "Exploiting the Neuroscience of Internet Addiction" describes the process in the following way:

[32] Wikipedia. 2017. Reinforcement. https://en.wikipedia.org/wiki/Reinforcement. Accessed 12 Nov 2017.

[33] Richtel, Matt. 2017. Are teenagers replacing drugs with smartphones? *The New York Times*, March 13. https://www.nytimes.com/2017/03/13/health/teenagers-drugs-smartphones.html. Accessed 11 Nov 2017.

> [A]chieving a goal or anticipating the reward of new content for completing a task can excite the neurons in the ventral tegmental area of the midbrain, which releases the neurotransmitter dopamine into the brain's pleasure centers. This in turn causes the experience to be perceived as pleasurable.[34]

Drugs such as alcohol and cocaine have long been considered to have a direct effect on the brain's dopamine system, and this perpetuates the direct comparisons between drug and smartphone use. (Consider this 2017 article from *The Independent*, which claims "giving your child a smartphone is like giving them a gram of cocaine."[35]) But it is not that drug use itself is inherently pleasurable, but that it invokes neurological processes that perceive it to be so, further capitalizing on the addictive properties of drugs. Although dopamine often is associated solely with pleasure, such as euphoric drug use, more recent research indicates that dopamine might also be present in less-than-desirable behavioral outcomes and disorders. A 2010 study of pathological gamblers found a "recruitment of brain reward circuitry by near-miss outcomes."[36] In other words, near-misses such as *almost* losing all of your money in a betting scenario triggers the same type of dopamine transmission that is triggered by a monetary win. In this example, a near-miss outcome is not necessarily desirable, but it is preferable to the alternate outcome of losing all of our money. Others have suggested that "abnormal dopaminergic signaling" might help explain neuropsychiatric disorders such as ADHD.[37] So, like our neurological processes, dopamine is complex and often misunderstood, yet it is widely cited as the central reason for our smartphone dependency, when in fact, Psychology Professors Christopher Ferguson

[34] Davidow, Bill. 2012. Exploring the neuroscience of internet addiction. *The Atlantic*, July 18. https://www.theatlantic.com/health/archive/2012/07/exploiting-the-neuroscience-of-internet-addiction/259820/. Accessed 11 Nov 2017.

[35] Pells, Rachael. 2017. Giving your child a smartphone is like giving them a gram of cocaine, says top addiction expert. *Independent*, June 7. http://www.independent.co.uk/news/education/education-news/child-smart-phones-cocaine-addiction-expert-mandy-saligari-harley-street-charter-clinic-technology-a7777941.html. Accessed 12 Nov 2017.

[36] Chase, Henry W. and Luke Clark. 2010. Gambling severity predicts midbrain response to near-miss outcomes. *Journal of Neuroscience* 30: 6180–6187.

[37] Li, Lizhuo, Yijun Bao, Songbai He, Gang Wang, Yanlei Guan, Dexuan Ma, Pengfei Wang, Xialong Huang, Shanwei Tao, Dewei Zhang, Qiwen Liu, Yunjie Wang and Jingyun Yang. 2016. The Association Between Genetic Variants in the Dopaminergic System and Posttraumatic Stress Disorder: A Meta-Analysis. *Medicine* 95: e3074. https://doi.org/10.1097/MD.0000000000003074.

and Patrick Markey contend that "on its own, the fact that a pleasurable activity involves dopamine release tells us nothing else about it."[38]

An article in *USA Today* titled "Why You're Addicted to Your Phone… And What to Do About It" is an example of the oversimplification of the dopaminergic process. In it, the author refers to a *60 Minutes* piece in which Anderson Cooper experiences physical effects as a result of not being able to respond to texts on his smartphone, which has been carefully positioned just out of his reach. The conclusion, according to the author of the article, was that "the anxiety was caused by withdrawal from an addiction." He goes on to say:

> But why are addicted in the first place? The answer is we get a massive thrill from what we are addicted to—a reward called dopamine. Dopamine is a brain chemical that literally makes us happy, and it is released every time we receive something on our phones. It could be a text from a loved one, a "like" on Facebook, or a bit of breaking news we find interesting. Dopamine feels good, so we keep checking our phones, hoping to get a little hit of it.[39]

To an extent, this is true, but it is more of an overly simplistic view of our smartphone behaviors than an accurate portrayal of how dependence works. Indeed, interacting with our smartphones can register an effect in our brain's reward center, but our dependency on these devices is more complex than this chemically-based explanation. For a deeper explanation, I spoke with Dr. Susan Weinschenk, chief behavioral scientist at The Team W, a consultancy firm that offers "deep insights on brain and behavioral science."[40] According to Weinschenk, we ought to think of dopamine as the "seeking chemical" rather than a pleasure-seeking one. She goes on to say, "Dopamine causes you to want, desire, seek out, and search… [it] fuels your searching for information."[41] Because we seek more often on

[38] Ferguson, Christopher J. and Patrick Markey. 2017. Video games aren't addictive. *The New York Times*, April 1. https://www.nytimes.com/2017/04/01/opinion/sunday/video-games-arent-addictive.html?_r=0&utm_campaign=Revue%20newsletter&utm_medium=Newsletter&utm_source=revue. Accessed 8 Aug 2017.

[39] Stibel, Jeff. 2017. Why you're addicted to your phone and what to do about it. *USA Today*, July 3. https://www.usatoday.com/story/money/columnist/2017/07/03/why-youre-addicted-your-phone-and-what-do/443448001/. Accessed 8 Aug 2017.

[40] The Team W. 2017. Web site. https://www.theteamw.com/. Accessed 12 Aug 2017.

[41] Weinschenk, Susan. 2018. The dopamine seeking-reward loop, or 'why I can't stop scrolling on my newsfeed.' *The Team W Blog*. https://www.blog.theteamw.com/2018/02/28/the-dopamine-seeking-reward-loop-or-why-cant-i-stop-scrolling-on-my-newsfeed/. Accessed 14 Mar 2018.

our devices than we are satisfied or pleased by them, it is the act of seeking that is pleasurable, not simply the outcome.

Even with a revised understanding of how dopamine works, the idea of smartphone addiction is often explained through a lens of chemical imbalance theory—that, like depression, behavior is dictated by disproportionate levels of specific chemicals in the brain. Take, for example, these news headlines from last year:

> "Kids Who Are Addicted to Smartphones May Have an Imbalance in the Brain"[42]
> "Addicted to Your Phone? It Could Throw Off Your Brain Chemistry"[43]
> "New Study Reveals Chemical Brain Imbalance in Smartphone Addicts"[44]

Characterizing our smartphone-checking behaviors as a neurological deficiency is reckless not simply because it is erroneous but also because it implies that our checking habits are fatalistic. Rather, according to Dr. Joseph Coyle, a Professor of Neuroscience at Harvard Medical School, "Chemical imbalance is sort of last-century thinking. It's much more complicated than that; it's really an outmoded way of thinking."[45] Dr. Weinschenk reiterated this perspective by telling me, "I don't think that when we talk about dopamine we are referring to a chemical imbalance. Our brain is awash in lots of brain chemical. Dopamine is one of them. It's not an imbalance; it's just how our brains work."

If we are to believe that our smartphone behaviors are the direct result of a chemical imbalance, it won't be long before a pharmaceutical response is developed, as has been done with depression and other neurological disorders such as attention deficit disorder (ADD) and attention deficit hyperactivity disorder (ADHD). In fact, studies are already beginning to

[42] Pawlowski, A. 2017. Kids who are addicted to smartphones may have an imbalance in the brain. *Today*, November 30. https://www.today.com/health/teen-smartphone-addicts-have-chemical-imbalance-brains-t119423. Accessed 12 Dec 2017.

[43] Specktor, Brandon. 2017. Addicted to your phone? It could throw off your brain chemistry. *Live Science*, December 1. https://www.livescience.com/61075-internet-smartphone-addiction-chemical-imbalance-brain.html. Accessed 12 Dec 2017.

[44] Friday, Francesca. 2017. New study reveals chemical brain imbalance in smartphone addicts. *Observer*, December 29. http://observer.com/2017/12/new-study-reveals-chemical-brain-imbalance-in-smartphone-addicts/. Accessed 30 Dec 2017.

[45] Spiegel, Alix. 2012. When it comes to depression, serotonin isn't the whole story. *NPR*, January 23. https://www.npr.org/sections/health-shots/2012/01/23/145525853/when-it-comes-to-depression-serotonin-isnt-the-whole-story. Accessed 12 Dec 2017.

denote these imbalances with regard to our mobile devices; a 2017 study published findings that young people who are addicted to their smartphones exhibit lower levels of gamma aminobutyric acid, or GABA, which results in a degradation of motor functions and control as well as the regulation of anxiety. Though the researchers recommend cognitive behavioral therapy as treatment, don't worry, you can also purchase a GABA supplement online to help restore your chemical balance.[46]

Phone Psychosis

The National Institute of Mental Health (NIMH) uses the word psychosis "to describe conditions that affect the mind, where there has been some loss of contact with reality… A person in a psychotic episode may also experience depression, anxiety, sleep problems, social withdrawal, lack of motivation, and difficulty functioning overall."[47] It might seem melodramatic to relate smartphone dependency to psychosis, and in some ways, it is. Suffering a psychotic break can be gravely serious and is triggered by mental illnesses like schizophrenia and bipolar disorder. So, in this sense, calling an overdependence on a smartphone a "psychosis" is admittedly hyperbolic. But ongoing research continues to reaffirm the many ways in which smartphone dependency parallels psychotic episodes and can result in long-term physical, psychological, physiological, and emotional ailment.

Public concern over sustained technology use is not new. In 1760, Italian physician Bernardino Ramazzini was the first to publicize occupational hazards in his textbook, *De Morbis Artificum Diatriba*, which translates to *Diseases of Workers*. Ramazzini's research documented the health hazards of perpetual exposure to harmful chemicals and other irritants that would later inform the first workplace safety standards that we have today; the Occupational Safety and Health Act (OSHA), first signed into law in 1970, governs the safety and welfare of public and private sector workers. Ramazzini also investigated workplace effects on individuals. In particular, he cautioned that those who earned a living as professional writers were especially susceptible to physical repercussion:

[46] Alban, Deane. n.d. GABA supplements for stress and anxiety relief. *Be Brain Fit*. https://bebrainfit.com/gaba-supplements-stress-anxiety/. Accessed 9 Jan 2018.

[47] National Institute of Mental Health. 2018. What is psychosis? https://www.nimh.nih.gov/health/topics/schizophrenia/raise/what-is-psychosis.shtml. Accessed 12 Jan 2018.

> Yet 'tis certain that in each City and Town, vast Numbers of Persons still earn their Bread by writing. The Diseases of Persons incident to this Craft arise from three Causes; first, constant Sitting; secondly, the perpetual Motion of the Hand in the same manner; and, thirdly, the Attention and Application of the Mind... In a word, Writers are depriv'd of all the Advantages arising from moderate and salutary Exercise. Constant writing also considerably fatigues the Hand and whole Arm, on account of the continual and almost tense Tension of the Muscles and Tendons. I knew a Man who, by perpetual writing, began first to complain of an excessive Weariness of his whole right Arm, which could be remov'd by no Medicines, and was at last Succeeded by a perfect Pally of the whole Arm. That he might sustain as little Loss as possible by the Accident, he learn'd to write with his left Hand, which was soon after seiz'd with the same Disorder.[48]

Ramazzini, who is widely considered the father of occupational and human ergonomics, feared that prolonged bodily motions would lead to a "disease of person." The Italian physician substantiated his argument by claiming that "certain violent and irregular motions, and unnatural postures of the body, by reason of which the natural structure of the vital machine is so impaired that serious diseases gradually develop therefrom." Ramazzini was among the first to point out that sustained movements that are "unnatural to the body" could manifest physical diseases, by which we understand to mean physical conditions in today's medical parlance. Ramazzini's account of the man who required amputation of his arm due to "excessive weariness" is undoubtedly a precipitous reaction to discomfort, and so this seems like an absurd scenario. For a more modern example, we might consider the case of an injurious epidemic that spread throughout white-collar office jobs in the early to mid-1990s: carpal tunnel syndrome.

The Mayo Clinic describes carpal tunnel syndrome (CTS) as a condition that causes numbness and tingling in the wrist, hand, and arm, due to "the anatomy of your wrist, health problems, and possible repetitive motions."[49] Interestingly, the term first appeared in medical literature in 1953, but the first treated case of CTS dates back to the mid-1800s. CTS

[48] Human Ergonomics. 2018. Bernardino Ramazzini on the Diseases of Writers. https://www.humanics-es.com/ramazzini.htm. Accessed 9 Jan 2018.

[49] Mayo Clinic. 2018. Carpal tunnel syndrome. https://www.mayoclinic.org/diseases-conditions/carpal-tunnel-syndrome/symptoms-causes/syc-20355603. Accessed 12 Jan 2018.

is caused by a compression of the median nerve that runs through a small opening in the carpal bones in the wrist, which then results in an inflammation and restriction of nerve impulses.[50] The CTS era, incidentally, coincided with the rise of the popularity of the personal computer. It was believed that the increase in the amount of time spent typing on a keyboard had a strong correlation with musculoskeletal problems in the wrist. In 1998 alone, the National Institute of Health reported that three in every 10,000 workers took medical leave from work due to carpal tunnel problems.[51] CTS diagnoses reached a crescendo a year later in 1999, when the Bureau of Labor Statistics reported CTS as having the highest number of median days away from work, outpacing other injuries and illnesses including fractures, bruises, contusions, sprains, strains, heat and chemical burns, cuts, and lacerations.[52] And then, CTS all but vanished.

Today, CTS affects approximately 2–3% of American workers, and we hardly ever hear the term used. So what happened to CTS? Perhaps it was the perception that CTS was idiopathic—that is, the syndrome was spawned out of spontaneity, and personal computers had just become newly ubiquitous. Or, perhaps it was that our newly ubiquitous devices certainly had to have an effect, and CTS made the most sense. Regardless, as computing gained ubiquity, CTS did not, therefore debunking the notion that typing or mouse-clicking lead to a physical disorder of the wrist. In 2006, *The Harvard Gazette* ran the headline, "Computer Use Deleted as Carpal Tunnel Syndrome Cause." The article concluded: "The popular belief that excessive computer use causes painful carpal tunnel syndrome has been contradicted by experts at Harvard Medical School. According to them, even as much as seven hours a day of tapping on a computer keyboard won't increase your risk of this disabling disorder."[53]

[50] WebMD. 2018. Carpal tunnel syndrome. https://www.webmd.com/pain-management/carpal-tunnel/carpal-tunnel-syndrome#1. Accessed 12 Jan 2018.

[51] NBC News. 2018. Why carpal tunnel cases are plummeting. http://www.nbcnews.com/id/23467703/ns/health-health_care/t/why-carpal-tunnel-cases-are-plummeting/#.Wp2-bxMbPOQ. Accessed 12 Jan 2018.

[52] Bureau of Labor Statistics. 2018. Days away from work highest for carpal tunnel syndrome. https://www.bls.gov/opub/ted/2001/apr/wk1/art01.htm. Accessed 12 Jan 2018.

[53] Cromie, William J. 2006. Computer use deleted as carpal tunnel syndrome cause. *The Harvard Gazette*, February 2. https://news.harvard.edu/gazette/story/2006/02/computer-use-deleted-as-carpal-tunnel-syndrome-cause/. Accessed 13 Jan 2018.

Moreover, a further investigation into the causes of CTS found that it originated mainly in workers in manufacturing jobs that require repetitive and unnatural movements for extended lengths of time, such as assembly line work and sewing. As it turns out, the computer keyboard was not the culprit, but it was most definitely blamed for all that lost productivity and workers' compensation cases. Instead, CTS was more likely to manifest itself in people with preexisting conditions such as rheumatoid arthritis and diabetes. The computer keyboard and mouse aggravated, not initiated, this physical condition.

What we ultimately learned from the CTS debacle was that people often use technology as an explanatory factor: Why are there school shootings? Video games. Why can't kids speak properly? Texting. Why are people so inattentive? Phones. The explanation is too easy. Instead, we might think of technology as an *accelerator*. And in some cases, technology (in this case, smartphones) can accelerate actual psychosis. More than one quarter of my survey respondents (27.7%) reported that they feel physical discomfort as a result of excessive smartphone use.

One physical manifestation of smartphone dependency is a condition referred to as "text neck,"[54] which is severe neck pain that results from constantly gazing down at a handheld screen. When a human head is angled downwards at 60°, or the approximate angle of vision when we look down at our smartphones, the weight on the cervical spine increases to roughly 60 pounds—five times the weight of an average adult head.[55] This added exertion on the spine can lead to early degeneration and require corrective surgery. In a 2017 article published in *The Spine Journal*, Drs. Cuellar and Landman testify, "As spine surgeons we have been noticing a rise of patients in our office complaining of neck and upper back pain… One thing they all seem to have in common is prolonged smart phone use."[56]

[54] Khazan, Olga. 2014. What texting does to the spine. *The Atlantic*, November 18. http://www.theatlantic.com/health/archive/2014/11/what-texting-does-to-the-spine/382890/. Accessed 13 Jan 2018.

[55] Bever, Lindsey. 2014. Text neck is becoming an epidemic and could wreck your spine. *The Washington Post*, November 20. https://www.washingtonpost.com/news/morning-mix/wp/2014/11/20/text-neck-is-becoming-an-epidemic-and-could-wreck-your-spine/?utm_term=.ec16c9b9d855. Accessed 13 Jan 2018.

[56] Cuéllar, Jason M. and Todd H. Landman. 2017. "Text neck": An epidemic of the modern era of cell phones? *The Spine Journal* 17: 901–902.

Dr. Dean Fishman is a chiropractor who is best known for his work in this specific area. Fishman founded the Text Neck Institute, and he has been featured on the daytime television show, *The Doctors*. His website, text-neck.com, claims that he was the first to use the term "text neck" and calls it a "global epidemic." In response, Fishman has developed an app for Android-based devices that alerts the smartphone user when the phone is positioned downward at a dangerous angle. The general consensus among physicians is to hold up your smartphone so that you are looking straight ahead, rather than down, when interacting with the device. A simple enough remedy, but a hard habit to break.

Aside from irreversible spine damage, our digital fixation might also threaten our vision. According to Common Sense Media, adults spend an average of ten hours per day in front of various screens—a potent combination of televisions, smartphones, laptop/desktops, and tablets.[57] There is now an abundance of literature in medical journals that suggests our digital gaze can have serious and long-term physical ramifications on our eyes. One condition that has been well-documented is computer vision syndrome (CVS).[58] From the American Optometric Association (AOA) website:

> Computer Vision Syndrome, also referred to as Digital Eye Strain, describes a group of eye and vision-related problems that result from prolonged computer, tablet, e-reader and cell phone use. Many individuals experience eye discomfort and vision problems when viewing digital screens for extended periods. The level of discomfort appears to increase with the amount of digital screen use.[59]

We cannot be entirely sure without having studied longitudinal effects, but there is compelling evidence that our devices contribute to physical discomfort. Chances are, you have probably experienced some or all of the

[57] Sheikh, Knvul. 2017. Most adults spend more time on their digital devices than they think. *Scientific American*, March 1. https://www.scientificamerican.com/article/most-adults-spend-more-time-on-their-digital-devices-than-they-think/. Accessed 13 Jan 2018.

[58] Wen, Patricia. 2013. Tiny screens can be a big strain on eyes. *Boston Globe*, December 16.http://www.bostonglobe.com/lifestyle/health-wellness/2013/12/16/all-that-squinting-tiny-screens-causing-physical-problems-for-some-but-there-are-ways-lessen-harm/14Nmdk9Znjnppv3TMqqg9K/story.html. Accessed 14 Jan 2018.

[59] American Optometric Association. 2018. Computer vision syndrome. https://www.aoa.org/patients-and-public/caring-for-your-vision/protecting-your-vision/computer-vision-syndrome. Accessed 14 Jan 2018.

symptoms associated with CVS, which include headaches, blurred vision, dry eyes, and neck and shoulder pain. Although, the AOA recognizes that "problems like farsightedness and astigmatism, inadequate eye focusing or eye coordination abilities, and aging changes of the eyes, such as presbyopia, can all contribute to the development of visual symptoms when using a computer or digital screen device." Here again, it is likely that this technology exacerbates and accelerates, rather than idiopathically causes, this syndrome.

Another key feature of psychosis is sleep disorder, which also is incurred from smartphone dependency. Despite the growing number of studies that show how smartphones are interrupting sleep patterns, which can lead to severe physical and mental health problems, the majority of smartphone users sleep with their smartphone within reach, which makes midnight texting, scrolling, and emailing possible.[60] Smartphone activity during normal sleep hours results in sleep difficulty, which can decrease academic performance in students,[61] increase morning depletion in workers,[62] and even lead to depression.[63] While some argue that it is the blue light emanating from the device that makes sleep difficult, others claim that smartphone interaction in the middle of the night interrupts the natural circadian rhythm of the body, resulting in carryover effects the next day. Simply put, late-night smartphone use means shorter sleep duration, worse sleep efficiency, and overall lower quality of sleep.[64]

Yet another physical malady that I will mention here is something all of us have probably sensed at one time or another. *Phantom vibration syn-*

[60] Khazan, Olga. 2015. How smartphones hurt sleep. *The Atlantic*, February 24. https://www.theatlantic.com/health/archive/2015/02/how-smartphones-are-ruining-our-sleep/385792/. Accessed 5 Jan 2018.

[61] Grover, Karan, Keith Pecor, Michael Malkowski, Lilia Kang, Sasha Machado, Roshni Lulla, David Heisey and Xue Ming. 2016. Effects of instant messaging on school performance in adolescents. *Journal of Child Neurology* 31: 850–857.

[62] Lanaj, Klodiana, Russell E. Johnson and Christopher M. Barnes. 2014. Beginning the workday yet already depleted? Consequences of late-night smartphone use and sleep. *Organizational Behavior and Human Decision Processes* 124: 11–23.

[63] Lemola, Sakari, Nadine Perkinson-Gloor, Serge Brand, Julia F. Dewald-Kaufmann and Alexander Grob. 2015. Adolescents' Electronic media use at night, sleep disturbance, and depressive symptoms in the smartphone age. *Journal of Youth and Adolescence* 44: 405–418.

[64] Christensen, Matthew A., Laura Bettencourt, Leanne Kaye, Sai T. Moturu, Kaylin T. Nguyen, Jeffrey E. Olgin, Mark J. Pletcher and Gregory M. Marcus. 2016. Direct Measurements of Smartphone Screen-Time: Relationships with Demographics and Sleep. *PLoS One* 11.

drome is the feeling or sensation that your smartphone is ringing, dinging, or vibrating in your pocket or purse when in fact it is not. While not officially designated as a "syndrome," the phenomenon occurs in a staggeringly high number of smartphone users. Studies vary in their estimation, but some have approximated 90% of smartphone users to have experienced a phantom vibration. According to University of Michigan researchers Daniel Kruger and Jaikob Djerf, the likelihood and intensity of experiencing a phantom vibration is "influenced by individual differences in personality, condition, and context."[65] More specifically, their study found a direct relationship between the frequency of perceived phantom vibrations and the level of psychological dependency on the smartphone. Dr. Robert Rosenberger of Georgia Institute of Technology, explains:

> [O]ur general relationships with contemporary technologies lead to significant levels of anxiety. For example, we get anxious as we wait in high anticipation for the next email, social media post, phone call, or text message. In this account, such anxiety causes any number of ill effects, just one of which—and a rather innocent one at that, at least for most users—is phantom vibrations.[66]

The more we pour ourselves into our devices, the more we expect from others, and when that doesn't happen, we are left with a technological angst. Phantom vibrations, according to Rosenberger, are "learned bodily and perceptual habits with the phone." That is, phantom sensations have less to do with the device itself and more with the cognitive anticipation for interaction with others. Our technologies are only vehicles for transmitting this anticipation, and when these vehicles are absent or incapacitated, so are we.

Nomophobia is the fear of being without one's smartphone or mobile device (think of it as no-mo-phone-phobia). If you've ever had a panicked moment of "Where did I leave my phone?," you have experienced nomophobia, at least briefly. A 2015 study conducted by researchers at Iowa State University validated a 20-item nomophobia questionnaire to help you determine your phobia severity. The self-report questionnaire, called the NMP-Q, includes statements such as:

[65] Kruger, Daniel J. and Jaikob M. Djerf. 2017. Bad vibrations? Cell phone dependency predicts phantom communication experiences. *Computers in Human Behavior* 70: 360–364.

[66] Rosenberger, Robert. 2015. An experiential account of phantom vibration syndrome. *Computers in Human Behavior* 52: 124–131.

- If I could not use my smartphone, I would be afraid of getting stranded somewhere
- If I could not check my smartphone for a while, I would feel a desire to check it
- If I did not have my smartphone with me, I would be worried because my family and/or friends could not reach me[67]

In their results, the researchers uncovered four dimensions related to nomophobia: (1) not being able to communicate, (2) losing connectedness, (3) not being able to access information, and (4) giving up convenience—all hallmarks of problematic smartphone use. The responses from this study's participants echoed much of the same sentiment I encountered in my own research. One response from a 20-year-old male college undergraduate reads: "My smartphone is a part of my everyday life. I use it for many reasons, and I am lost without it." For some, the smartphone has become a compass for their lives.

Tangential to nomophobia is another phenomenon common to smartphone users: FOMO, or the fear of missing out. FOMO can assume a variety of different meanings, but it essentially refers to a sense of regret that results from an exclusion from an activity or experience. If you have ever attended an outdoor music festival, you will know that concert goers often have to choose between musical acts performing at the same time on different stages. Festival organizers in Australia countered this problem at their annual FOMO Festival, which uses the tagline: "One stage. No clashes. Party together." Our social media lives fuel our fear of missing out, streaming the activities of our family and friends directly to our smartphones. But FOMO is more likely a function of social anxiety than a uniquely digital disorder. Dr. Barbara Kahn, a Professor at University of Pennsylvania who studies decision-making processes, explains further:

> [T]he thing that [generates] FOMO, the feelings of fear of missing out, it isn't really a fear. It's like a social anxiety, and it's really more about what are your friends doing in building up their social group history that you're missing out on. So it's not really about the experience per se… In all of our experiments, we found that it was really more function of an anxiety that

[67] Yildirim, Caglar and Ana-Paula Correia. 2015. Exploring the dimensions of nomophobia: Development and validation of a self-reported questionnaire. *Computers in Human Behavior* 49: 130–137.

> something might happen in a group experience that will shape the group history in the future that you may not be part of. And that will undermine your group belongingness.[68]

FOMO has existed long before the smartphone era, but our devices have brought it to the forefront of our social consciousness. We experience FOMO more often because we are more aware of that on which we are missing out.

In addition to the physical costs of overdependence, our love affair with smartphones can produce latent psychological and physiological effects as well. There is overwhelming evidence that mobile devices might alter our personalities. For instance, studies have found relationships between heavy smartphone usage and increased prevalence of extraversion,[69] social interaction anxiety,[70] and neuroticism.[71] Researchers have shown that heavy smartphone users can demonstrate observable symptoms of separation anxiety when forced to detach from their devices.[72] We are even affected by our smartphones when we are not explicitly interacting with them. The mere presence of a smartphone has even been correlated with lower levels of empathy; this has been deemed the "iPhone effect."[73]

As the consequential effect of smartphones on our health becomes evident, so too does their non-neutrality. Often, research studies that examine the physical, emotional, psychological, or physiological effects of

[68] Vedantam, Shankar. 2017. When it comes to our lives on social media, 'There's always another story.' *NPR*, April 17. https://www.npr.org/templates/transcript/transcript.php?storyId=524005057. Accessed 18 Jan 2018.

[69] Montag, Christian, Konrad Blaszkiewicz, Bernd Lachmann, Ionut Andone, Rayna Sariyska, Boris Trendafilov, Martin Reuter and Alexander Markowetz. 2014. Correlating personality and actual phone usage. *Journal of Individual Differences* 35: 158–165. https://doi.org/10.1027/1614-0001/a000139.

[70] Lee, Yu-Kang, Chun-Tuan Cheng, You Lin and Zhao-Hong Cheng. 2014. The dark side of smartphone usage: Psychological traits, compulsive behavior and technostress. *Computers in Human Behavior* 31: 373–383. https://doi.org/10.1016/j.chb.2013.10.047.

[71] Ehrenberg, Alexander, Suzanna Juckes, Katherine M. White and Shari P. Walsh. 2008. Personality and self-esteem as predictors of young people's technology use. *Cyberpsychology & Behavior* 11: 739–741. https://doi.org/10.1089/cpb.2008.0030.

[72] Cheever, Nancy A., Larry Rosen, L. Mark Carrier and Amber Chavez. 2014. Out of sight is not out of mind: The impact of restricting wireless mobile device use on anxiety levels among low, moderate, and high users. *Computers in Human Behavior* 37: 290–297.

[73] Misra, Shalini, Lulu Cheng, Jamie Genevie and Miao Yuan. 2014. The iPhone effect: The quality of in-person social interactions in the presence of mobile devices. *Environment and Behavior*: 1–24. https://doi.org/10.1177/0013916514539755.

smartphones get distilled into a soundbite. Facebook makes you unhappy. Texting will ruin your neck. The screen will ruin your eyes. And while these things may be true to an extent, they are highly dependent on a complex makeup of physical, emotional, psychological, and physiological variables. The smartphone has latency—it has the ability to unlock the worst in us, but that doesn't mean necessarily that it will.

References

Ackerman, Dan. 2016. *The Tetris Effect: The Game that Hypnotized the World*. New York: PublicAffairs.

Alban, Deane. n.d. GABA supplements for stress and anxiety relief. *Be Brain Fit*. Accessed January 9, 2018. https://bebrainfit.com/gaba-supplements-stress-anxiety/.

American Optometric Association. 2018. Computer vision syndrome. Accessed January 14, 2018. https://www.aoa.org/patients-and-public/caring-for-your-vision/protecting-your-vision/computer-vision-syndrome.

American Psychiatric Association [APA]. 2013. *Diagnostic and Statistical Manual of Mental Disorders*. 5th ed. Arlington, VA: American Psychiatric Association.

American Psychiatric Association. 2017. *What Is Addiction?* Accessed December 9, 2017. www.psychiatry.org/patients-families/addiction/what-is-addiction.

Andrews, Sally, David A. Ellis, Heather Shaw, and Lukasz Piwek. 2015. Beyond self-report: Tools to compare estimated and real-world smartphone use. *PLoS One* 10 https://doi.org/10.1371/journal.pone.0139004.

Bernroider, Edward W.N., Barbara Krumay, and Sebastian Margiol. 2014. Not without my smartphone! Impacts of smartphone addiction on smartphone usage. *Semantic Scholar*. Accessed January 12, 2018. https://pdfs.semanticscholar.org/76df/ba5bbb987a46d2abc61d746f766695422bc4.pdf.

Bever, Lindsey. 2014. Text neck is becoming an epidemic and could wreck your spine. *The Washington Post*, November 20. Accessed January 13, 2018. https://www.washingtonpost.com/news/morning-mix/wp/2014/11/20/text-neck-is-becoming-an-epidemic-and-could-wreck-your-spine/?utm_term=.ec16c9b9d855.

Billieux, Joel, Adriano Schimmenti, Yasser Khazaal, Pierre Maurage, and Alexandre Heeren. 2013. Are we overpathologizing everyday life? A tenable blueprint for behavioral addiction research. *Journal of Behavioral Addictions* 4: 119–123.

Block, J.J. 2007. Lessons from Columbine: Virtual and real rage. *American Journal of Forensic Psychiatry* 28. Accessed February 9, 2018. http://murderpedia.org/male.H/images/harris-eric/lessons-from-columbine.pdf.

Brewer, Judson. 2017. *The Craving Mind: From Cigarettes to Smartphones to Love—Why We Get Hooked and How We Can Break Bad Habits*. New Haven, CT: Yale University Press.

Bureau of Labor Statistics. 2018. Days away from work highest for carpal tunnel syndrome. Accessed January 12, 2018. https://www.bls.gov/opub/ted/2001/apr/wk1/art01.htm.

Carey, Tanith. 2017. What will happen if I take my child's phone away? *The Telegraph*, January 16. Accessed January 29, 2018. http://www.telegraph.co.uk/women/family/will-happen-take-childs-phone-away/.

Chase, Henry W., and Luke Clark. 2010. Gambling severity predicts midbrain response to near-miss outcomes. *Journal of Neuroscience* 30: 6180–6187.

Cheever, Nancy A., Rosen Larry, L. Mark Carrier, and Amber Chavez. 2014. Out of sight is not out of mind: The impact of restricting wireless mobile device use on anxiety levels among low, moderate, and high users. *Computers in Human Behavior* 37: 290–297.

Christensen, Matthew A., Laura Bettencourt, Leanne Kaye, Sai T. Moturu, Kaylin T. Nguyen, Jeffrey E. Olgin, Mark J. Pletcher, and Gregory M. Marcus. 2016. Direct measurements of smartphone screen-time: Relationships with demographics and sleep. *PLoS One* 11: e0165331.

Coupofy. 2017. Millennials & their smartphone habits. Accessed November 11, 2017. http://www.coupofy.com/millennials-smartphone-behavior-report-2016/#infographics-title.

Cromie, William J. 2006. Computer use deleted as carpal tunnel syndrome cause. *The Harvard Gazette*, February 2. Accessed January 13, 2018. https://news.harvard.edu/gazette/story/2006/02/computer-use-deleted-as-carpal-tunnel-syndrome-cause/.

Cuéllar, Jason M., and Todd H. Landman. 2017. "Text neck": An epidemic of the modern era of cell phones? *The Spine Journal* 17: 901–902.

Davidow, Bill. 2012. Exploring the neuroscience of internet addiction. *The Atlantic*, July 18. Accessed November 11, 2017. https://www.theatlantic.com/health/archive/2012/07/exploiting-the-neuroscience-of-internet-addiction/259820/.

Deloitte. 2018. There's no place like phone. Accessed February 4, 2018. https://drive.google.com/file/d/0B5buBct5cGDZN1d2T1BWQXF3ck0/view.

Ehrenberg, Alexander, Suzanna Juckes, Katherine M. White, and Shari P. Walsh. 2008. Personality and self-esteem as predictors of young people's technology use. *Cyberpsychology & Behavior* 11: 739–741. https://doi.org/10.1089/cpb.2008.0030.

Ferguson, Christopher J., and Patrick Markey. 2017. Video games aren't addictive. *The New York Times*, April 1. Accessed August 8, 2017. https://www.nytimes.com/2017/04/01/opinion/sunday/video-games-arent-addictive.html?_r=0&utm_campaign=Revue%20newsletter&utm_medium=Newsletter&utm_source=revue.

Friday, Francesca. 2017. New study reveals chemical brain imbalance in smartphone addicts. *Observer*, December 29. Accessed December 30, 2017. http://

observer.com/2017/12/new-study-reveals-chemical-brain-imbalance-in-smartphone-addicts/.

Goleman, Daniel. 2012. *Emotional Intelligence: Why It Can Matter More Than IQ.* Random House, LLC.

Greenfield, David. 2017. Are smartphones really so smart? *The Huffington Post*, March 24. Accessed November 11, 2017. https://www.huffingtonpost.com/dr-david-greenfield/are-smartphones-really-so-smart_b_9526956.html.

Griffiths, Mark D. 1996. Gambling on the Internet: A brief note. *Journal of Gambling Studies* 12: 471–473.

Grover, Karan, Keith Pecor, Michael Malkowski, Lilia Kang, Sasha Machado, Roshni Lulla, David Heisey, and Ming Xue. 2016. Effects of instant messaging on school performance in adolescents. *Journal of Child Neurology* 31: 850–857.

Guernsey, Lisa. 2017. Don't take you're your teen's phone. *Slate*, August 10. Accessed September 1, 2017. http://www.slate.com/articles/technology/future_tense/2017/08/smartphones_haven_t_destroyed_a_generation.html.

Human Ergonomics. 2018. Bernardino Ramazzini on the diseases of writers. Accessed January 9, 2018. https://www.humanics-es.com/ramazzini.htm.

Khazan, Olga. 2014. What texting does to the spine. *The Atlantic*, November 18. Accessed January 13, 2018. http://www.theatlantic.com/health/archive/2014/11/what-texting-does-to-the-spine/382890/.

———. 2015. How smartphones hurt sleep. *The Atlantic*, February 24. Accessed January 5, 2018. https://www.theatlantic.com/health/archive/2015/02/how-smartphones-are-ruining-our-sleep/385792/.

Kooijmans, Thomas A. 2004. Effects of video games on aggressive thoughts and behaviors during development. *Personality Research*. Accessed February 3, 2018. http://www.personalityresearch.org/papers/kooijmans.html.

Krstic, Ivan. 2016. How iOS security really works. *Apple, Inc.* Accessed January 2, 2018. http://devstreaming.apple.com/videos/wwdc/2016/705s57mrvm8so193i8c/705/705_how_ios_security_really_works.pdf.

Kruger, Daniel J., and Jaikob M. Djerf. 2017. Bad vibrations? Cell phone dependency predicts phantom communication experiences. *Computers in Human Behavior* 70: 360–364.

Kuss, Daria, Thomas J. Dunn, Klaus Wölfling, Kai W. Müller, Marcin Hędzelek, and Jerzy Marcinkowski. 2017. Excessive Internet use and psychopathology: The role of coping. *Clinical Neuropsychiatry* 14: 73–81.

Lanaj, Klodiana, Russell E. Johnson, and Christopher M. Barnes. 2014. Beginning the workday yet already depleted? Consequences of late-night smartphone use and sleep. *Organizational Behavior and Human Decision Processes* 124: 11–23.

Lee, Yu-Kang, Chun-Tuan Cheng, You Lin, and Zhao-Hong Cheng. 2014. The dark side of smartphone usage: Psychological traits, compulsive behavior and technostress. *Computers in Human Behavior* 31: 373–383. https://doi.org/10.1016/j.chb.2013.10.047.

Leiva, Luis, Matthias Böhmer, Sven Gehring, and Antonio Krüger. 2012. Back to the app: The costs of mobile application interruptions. In *Proceedings of the 14th International Conference on Human-Computer Interaction with Mobile Devices and Services—Mobile HCI 12*, 291–294.

Lemola, Sakari, Nadine Perkinson-Gloor, Serge Brand, Julia F. Dewald-Kaufmann, and Alexander Grob. 2015. Adolescents' electronic media use at night, sleep disturbance, and depressive symptoms in the smartphone age. *Journal of Youth and Adolescence* 44: 405–418.

Li, Lizhuo, Yijun Bao, Songbai He, Gang Wang, Yanlei Guan, Dexuan Ma, Pengfei Wang, et al. 2016. The association between genetic variants in the dopaminergic system and posttraumatic stress disorder: A meta-analysis. *Medicine* 95: e3074. https://doi.org/10.1097/MD.0000000000003074.

Lin, Yu-Hsuan, Li-Ren Chang, Yang-Han Lee, Hsien-Wei Tseng, Terry B.J. Kuo, and Sue-Huei Chen. 2014. Development and validation of the Smartphone Addiction Inventory (SPAI). *PLoS One* 9: e98312. https://doi.org/10.1371/journal.pone.0098312.

Lin, Yu-Hsuan, Chih-Lin Chiang, Po-Hsien Lin, Li-Ren Chang, Chih-Hung Ko, Yang-Han Lee, and Sheng-Hsuan Lin. 2016. Proposed diagnostic criteria for smartphone addiction. *PLoS One* 11. https://doi.org/10.1371/journal.pone.0163010.

Mayo Clinic. 2018. Carpal tunnel syndrome. Accessed January 12, 2018. https://www.mayoclinic.org/diseases-conditions/carpal-tunnel-syndrome/symptoms-causes/syc-20355603.

McCoy, Bernard R. 2016. Digital distractions in the classroom, Phase II: Student classroom use of digital devices for non-class related purposes. *Journal of Media Education* 7: 5–32.

Misra, Shalini, Lulu Cheng, Jamie Genevie, and Miao Yuan. 2014. The iPhone effect: The quality of in-person social interactions in the presence of mobile devices. *Environment and Behavior*: 1–24. https://doi.org/10.1177/0013916514539755.

Montag, Christian, Konrad Blaszkiewicz, Bernd Lachmann, Ionut Andone, Rayna Sariyska, Boris Trendafilov, Martin Reuter, and Alexander Markowetz. 2014. Correlating personality and actual phone usage. *Journal of Individual Differences* 35: 158–165. https://doi.org/10.1027/1614-0001/a000139.

National Institute of Mental Health. 2018. What is psychosis? Accessed January 12, 2018. https://www.nimh.nih.gov/health/topics/schizophrenia/raise/what-is-psychosis.shtml.

NBC News. 2018. Why carpal tunnel cases are plummeting. Accessed January 12, 2018. http://www.nbcnews.com/id/23467703/ns/health-health_care/t/why-carpal-tunnel-cases-are-plummeting/#.Wp2-bxMbPOQ.

Oulasvirta, Antti, Tye Rattenbury, Lingyi Ma, and Eeva Raita. 2012. Habits make smartphone use more pervasive. *Personal and Ubiquitous Computing* 16: 105–114.

Pawlowski, A. 2017. Kids who are addicted to smartphones may have an imbalance in the brain. *Today*, November 30. Accessed December 12, 2017. https://www.today.com/health/teen-smartphone-addicts-have-chemical-imbalance-brains-t119423.

Pells, Rachael. 2017. Giving your child a smartphone is like giving them a gram of cocaine, says top addiction expert. *Independent*, June 7. Accessed November 12, 2017. http://www.independent.co.uk/news/education/education-news/child-smart-phones-cocaine-addiction-expertmandy-saligari-harley-street-charter-clinic-technology-a7777941.html.

Psychiatric News. 2018. Media violence can harm children, Borenstein says. Accessed February 2, 2018. http://psychnews.org/pnews/00-10-06/media.html.

Richtel, Matt. 2017. Are teenagers replacing drugs with smartphones? *The New York Times*, March 13. Accessed November 11, 2017. https://www.nytimes.com/2017/03/13/health/teenagers-drugs-smartphones.html.

Rosenberger, Robert. 2015. An experiential account of phantom vibration syndrome. *Computers in Human Behavior* 52: 124–131.

Sheikh, Knvul. 2017. Most adults spend more time on their digital devices than they think. *Scientific American*, March 1. Accessed January 13, 2018. https://www.scientificamerican.com/article/most-adults-spend-more-time-on-their-digital-devices-than-they-think/.

Skinner, B.F. 1938. *The Behavior of Organisms*. New York: Appleton-Century-Crofts.

Specktor, Brandon. 2017. Addicted to your phone? It could throw off your brain chemistry. *Live Science*, December 1. Accessed December 12, 2017. https://www.livescience.com/61075-internet-smartphone-addiction-chemical-imbalance-brain.html.

Spiegel, Alix. 2012. When it comes to depression, serotonin isn't the whole story. *NPR*, January 23. Accessed December 12, 2017. https://www.npr.org/sections/health-shots/2012/01/23/145525853/when-it-comes-to-depression-serotonin-isnt-the-whole-story.

Stern, Joanna. 2013. Cellphone users check phones 150×/day and other internet fun facts. *ABC News*, May 29. Accessed January 9, 2018. https://abcnews.go.com/Technology/cellphone-users-check-phones-150xday-and-other-internet-fun-facts/blogEntry?id=19283674.

Stibel, Jeff. 2017. Why you're addicted to your phone and what to do about it. *USA Today*, July 3. Accessed August 8, 2017. https://www.usatoday.com/story/money/columnist/2017/07/03/why-youre-addicted-your-phone-and-what-do/443448001/.

The Team W. 2017. Web site. Accessed August 12, 2017. https://www.theteamw.com/.

Vedantam, Shankar. 2017. When it comes to our lives on social media, 'There's always another story.' *NPR*, April 17. Accessed January 18, 2018. https://www.npr.org/templates/transcript/transcript.php?storyId=524005057.

Ward, Mark. 2001. Columbine families sue computer game makers. *BBC News*, May 1. Accessed February 2, 2018. http://news.bbc.co.uk/2/hi/science/nature/1295920.stm.

WebMD. 2018. Carpal tunnel syndrome. Accessed January 12, 2018. https://www.webmd.com/pain-management/carpal-tunnel/carpal-tunnel-syndrome#1.

Weinschenk, Susan. 2018. The dopamine seeking-reward loop, or 'why I can't stop scrolling on my newsfeed'. *The Team W Blog*. Accessed March 14, 2018. https://www.blog.theteamw.com/2018/02/28/the-dopamine-seeking-reward-loop-or-why-cant-i-stop-scrolling-on-my-newsfeed/.

Wen, Patricia. 2018. Tiny screens can be a big strain on eyes. *Boston Globe*, December 16. Accessed January 14, 2018. http://www.bostonglobe.com/lifestyle/health-wellness/2013/12/16/all-that-squinting-tiny-screens-causing-physical-problems-for-some-but-there-are-ways-lessen-harm/14Nmdk9Znjnppv3TMqqg9K/story.html.

Wikipedia. 2017. Reinforcement. Accessed November 12, 2017. https://en.wikipedia.org/wiki/Reinforcement.

Winnick, Michael. 2016. Putting a finger on our phone obsession. *dscout*. Accessed May 4, 2017. https://blog.dscout.com/mobile-touches.

World Health Organization. 2018. Accessed May 4, 2018. https://icd.who.int/dev11/l-m/en#/http%3a%2f%2fid.who.int%2ficd%2fentity%2f1041487064.

Yildirim, Caglar, and Ana-Paula Correia. 2015. Exploring the dimensions of nomophobia: Development and validation of a self-reported questionnaire. *Computers in Human Behavior* 49: 130–137.

Zichermann, Gabe. 2018. Stop blaming Apple and take responsibility for tech addiction. *TechCrunch*, February 4. Accessed February 7, 2018. https://techcrunch.com/2018/02/04/stop-blaming-apple-and-take-responsibility-for-tech-addiction/.

CHAPTER 4

Use. Gratify. Repeat.

Uses and gratifications theory (UGT) is a mass communications theory that explains how consumers select, use, and are gratified by media. The origins of this theory can be traced back to the early 1940s when researchers sought to better understand the habits of radio listeners. Over time, the theory has been applied to various forms of media as it has reached ubiquity, including telephones, television, computer use, Internet use, and now smartphone use. Uses and Gratifications Theory determines how media is consumed (the *use*) and why it is sought after and obtained (the *gratification*). We can use UGT to better understand how and why we use our smartphones, which have a wide range of uses and functions.

While there are many different types of uses and gratifications associated with each use (which I will discuss in this chapter), we might broadly characterize all smartphone usage as being either *process* or *social*.[1] Process use is primarily nonsocial; this includes information-seeking, entertainment, and productivity tasks. Social use, as it implies, includes any behavior with social engagement features, such as social media apps or messaging. (Voice calling would be included in the social use category, though this usage is vastly different from the typical smartphone uses. Research on this feature is an entirely different animal, and so we will exclude voice calling from our analysis of usage and gratification.) With the seemingly endless

[1] Elhai, Jon D., Jason C. Levine, Robert D. Dvorak and Brian J. Hall. 2017. Non-social features of smartphone use are most related to depression, anxiety, and problematic smartphone use. *Computers in Human Behavior* 69: 75–82.

A. J. Reid, *The Smartphone Paradox*,
https://doi.org/10.1007/978-3-319-94319-0_4

combinations of process and social use, each user develops a unique signature for his or her smartphone usage; just imagine the differences between usage patterns of a 40-year-old and a 14-year-old. This variability makes it impossible to make generalizations to the entire population.

Just as there are many uses for smartphones, there are different combinations of gratifications that can be obtained. A 2014 study[2] characterized gratifications obtained from smartphones into four categories: cognitive, hedonic, integrative, and social interactive. Cognitive gratification relates to information acquisition (e.g. Googling the answer to a question); hedonic gratification includes entertainment and joy-seeking experiences (e.g. watching YouTube videos for enjoyment); integrative and social interactive gratifications are similar in that both involve social networks, but integrative gratification is more individual-centered (e.g. updating statuses for identity-forming), whereas social interactive gratifications are derived from interacting with others online (e.g. scrolling social media feeds). Our smartphone behaviors will toggle between the process and the social, thereby informing the various gratifications sought and obtained. Uses and Gratifications Theory is a common language that provides a clear framework for understanding our habits of how we consult our smartphones, why we do it, and what we gain from it.

Sometimes, we engage with our devices with a goal-directed behavior in mind, but often, we are just pulled into their gravitational orbit. This usually is the result of either an endogenous or an exogenous interruption. Endogenous interruptions occur "when the user's own thoughts drift toward a smartphone-related activity," whereas exogenous interruptions are triggered by audible and visual cues from the smartphone.[3] Endogenous interruptions are intrinsic, making them harder to understand why we sometimes gravitate towards our devices without being prompted. Sherry Turkle laments, "When people are alone, even for a few moments, they fidget and reach for a device."[4] These self-inflicted interruptions usually are not goal-directed. Exogenous interruptions, on the other hand, are

[2] Ha, Young Wook, Jimin Kim, Christian Fernando Libaque-Saenz, Younghoon Chang and Myeong Cheol Park. 2014. Use and gratifications of mobile SNSs: Facebook and KakaoTalk in Korea. *Telematics and Informatics* 32: 425–438.

[3] Wilmer, Henry H. and Jason M. Chein. 2016. Mobile technology habits: Patterns of association among device usage, intertemporal preference, impulse control, and reward sensitivity. *Psychonomic Bulletin & Review* 23: 1607–1614.

[4] Turkle, Sherry. 2013. *Alone Together: Why We Expect More From Technology and Less From Each Other*. Cambridge, MA: Perseus.

purposeful. Notifications let us know when we have received a text message, an email, or if someone liked our post on social media, which positively reinforces our checking behaviors. Or, as Nicholas Carr puts it, "We want to be interrupted, because each interruption brings us a valuable piece of information." He further likens us to "lab rats constantly pressing levers to get tiny pellets of social or intellectual nourishment."[5] It's simple, really. Our smartphone beguiles us with what we perceive to be important, and our human nature compels us to pursue it. A 2016 study that examined smartphone usage and gratification concludes:

> In considering the question "What drives people to engage with their smartphones?", one might offer two seemingly reasonable answers: (1) individuals are unable to withhold the impulse to check, whether driven by endogenous thoughts or exogenous cues, and (2) individuals engage with their phones in an attempt to seek out a rewarding stimulus. Ultimately, the present evidence leads us to the conclusion that mobile technology habits, such as frequent checking, are driven most strongly by uncontrolled impulses and not by the desire to pursue rewards.[6]

When it comes to our smartphone usage, we are impulsive rather than deliberate. Receiving exogenous interruptions and notifications confirms that we are in fact desirable to someone else, and this makes us feel good and keeps us coming back for more. But it is not just this bite-sized reward that we find pleasurable; checking our phones and discovering that we have not missed anything also provides us with a gratification, momentarily wiping the slate clean and temporarily extending our analog lives until we feel the next impulse to check.

Instant Gratification

Researchers have been studying the benefits of delayed gratification since the 1960s. While at Stanford University, Walter Mischel conducted a study in which he gave the 4–6-year-old participants a choice: they could have a marshmallow in that instant (an impulsive, small reward), or they could

[5] Carr, Nicholas G. 2011. *The Shallows: What the Internet is Doing to Our Brains.* New York: W.W. Norton & Company.

[6] Wilmer, Henry H. and Jason M. Chein. 2016. Mobile technology habits: Patterns of association among device usage, intertemporal preference, impulse control, and reward sensitivity. *Psychonomic Bulletin & Review* 23: 1607–1614.

wait approximately 15 minutes and receive two marshmallows (a delayed, larger reward). This study has been recreated many times over the years among different populations and using different types of rewards. The finding is generally consistent; a correlation exists between the ability to self-regulate willpower by deferring to the second reward and success later in life, as measured by higher SAT scores,[7] a disinclination towards aggressiveness,[8] and interpersonal relationships.[9] So delaying gratification presumably indicates self-control, which is a highly desirable quality. But some argue that delaying gratification is not always best. For example, a 2004 study[10] found that the effect of delayed gratification hinges on the perceived enjoyment of the product being consumed. In her article titled "What's So Bad About Instant Gratification?," Alexandra Samuel surmises that if a product is highly desirable, the delay time enhances the enjoyment payoff, but if the product or outcome is less desirable, delaying its arrival only "imposes all the aggravation of waiting without the ultimate payoff." Although we can use our smartphones in deliberate and pragmatic ways, often, we defer to them as tools of preoccupation, aimlessly scrolling, swiping, and tapping. In this attention economy, where our devices constantly push notifications, it is important to manage our expectations to be gratified. Perhaps waiting to read that text message or comment on social media would be more enjoyable if delayed. Then again, this is only the case if that message is a desirable one. I wonder if Professor Mischel could have predicted a society where everyone is receiving a constant barrage of notifications coming right from their pockets. Indeed, the majority (61.4%) of respondents in my survey agreed that they felt a sense of gratification after checking their phone and seeing a notification of any kind. We are getting fat on marshmallows.

[7] Shoda, Yuichi, Walter Mischel and Philip K. Peake. 1990. Predicting adolescent cognitive and self-regulatory competencies from preschool delay of gratification: Identifying diagnostic conditions. *Developmental Psychology* 26: 978–986.

[8] Winderman, Lea. 2014. Acing the marshmallow test. *American Psychological Association*, December 2014. http://www.apa.org/monitor/2014/12/marshmallow-test.aspx. Accessed 2 Feb 2018.

[9] Ayduk, Ozlem, Rodolfo Mendoza-Denton, Walter Mischel, Geraldine Downey, G., Philip K. Peake and Monica Rodriguez. 2000. Regulating the interpersonal self: Strategic self-regulation for coping with rejection sensitivity. *Journal of Personality and Social Psychology* 79: 776–792.

[10] Nowlis, Stephen, Naomi Mandel and Deborah Brown McCabe. 2004. The effect of a delay between choice and consumption on consumption enjoyment. *Journal of Consumer Research* 31: 502–510.

Perhaps we should embrace the idea of slowness instead. Milan Kundera is a Czech-born French novelist whose popularity climaxed in the United States during the early 1980s when his most notable work, *The Unbearable Lightness of Being*, was translated from French to English. Kundera is viewed as a sort of diet-Nietzsche, writing about politics, love, and society through a philosophical lens, and he has been described as "a writer in love with paradox,"[11] perfectly situating him within the argument of this book. A common theme that runs throughout his body of work is man's struggle with modernity; in particular, his novel, *Slowness*, explores its characters' relationships with the gratification that modern technologies provide. Eerily foreshadowing our imminent coexistence with the Internet, Kundera's 1995 publication of *Slowness* coincided with the release of the popular web browser, Netscape (which would later become Internet Explorer). By the mid-1990s, people had just begun to log on for the first time, galvanizing a new way of life.

In the opening chapter of *Slowness*, the narrator asks "Why has the pleasure of slowness disappeared? … a person with nothing to do is frustrated, bored, is constantly searching for the activity he lacks."[12] The narrative thread that runs throughout the novel is the contemplation of technology's impact on *speed*. The narrator, who is en route to a French chateau, laments:

> Speed is the form of ecstasy the technical revolution has bestowed on man. As opposed to a motorcyclist, the runner is always present in his body, forever required to think about his blisters, his exhaustion; when he runs he feels his weight, his age, more conscious than ever of himself and of his time of life. This all changes when man delegates the faculty of speed to a machine: from then on, his own body is outside the process, and he gives over to a speed that is noncorporeal, nonmaterial, pure speed, speed itself, ecstasy speed.

With modernization comes speed, but it seems we are never fully satisfied. In transportation, steam-powered engines enabled safer and more efficient travel than horses could provide, but the locomotive eventually was replaced by the automobile and the internal combustion engine. Traveling

[11] Rosen, Jonathan. 2015. Does Milan Kundera still matter? *The Atlantic*, July/August 2015. https://www.theatlantic.com/magazine/archive/2015/07/does-milan-kundera-still-matter/395237/. Accessed 2 Feb 2018.

[12] Kundera, Milan. 1995. *Slowness*. New York: HarperCollins Publishers.

across country would have taken months in the early 1800s,[13] but newer forms of transportation made it possible in mere days. Today, we bristle at the thought of a 6-hour flight from New York City to Los Angeles. Subsequently, five different American airlines have vowed supersonic air travel by 2023, which would cut air travel times in half. The Virgin Concorde promises a cruising speed of Mach 2.2, allowing it to complete a flight between New York and Paris in only three-and-a-half hours.[14] In California and Nevada, capitalists are pioneering Hyperloop transportation, which would circumvent aboveground traffic congestion by hurling individual pods, known as "electric skates," through underground tunnels at speeds in excess of 700 miles per hour. But our need for speed is not unique to transportation; nearly every aspect of our lives is on-demand.

Our food is on-demand. The emergence of fast food restaurants led to the installation of drive-thrus, which now have two lanes for faster service. Smartphone apps from restaurants like McDonald's and Wendy's allow customers to pre-order their food and pick it up on-site. If that is too time-consuming, Grubhub and Postmates excise the inconvenience of the drive-thru by delivering food right to your doorstep. Postmates even goes beyond food delivery; their tagline is "Anything, anywhere, anytime. We get it."

Our entertainment is on-demand. Streaming content services like Netflix, Hulu, Spotify, and iTunes mean that for a small subscription fee, we can purchase our way out of having to wait for our favorite shows or our favorite songs to show up on the television or the radio. We are no longer at the mercy of broadcast companies and radio programmers. If we want to watch it or listen to it, we can do so, uninterrupted and commercial-free. In fact, why wait for the weekly installment of *Downton Abbey* one episode at a time when you can binge-watch the entire season in one night and have Postmates deliver your dinner and a bottle of wine?

Our shopping is on-demand. A Pew Research Center study has found that nearly 8 in 10 Americans shop online, with more than half doing so

[13] Richard, Michael G. 2012. How fast could you travel across the U.S. in the 1800s? *Mother Nature Network*, December 26. https://www.mnn.com/green-tech/transportation/stories/how-fast-could-you-travel-across-the-us-in-the-1800s. Accessed 21 Jan 2018.

[14] Reid, David. 2017. Supersonic flight promised by 2023 as Boom announces airline orders. *CNBC*, June 20. https://www.cnbc.com/2017/06/20/supersonic-flight-2023-as-boom-announces-airline-orders.html. Accessed 30 Jan 2018.

from a mobile device.[15] In 2017, Amazon was responsible for nearly half of all e-commerce sales, which amount to roughly 4% of total retail sales in the United States.[16] A Prime Membership with Amazon will guarantee free 2-day shipping on Prime eligible items and free same-day delivery for some zip codes. Amazon currently is experimenting with its even fast service, Prime Air, which is "a delivery system from Amazon designed to safely get packages to customers in 30 minutes or less using unmanned aerial vehicles, also called drones." And who needs the local grocery store when you can use AmazonFresh, which has thousands of household products readily available for same-day or next-day delivery straight to your door. Local and global marketplaces are just a tap away.

Our information is on-demand. In 2016, Google commissioned a study of more than 10,000 mobile websites and found that more than half (53%) of mobile sites are abandoned if taking longer than three seconds to load.[17] Website loading speed, the study argues, is directly related to revenue. If the user cannot see the webpage in under five seconds, he or she likely will navigate to another page, which incentivizes online retailers and ad providers to make every second count. Mobile users are especially notorious for expecting near instantaneous responses from their devices.

And lastly, our education is on-demand. ECPI University is located throughout the southeast in Virginia, North Carolina, South Carolina, and Florida. In 2018, the fully online program was ranked in the top 10% of all online schools by *U.S. News & World Report*, and *Military Times* named it one of the nation's best colleges for active duty and veteran students. According to its website, ECPI offers a four-year bachelor's degree in only two and a half years. The program, referred to as Zero to Bachelor's in 2.5, is described as such:

> At ECPI University, we operate on an accelerated schedule. This allows you the opportunity to earn a Bachelor's Degree in 2.5 years or an Associate's in just 1.5 years. The benefit to you is obvious: you could finish college sooner

[15] Smith, Aaron and Monica Anderson. 2016. Online shopping and e-commerce. *Pew Research Center*. http://www.pewinternet.org/2016/12/19/online-shopping-and-e-commerce/. Accessed 3 Feb 2018.

[16] Thomas, Lauren. 2018. Amazon grabbed 4 percent of all US retail sales in 2017, new study says. *CNBC*, January 3. https://www.cnbc.com/2018/01/03/amazon-grabbed-4-percent-of-all-us-retail-sales-in-2017-new-study.html. Accessed 5 Jan 2018.

[17] Double Click. 2018. The need for mobile speed. How mobile latency impacts publisher revenue. https://www.doubleclickbygoogle.com/articles/mobile-speed-matters/. Accessed 12 Jan 2018.

> and begin earning a professional salary. It's simple. At most colleges and universities, there is a tremendous amount of "down time"—fall break, holiday break, spring break, and summer vacation. It all adds up. Sure, it's nice to have time off, but ECPI University students aren't interested in long breaks. They want to earn their degree as soon as possible so they can begin their careers.[18]

If two and a half years is too long, there are even faster options. DegreeQuery.com lists three online schools at which you can earn a four-year degree in as little as nine months.[19] But the fundamental problem with accelerated learning programs is that education is an intellectual maturation process that cannot be sped up. Like our physical growth, mental growth takes time, and this is a dilemma in a culture of demand and impatience. It is not surprising then that companies like Kernel are exploring brain hacking solutions for "cognitive enhancement."[20] The company's founder, Bryan Johnson, has invested $100 million into the intelligence-boosting project and asks the question, "Could we learn a thousand times faster?"[21]

All of this on-demand catering has triggered a revitalization of slowness. Slow Food is an international organization that derides the "folly of fast life" and is committed to quality over efficiency. According to the group's manifesto, "We are enslaved by speed and have all succumbed to the same insidious virus: *Fast Life*, which disrupts our habits, pervades the privacy of our homes and forces us to eat Fast Foods."[22] In Norway, viewers tune in to slow television: public broadcasting that streams commercial-free programming of extremely boring activities such as sheep-shearing, knitting, and salmon swimming upstream.[23] The television events sometimes last for

[18] ECPI University. 2018. ECPI University students go from zero to Bachelor's in 2.5 years (or less)! https://www.ecpi.edu/zero-to-bachelors. Accessed 3 Feb 2018.

[19] Dodge, Krystle. 2017. 25 fastest online Bachelor's degree programs. *Degree Query*, June 24. https://www.degreequery.com/fastest-online-bachelors-degree/. Accessed 12 Dec 2017.

[20] Kernal. 2018. https://kernel.co/. Accessed 3 Jan 2018.

[21] Hamzelou, Jessica. 2016. $100 million project to make intelligence-boosting brain implant. *New Scientist*, October 20. https://www.newscientist.com/article/2109868-100-million-project-to-make-intelligence-boosting-brain-implant/. Accessed 12 Dec 2017.

[22] Slow Food USA. 2018. The slow food manifesto. https://www.slowfoodusa.org/manifesto. Accessed 3 Feb 2018.

[23] CBS News. 2017. Norway's slow tv: Fascinating viewers for hours of days at a time. *CBS News*, May 7. https://www.cbsnews.com/news/norways-slow-tv-fascinating-viewers-for-hours-or-days-at-a-time/. Accessed 12 Dec 2017.

days, and viewership is through the roof. In the United Kingdom, an organization called Slow Shopping® offers "a safe dedicated shopping session" for anyone who "may find shopping stressful or challenging."[24] The Slow Media Institute is a collaborative online project that began in 2010 and advocates for a more "resilient digital society" in which we curate our news and information rather than receive it in rapid-fire bursts. The group's manifesto, which was originally published in German, has been translated into more than 30 languages. The preamble states:

> The first decade of the 21st century, the so-called 'naughties', has brought profound changes to the technological foundations of the media landscape. The key buzzwords are networks, the Internet and social media. In the second decade, people will not search for new technologies allowing for even easier, faster and low-priced content production. Rather, appropriate reactions to this media revolution are to be developed and integrated politically, culturally and socially. The concept "Slow", as in "Slow Food" and not as in "Slow Down", is a key for this.[25]

Slowness has pervaded academia as well. In *The Slow Professor*, authors Maggie Berg and Barbara Seeber propose that "Slow professors advocate deliberation over acceleration. We need time to think, and so do our students. Time for reflection and open-ended inquiry is not a luxury but it is crucial to what we do… the Slow Professor takes back the intellectual life of the university." If modernity yields speed, then we are beginning to experience a postmodern phase of deliberate slowness.

Waiting is foreplay for the mind, and it strengthens us. In some ways, waiting breeds anticipation; for example, when I order something from Amazon, I anxiously await its arrival on my doorstep. This suspense is noticeably absent from an impulsive or immediate purchase, which does not feel quite as satisfactory as a delayed transaction. Waiting also increases our mental fortitude. Avid golfers often will talk about the mental demands of the game; legendary golfer Bobby Jones once said, "Golf is a game that is played on a five-inch course—the distance between your ears." In addition to the physical ability, golf requires forethought, planning, self-monitoring, and reflection before and after every shot. A new trend called "speed golf" compromises all of this, reducing golf to its physical component only. According to USAspeedgolf.com, the sport offers a "fun,

[24] Slow Shopping. 2018. http://www.slowshopping.org.uk/. Accessed 14 Dec 2017.
[25] Slow Media. 2010. http://en.slow-media.net/manifesto. Accessed 14 Dec 2017.

faster…alternative to the traditional game…played in a fraction of the time."[26] In 2017, the United States officially joined the National SpeedGolf Association, which includes six other countries that host an annual SpeedGolf championship. US speedgolfers Mark McLain and Lauren Cupp claimed the men's and women's inaugural season titles, respectively, by playing 18 holes in the fastest time with the lowest score. On the 18-hole course, which takes approximately four hours to play at a normal pace, the men's division averaged 82 strokes in just under an hour (58 minutes); women averaged 92 strokes in 72 minutes.[27]

Despite our constant efforts to extinguish it, the practice of waiting, whether it is on horseback, in a fast food drive-thru, or during a television commercial break, has always been engrained in the human experience. Jason Farman is an Associate Professor at the University of Maryland, College Park whose latest book, *Waiting for Word: How Message Delays Have Shaped Love, History, Technology, and Everything We Know*, examines "how societies have worked to eliminate waiting in communication and interpreted those times' meanings."[28] To eliminate waiting is to diminish our satisfaction, ultimately. As Farman notes, "Waiting is such a powerful part of our relationships (to people that we long for, to objects like iPhones that we may long for) because that's where imagination does its work."[29] Waiting encourages thoughtfulness, reflection, and self-consciousness, but the smartphone destroys waiting. It works primarily to accelerate our lives, inherently promoting opportunities for gratification, whether it be for communication, information, shopping, or entertainment. The blueprint for the smartphone is the antithesis of slowness.

Smartphone compulsivity is driven by gratification. In one particular study, researchers at three Chinese universities found that instant gratification derived from a smartphone increases the likelihood of problematic smartphone use such as compulsivity and even addiction later on. Specifically, the study found that instant gratification is positively associated with the flow experience. Flow theory, as you'll recall from Chap. 1,

[26] SpeedGolf USA. 2018. http://www.usaspeedgolf.com/. Accessed 29 Dec 2017.

[27] SpeedGolf USA. 2018. http://www.usaspeedgolf.com/uschamps. Accessed 29 Dec 2017.

[28] Farman, Jason. 2017. The book. *Waiting for Word. Waiting for Word*, April 30. http://www.waitingforword.com/the-book/. Accessed 11 Nov 2017.

[29] Farman, Jason. 2017. How buffer icons shape our sense of time and our practices of waiting. *Waiting for Word*, June 16. http://www.waitingforword.com/loading-how-buffer-icons-shape-our-sense-of-time-and-our-practices-of-waiting/. Accessed 11 Nov 2017.

was established by Csikszentmihalyi and describes a state of being "completely involved in something to the point of forgetting time, fatigue, and everything else but the activity itself." The researchers argue that flow is an intrinsic motivational reward that is sought after by smartphone users, and when attained, the reward strengthens the desire to achieve the flow state again and again. Of course, this depends on the type of user, too. The study categorizes participants according to their behavioral activation systems (BAS) which "demonstrates users' predisposition to the rewarding experience of flow."[30] Those with strong BAS personality traits exhibit a high level of sensitivity to reward and punishment, making them more susceptible to extended and compulsive use of the smartphone. In short, if we have strong emotional reactions to being rewarded or punished, we are more vulnerable to using our smartphones as a gratification-seeking device. The unending cycle of seek-use-gratify-repeat is emboldened each time we are positively rewarded by the screen. Delaying gratification obtained from our devices certainly can help preserve our autonomy, but as William Poundstone asserts, "No one is saying that you should always defer gratification…The key thing is to be able to strike a balance."[31]

The How and the Why

Think of the most recent time that you have interacted with your smartphone. Was it a check? Did you have a notification waiting for you? Did you have a directed goal in mind? If so, did you consult your phone to satisfy a social, communicative, entertainment, or some other type of need? How did it make you feel? Did you unlock your phone and get sidetracked for a little while? How long were you on your phone? How long had it been since your last interaction?

Throughout the course of each day, we use our smartphones in very different ways and for very different purposes. We might think of this as a *smartphone schedule*. The general pattern of my smartphone schedule remains relatively consistent; within the first ten minutes of waking up, I check my phone to see if I have any important notifications pending. (An important

[30] Chen, Chongyang, Kem Zhang, Xiang Gong, Sesia J. Zhao, Matthew K.O. Lee and Liang Liang. 2017. Understanding compulsive smartphone use: An empirical test of a flow-based model. *International Journal of Information Management* 37: 438–454.

[31] Poundstone, William. 2017. *Head in the Cloud: Dispatches from a Post-fact World*. S.l., OneWorld Publications.

notification might consist of an email from a colleague or a student that requests something from me, or a text message conversation that I missed out on after going to bed.) During the midday hours, my smartphone use is fairly dormant, using it mostly to listen to music or podcasts during drive time, though I closely monitor emails, phone calls, and texts by checking my screen regularly. If something important surfaces, I usually will interrupt whatever task I am doing at the time and respond, depending on my perceived importance of the message. I engage in heavier smartphone usage in the evening. I use this time to catch up on the day's news headlines, exhaust my Twitter feed, and when I feel really motivated, to grade student work in the Canvas app. Although the reasons for and time spent using my phone fluctuate, I rarely find myself without my phone at my side. And I'm not alone; a key reason for using our smartphones is their convenience; a 2013 Facebook-sponsored research study found that 79% of smartphone owners have their devices on them or near them for 22 hours per day.[32]

The variability in usage and the reasons for usage gives each one of us a signature smartphone profile. According to the Pew Research Center, the most frequent usage of smartphones relates to following breaking news (this is a cognitive gratification-seeking behavior) and sharing to social media (this is integrative and social interactive gratification-seeking behavior).[33] Among the 18–29-year-old smartphone user demographic, "social networking, video consumption, and music/podcasts are especially popular." But perhaps more interesting is that the Pew Research study asked the disparate populations under what circumstances they used their smartphones that week. 93% and 47% of the 18–29-year-old respondents used their devices to avoid boredom and to avoid others around them, respectively. Those in the 30–49-year-old demographic also reported using their smartphones to avoid being bored (82%) and to avoid others (32%). Over half of the older smartphones users, aged 50 and over, also acknowledged using their phones to combat boredom. Who can blame them? With the entire record of collective human intelligence at our fingertips, it seems boredom is no match for the smartphone. In 2017, it was estimated that YouTube users watched over one billion hours of videos per

[32] Facebook. 2017. Always connected: How smartphones and social keep us engaged. https://www.nu.nl/files/IDC-Facebook%20Always%20Connected%20%281%29.pdf. Accessed 1 Nov 2017.

[33] Smith, Aaron. 2015. U.S. smartphone use in 2015. *Pew Research Center*. http://www.pewinternet.org/2015/04/01/us-smartphone-use-in-2015/. Accessed 1 Nov 2017.

day,[34] with smartphone users accounting for more than one billion views per day.[35] It is becoming increasingly evident, however, that the majority of our smartphone interaction habits are not making us better or more informed; they are making us unhappy.

Time Well Spent is a nonprofit initiative that seeks to build an awareness campaign of technology users "to stop technology platforms from hijacking our minds."[36] The public advocacy group studied 200,000 iPhone users and ranked the apps that made users the most happy and the most unhappy. Social media and games accounted for the majority of the apps that left users feeling the most unhappy and filled with regret for spending time using them. Yet these social apps also ranked highest in terms of time spent, compared to the process apps that make users feel the most happy, which included (among others) Google Calendar, Weather, Podcasts, and Spotify. The distinction is clear; our process use of apps tends to make us happier than our social use of apps, which we often employ to fill the voids in our daily lives. So why, then, do we spend the majority of our time on the things that make us most unhappy? Perhaps it is that our devices are intentionally designed to be persuasive and manipulate our time and attention.

Tristan Harris is formerly the Design Ethicist for Google and the founder of the Center for Humane Technology, which directly inspired the Time Well Spent movement. Harris, who has been described as "the closest thing Silicon Valley has to a conscience,"[37] has been a vocal critic of the current ecosystem of technologies, pointing out that technology companies have sneakily monetized our attention. In a podcast series titled *Waking Up with Sam Harris*, Tristan Harris (no relation to Sam) explains how technology companies profit from our usage:

> It comes down to advertising and time. Because of the link that more of your attention and more of your time equals more money, [tech companies]

[34] Etherington, Darrell. 2017. People now watch 1 billion hours of YouTube per day. *TechCrunch*, February 28. https://techcrunch.com/2017/02/28/people-now-watch-1-billion-hours-of-youtube-per-day/. Accessed 12 Nov 2017.

[35] MerchDope. 2018. YouTube statistics—2018. https://fortunelords.com/youtube-statistics/. Accessed 28 Apr 2018.

[36] Time Well Spent. 2018. http://www.timewellspent.io/. Accessed 1 Apr 2018.

[37] Bosker, Bianca. 2016. The binge breaker. *The Atlantic*, November 2016. https://www.theatlantic.com/magazine/archive/2016/11/the-binge-breaker/501122/. Accessed 12 Nov 2017.

> have an infinite appetite in getting more of your time… The whole goal is to maximize time on site… We only have so much time. What people miss about this is that it's not by accident. The web will continue to evolve to be more engaging and to take more time because that is the business model.

Unlike traditional brick-and-mortar businesses, which profit from the sale of goods and services, social apps like Facebook and Twitter profit from the time spent on their platforms, or user engagement. This incentivizes companies to employ stronger and stronger persuasive technology techniques to keep you mindlessly scrolling for as long as possible.

A company formerly named Dopamine Labs specializes in such behavior. The company, which refers to itself as a group of "hacker neuroscientists,"[38] offers app-building services to its clients using its artificial intelligence software named *Skinner* (yes, after the behavioral psychologist, B.F. Skinner). When the proprietary code is built into an app, the company promises a boost in engagement and retention of app visitors. In an earlier iteration of its website, Dopamine Labs advertised its software with the message: "Dopamine makes your app addictive."[39] But following a rocky interview on *60 Minutes*, and a flurry of bad press on social media (including a condemnatory tweet from the Francois Chollet, a Google engineer and AI expert), Dopamine Labs officially rebranded itself as Boundless Mind and its *Skinner* software as *Delight*—a much softer image with a more nuanced message on its website: "Boundless Mind makes it easy to hook your users."[40]

Whistleblowers like Tristan Harris and the aforementioned Tony Fadell are leading a burgeoning movement to pull back the curtain on technology companies in order to reveal their real intentions. Sean Parker, co-founder of Napster and the first president of Facebook, has joined the ranks of these technology dissidents by publicly acknowledging that the social media framework is deliberately designed to exploit "a vulnerability in human psychology"[41] by relying on social-validation feedback loops. In

[38] Boundless Mind. 2018. https://www.boundless.ai/about-us/. Accessed 13 Nov 2017.

[39] Shieber, Jonathan. 2017. Meet the tech company that wants to make you even more addicted to your phone. *TechCrunch*, September 8. https://techcrunch.com/2017/09/08/meet-the-tech-company-that-wants-to-make-you-even-more-addicted-to-your-phone/. Accessed 12 Nov 2017.

[40] Boundless Mind. 2018. https://www.boundless.ai/. Accessed 12 Nov 2017.

[41] Allen, Mike. 2017. Sean Parker unloads on Facebook: 'God only knows what it's doing to our children's brains.' *Axios*, November 9. https://www.axios.com/sean-parker-unloads-

a 2017 interview with Axios, Parker further admitted that "The inventors, creators—it's me, it's Mark [Zuckerberg], it's Kevin Systrom on Instagram, it's all of these people—understood this consciously. And we did it anyway." According to Parker, "The thought process that went into building these applications, Facebook being the first of them, was all about: 'How do we consume as much of your time and conscious attention as possible?'"[42] Parker is now a billionaire as a result of his work with Facebook, Friendster, Spotify, and a handful of other tech start-ups, but the damage has been done; habit loops have been formed.

Consider some of the design tactics that are intentionally employed to keep users tethered to their devices. Instagram videos automatically play when they appear in frame. YouTube concludes all of its videos with an "Up Next" screen that gives the user a ten-second countdown before autoplaying a related video based on an algorithmic expression. Twitter has expanded its use of its mobile notifications, a feature of which users cannot totally opt out, presumably to get users to visit the app more often. On a more granular level, design staples like the iMessage typing bubble let us know that someone on the other end is formulating a response to our text. This basic exploitation of social reciprocity entices us to hang on until we receive that message. And, the presence of this icon as it relates to the time it takes to respond can assume its own rhetoric.

Semiotics is the study of signs and symbols and their intended use or interpretation in communicative practices. A subfield, Mobile Semiotics, examines the symbols used in human-computer interfaces and their meaning. The iMessage typing bubble, as well as any variation of it that is used in a number of social applications, is a signifier that the user needs to wait. In this sense, the digital screen acts as a rhetorical interface between the human, the screen, and the human on the other end of the chat. (For a cruel social experiment to observe the power of the typing bubble, visit miscellaneousmischief.com/textinginprogress.html, download a GIF of the typing bubble, and text it to a friend). We understand the three blinking dots to mean someone is crafting a reply, and we even begin to scrutinize the forthcoming message based on the amount of time we see those

on-facebook-god-only-knows-what-its-doing-to-our-childrens-brains-1513306792-f855e7b4-4e99-4d60-8d51-2775559c2671.html. Accessed 12 Nov 2017.

[42] Allen, Mike. 2017. Sean Parker unloads on Facebook: 'God only knows what it's doing to our children's brains.' *Axios*, November 9. https://www.axios.com/sean-parker-unloads-on-facebook-god-only-knows-what-its-doing-to-our-childrens-brains-1513306792-f855e7b4-4e99-4d60-8d51-2775559c2671.html. Accessed 12 Nov 2017.

blinking dots. A 2014 article in *The New York Times* identifies different bubble-typing scenarios that induce anxiety: "There's the giving-away-too-much-without-actually-saying-anything pause, when you start to type and then decide to edit your response." Then, there's "the text you want to pretend you haven't read yet—but then find that your pocket has pressed against the cursor, which is now in the response tab and, damn, now he knows that you've seen it and your whole plan is foiled."[43] And if you have ever had an emotionally charged conversation via text, or sent a weighty message like "I love you," you'll understand that the outcome might well be predicated on the response time and those three blinking dots.

In some cases, digital interfaces are deliberately slowed down in order to manipulate our perceived credibility. In 2016, Fast Company reported that websites for companies that approve mortgage lending intentionally paused before approving a consumer's request for a loan; the added wait time made the experience feel more legitimate for the user, despite the fact that the mortgage calculator tool could provide near instantaneous results. A spokesperson for the tool said, "As subversive as this sort of design sounds, when used properly, consumers actually prefer the user experience of these white lies that take their time."[44] Similarly, Wells Fargo has admitted to slowing down its eye-scanning technology for user logins on mobile devices: "[The eye-scanning technology] worked so quickly that the developers had to slow it down by a few seconds so customers knew it had actually registered their identities."[45]

A manipulation of design is a manipulation of the user. This simple concept dismantles the argument that our smartphones are neutral tools; rather, the smartphone has enveloped our daily rituals. The rhetorical interface of the smartphone beckons interactivity and sustained use. We know this because technology developers tell us so. Professor Pedro Xavier Mendonça extends this point in his article, "Towards a Material Semiotics Rhetoric: Persuasion and Mobile Technologies":

[43] Bennet, Jessica. 2014. Bubbles carry a lot of weight. *The New York Times*, August 29. https://www.nytimes.com/2014/08/31/fashion/texting-anxiety-caused-by-little-bubbles.html. Accessed 12 Nov 2017.

[44] Wilson, Mark. 2016. The UX secret that will ruin apps for you. *Fast Co Design*, July 6. https://www.fastcodesign.com/3061519/the-ux-secret-that-will-ruin-apps-for-you. Accessed 11 Nov 2017.

[45] Corkery, Michael. 2016. Goodbye, password. Banks opt to scan fingers and faces instead. *The New York Times*, June 21. https://www.nytimes.com/2016/06/22/business/dealbook/goodbye-password-banks-opt-to-scan-fingers-and-faces-instead.html?smprod=nytcore-iphone&smid=nytcore-iphone-share. Accessed 10 Nov 2017.

> The materiality of technological artefacts, such as cell phones, is not neutral to the purposes that frame their construction. The need to have persuasive features helps in the creation of these features. In this sense, the rhetorical frame is a dynamic process that forms a significant part of the possibilities of action of a human being's daily life[46]

Mendonça sees the smartphone not as a communications device, but as a "material transformation of daily life." Because we have acquiesced ourselves to this technology, we are at the mercy of designers and engineers and, to a certain extent, exposed, vulnerable, and manipulated. At some point, our digital existence can even become preferable to our analog one. In the article, "Tech Companies Design Your Life, Here's Why You Should Care," Tristan Harris warns that our phones breed impatience and dissatisfaction with real life: "Our phone puts a new choice on life's menu, in any moment, that's 'sweeter' than reality," which then "can't live up to our expectations."

Outspoken critics like Tristan Harris, Tony Fadell, and Sean Parker place the blame squarely on tech companies, rather than individual users, for the intentional design of rewards-based mobile architecture. According to Harris, our personal dependence on smartphones is "*a design problem*, not just a personal responsibility problem." We hold cigarette and alcohol companies to higher standards and regulate them more prohibitively compared to other manufacturers because their products are highly addictive and potentially ruinous. The ongoing argument that the tech industry should have an ethical and moral obligation to its users draws eerie parallels to much of the same rhetoric used to hold Philip Morris accountable for its harmful product. As the largest cigarette manufacturer in the United States slowly hemorrhages from individual and class action lawsuits, one has to wonder whether or not tech companies ultimately will be held responsible for engineering an entire society's transfixation on their devices and the effects that metastasize. Just as Philip Morris peddled, enabled, and glamorized cigarette smoking throughout the twentieth century, twenty-first-century tech companies are profiteering from a new crop of habitual, compulsive, and addicted technology users.

Still, according to some, the onus falls on the individual user. Dr. Bryan Vartabedian is a pediatrician at Baylor College of Medicine and described

[46] Mendonça, Pedro Xavier. 2014. Towards a material semiotics' rhetoric: Persuasion and mobile technologies. *Techne: Research In Philosophy & Technology* 18: 183–202.

as "one of health care's influential voices on technology and medicine."[47] In his self-explanatory titled blog post, "There Is No Bad Technology, Only Bad Technology Habits," he likens technology to healthy living: "Of course there are bad foods. And they taste really good. But no one forces you to eat them. Similarly, technology is less of a problem than the way we relate to it. No one forces you to connect." This viewpoint that our personal technologies are neutral is a modern update of Lynn White's metaphor that devices open doors but do not compel us to enter. I agree with Vartabedian that our technology habits certainly shape our usage of technology, and consequently, our lives, but I cannot subscribe to his argument that "at the end of the day, our use is our own issue. The problem, it seems, is us." Nor does the burden fall entirely upon technology companies to look out for consumers' best interests. The answer lies somewhere in between.

Like food companies, technology companies respond to profits. When fast food restaurants began to offer healthier food options, it was not because they felt a social obligation to do so; it was the consumer's "general distaste for industrially produced and high processed food"[48] combined with an entrepreneurial move to rebrand entire sections of the menu as artisan, natural, and organic. No, this pivot towards more health-conscious menus was not a compassionate response to a growing epidemic of obesity; it was the seizure of a new business opportunity. Similarly, we should not expect technology companies to sacrifice their bottom line in order to act as moral agents. Technology companies can and should be pressured into offering healthier technology options since, like food, we need technology to function. Because disconnection simply is not an option for many of us, it stands to reason that we must demand alternatives to the habit-making technologies, devices, and apps that dominate the current digital landscape. But we also must understand that these friendly apps are not innocuous; they are ruthless businesses with investors and shareholders. We ought to be weary of businesses like Facebook that simultaneously hook us on to their product and then claim to want well-being for its users—Facebook is offering us the drug and the antidote.

[47] Vartabedian, Bryan. 2017. There is no bad technology, only bad technology habits. *33 Charts*, December 9. https://33charts.com/technology-habits/. Accessed 12 Dec 2017.

[48] Specter, Michael. 2015. Freedom from fries. *The New Yorker*, November 2. https://www.newyorker.com/magazine/2015/11/02/freedom-from-fries. Accessed 9 Nov 2017.

In 2017, Facebook made changes to the algorithm for its news feed so that users see more posts from friends and family and fewer posts from advertisers and paid publisher content. The move was inspired by a 2015 paper in the *Journal of Experimental Psychology* that found passive (or undirected) Facebook usage directly undermines personal sense of well-being.[49]

The modification caused a reduction of total time spent on the site by 5% (this equates to 50 million hours per day[50]) and a dip in earnings. CEO Mark Zuckerberg announced the change in a November 2017 Facebook post: "I want to be clear what our priority is: protecting our community is more important than maximizing our profits."[51] In the same Facebook post, Zuckerberg even co-opts the phrase most closely associated with Tristan Harris and his digital mindfulness movement: "Research shows that interacting with friends and family on social media tends to be more meaningful and can be good for our well-being, and that's ***time well spent*** [emphasis added]." But Facebook's moral pivot has some users skeptical. Some see this as a thinly veiled attempt to keep users from rebelling against the social networking site altogether, just as researchers continue to raise flags about excessive smartphone use.

We ought to be skeptical of entities that claim to have the solution to the very problem it helped to create. Philip Morris, an international cigarette and tobacco manufacturing company, recently announced the Foundation for a Smoke-Free World, which hopes "to improve global health by ending smoking in this generation."[52] The company says, "It's the biggest shift in our history. And it's the right one for our consumers, our company, our shareholders, and society."[53] This is quite an admirable shift in ethical responsibility that will certainly impact the company's bot-

[49] Verduyn, Philippe, David Seungjae Lee, Jiyoung Park, Holly Shablack, Ariana Orvell, Joseph Bayer, Oscar Ybarra, John Jonides and Ethan Kross. 2015. Passive Facebook usage undermines affective well-being: Experimental and longitudinal evidence. *Journal of Experimental Psychology: General* 144: 480–488.

[50] Constine, Josh. 2018. Facebook's U.S. user count declines as it prioritizes well-being. *TechCrunch*, January 31. https://techcrunch.com/2018/01/31/facebook-time-spent/. Accessed 4 Feb 2018.

[51] Zuckerberg, Mark. 2017. https://www.facebook.com/zuck/posts/10104146268321841. Accessed 12 Jan 2018.

[52] Foundation for a Smoke-Free World. 2018. https://www.smokefreeworld.org/about-us. Accessed 29 Jan 2018.

[53] Philip Morris. 2018. https://www.pmi.com/faq-section/faq/why-do-you-want-to-replace-cigarettes. Accessed 29 Jan 2018.

tom line. Luckily, Philip Morris now offers four different brands of e-cigarettes, which it views as an alternative to tobacco products. In other words, they offer consumers both the drug and the antidote.

The purveyors of technology benefit from our use of that technology. We naively assume that technology companies are harmless agents of change, propelling us towards our exciting technological destiny. A concept known as the technological imperative argues that new technologies are inevitable, and therefore, they must be accepted for the good of society.[54] We often talk about technology as a solution. In the novel *Things to Come* (1933), H.G. Wells adopts an optimistic view of technology, arguing that the principles of science and radical new technologies ultimately will conquer tyranny. Yet, it was Jorge Luis Borges, Argentine writer and poet, who in his review of *Things to Come*, retorted "[T]he power of almost all tyrants arises from their control of technology." While Wells and Borges were referencing the tyrannical regime of Nazi Germany, we might consider who has control over our technology, and whether it is ourselves or whether it is cognitive tyrants with a vested interest in our data, our attention, and our time.

News.0

The phrase *fake news* has become so widely used that it was recognized by Collins Dictionary as the 2017 Word of the Year,[55] but it did not originate on the 2016 presidential campaign trail. Fake news has always existed in the propagandist's toolbox. Ahead of the 1944 presidential election, southern newspapers perpetuated the rumors that men and women of color were physically preparing for a race riot in order to upend the institutional racism of the south. In an effort to vilify the incumbent Franklin D. Roosevelt, it was falsely reported that his wife, Eleanor Roosevelt, was recruiting young black women to organize a revolt against whites; the First Lady's "Eleanor Clubs" purportedly subscribed to the motto: "A white woman in the

[54] PC Mag. 2018. Technology imperative. https://www.pcmag.com/encyclopedia/term/64252/technology-imperative. Accessed 2 Feb 2018.

[55] Hunt, Julia. 2017. 'Fake news' named Collins Dictionary's official word of the year. *Independent*, November 2. http://www.independent.co.uk/news/uk/home-news/fake-news-word-of-the-year-2017-collins-dictionary-donald-trump-kellyanne-conway-antifa-corbynmania-a8032751.html. Accessed 4 Feb 2018.

kitchen by 1943."[56] This was factually untrue, but it did not prevent large swaths of the southern electorate from believing it and casting votes for Roosevelt's Republican challenger, Thomas Dewey. Roosevelt survived the assault on truth, but unlike in the 1940s, when fake news headlines creeped along primarily by word of mouth, smartphones have expedited the misinformation highway directly into our pockets, blurring the line between factual and non-factual, truth and falsehood, and what is any combination thereof.

A 2016 study found that time is a major factor in news consumption; the group most interested in reading political news does so on their mobile devices and is the most constrained for time.[57] In other words, political news often is consumed on-the-go, skimmed in sips, which is the perfect fertilization for fake news headlines to germinate. For example, the following headline was crafted by a Toledo-based broadcasting company, WTO5, and shared on Facebook: "Pope Francis Shocks the World, Endorses Donald Trump for President." Although the company later admitted to fabricating the content, the headline reached more than 960,000 engagements on Facebook in the months prior to the general election and was the top fake news story of the 2016 presidential campaign. In fact, a post-analysis of articles shared on Facebook reveals that the most popular fake news stories were shared more often than the most popular mainstream stories and that the fake news tended to favor Donald Trump over Hillary Clinton.[58] The contamination of authentic news with fake news stories such as this one likely played a significant role in shaping the public opinion, and consequently, the results of the US presidential election. Thus, *fake news* is not innocuous; instead, as Nigeria's Nobel Laureate, Wole Soyinka, describes, fake news has become "a permanent weaponry of power."[59]

[56] Zeitz, Joshua. 2017. Lessons from the fake news pandemic of 1942. *Politico*, March 12. https://www.politico.com/magazine/story/2017/03/lessons-from-the-fake-news-pandemic-of-1942-214898. Accessed 4 Feb 2018.

[57] Xiaoqun, Zhang and Louisa Ha. 2016. Mobile news consumption and political news interest: A time budget perspective. *Journal of Applied Journalism and Media Studies* 5: 277–295.

[58] Silverman, Craig. 2016. This analysis shows how fake election news stories outperformed real news on Facebook. *BuzzFeed News*, November 16. https://www.buzzfeed.com/craigsilverman/viral-fake-election-news-outperformed-real-news-on-facebook?utm_term=.lvrrv6YzJ#.nbExGbJAl. Accessed 4 Feb 2018.

[59] Chutel, Lynsey. 2017. Wole Soyinka is worried about the threat of fake news but things technology will still help us. *Quartz*, November 4. https://qz.com/1119907/wole-soyinka-is-embracing-technology-well-its-creative-potential-anyway/. Accessed 8 Feb 2018.

Donald J. Trump's preferred weapon is Twitter. One of the many rhetorical devices used by Trump, both as a presidential candidate and as president, is his relentless branding of news sources and media outlets, specifically those with which he does not agree, as being *fake*. He refers to *The New York Times* as the "failing @ny times" on Twitter, and he consistently uses the phrase "Fake News Media" to refer to the major media outlets, sans Fox News. He has more than 300 tweets that attack and undermine specific news publications and individual journalists.[60] Trump repeatedly has called the media the "enemy of the American people,"[61] and he even has gone so far as to suggest the revocation of NBC's broadcasting license, tweeting, "With all of the Fake News coming out of NBC and the Networks, at what point is it appropriate to challenge their License? Bad for country!"[62] Despite the fact that the office of the president does not actually possess the authority to censor a commercial television network, the tweet was liked more than 97,000 times and retweeted more than 22,000 times. But the factual accuracy of this statement is irrelevant; Trump's supporters interpret this as the president socking it to the Fake News Media, and his opponents view it as an attempt to suppress the first amendment. Instead, President Trump's tweet merely plants a seed that the integrity of the NBC news network is questionable, and this is an effective strategy for the majority of the American public who only have the time or attention span for bite-sized pieces of information. Still, the president's words, and tweets, matter. Describing the institution of the free press as *fake* destabilizes this cornerstone of democracy. General Michael Hayden, former director of the CIA and the NSA, has said of Trump's slanderous words on Twitter: "Until now it was not possible for me to conceive of an American President capable of such an outrageous assault on truth, a free press or the first amendment."

Whether intentional or not, Trump's strategy is masterful: create disruption by way of an inflammatory statement, which perfectly complements the need to fill a 24-hour news cycle. An article in *The New York Times* described this as "Trump's greatest trick: His tornado of news-making has

[60] Trump Twitter Archive. 2018. http://www.trumptwitterarchive.com/. Accessed 6 May 2018.

[61] Grynbaum, Michael M. 2017. Trump calls the news media the 'enemy of the American people.' *The New York Times*, February 17. https://www.nytimes.com/2017/02/17/business/trump-calls-the-news-media-the-enemy-of-the-people.html. Accessed 4 Apr 2018.

[62] Trump, Donald J. 2017. https://twitter.com/realdonaldtrump/status/918112884630093825?lang=en. Accessed 4 Feb 2018.

scrambled Americans' grasp of time and memory, producing a sort of sensory overload that can make even seismic events—of his creation or otherwise—disappear from the collective consciousness and public view."[63] And this illusory redirection usually requires no more than 140 characters; Twitter boasts 330 million active monthly users and Donald Trump (@realDonaldTrump) personally has 42 million Twitter followers. To date, Trump has tweeted the phrase "fake news" more than 300 times, with more than 200 of these tweets having originated since being elected president.[64] At the time of this writing, his most retweeted and second-most favorited tweet features a video meme of Donald Trump in a World Wrestling Entertainment (WWE) appearance tackling a wrestler with the CNN logo superimposed on his head. The hashtag reads #FraudNewsCNN. This president's outward disdain for the oppositional media is unprecedented. By comparison, President John F. Kennedy, amidst being heavily criticized by the media for his political and personal flaws, characterized the press as "invaluable." He stated, "Even though we never like it, and even though we wish they didn't write it, and even though we disapprove, there isn't any doubt that we could not do the job at all in a free society without a very, very active press."[65] Ironically, Kennedy's statement was in response to a question posed by Sander Vanocur, a correspondent for NBC News, or as Trump now refers to them on Twitter, Fake@NBCNews.

The majority of monthly active Twitter users now access the platform from their mobile devices, making it the primary conduit between President Trump and the American people.[66] But ten years ago, when Twitter was first launched, it was not well-received. Founder Biz Stone has even admitted to a complete lack of a business plan in the beginning. Before Twitter, the hashtag (or the octothorpe), was known as a pound sign instead, and it was used mostly in computer programming language. Now, hashtags are ubiquitous, and Twitter is at the center of the political

[63] Flegenheimer, Matt. 2017. The year the news accelerated to Trump speed. *The New York Times*. December 29. https://www.nytimes.com/2017/12/29/us/politics/trump-news-overload.html. Accessed 2 Feb 2018.

[64] Trump Twitter Archive. 2018. http://www.trumptwitterarchive.com/. Accessed 6 May 2018.

[65] John F. Kennedy Presidential Library and Museum. 2018. John F. Kennedy and the press. https://www.jfklibrary.org/JFK/JFK-in-History/John-F-Kennedy-and-the-Press.aspx. Accessed 12 Feb 2018.

[66] Smith, Craig. 2018. Twitter mobile statistics and facts (February 2018). https://expandedramblings.com/index.php/twitter-mobile-statistics/. Accessed 5 May 2018.

universe. To date, President Trump has tweeted 2103 times from his official presidential account (@POTUS) and more than 36,000 times from his personal Twitter handle, though there is a substantial overlap between various retweets and reposts from the two accounts. By comparison, it took his predecessor, President Obama, one and a half of his two presidential terms before he sent his first tweet, which read: "Hello, Twitter! It's Barack. Really! Six years in, they're finally giving me my own account." Over the course of his entire presidency, Obama sent 352 tweets—a number that Trump surpassed in the short time between being elected on November 8 to the Inauguration on January 20. The president has referred to the microblogging platform as his "own form of media" and has said that "I wouldn't be here if it wasn't for Twitter…"[67] In an interview with *The New York Times*, Twitter's co-founder, Evan Williams, responded, "It's a very bad thing, Twitter's role in that … If it's true that he wouldn't be president if it weren't for Twitter, then yeah, I'm sorry."[68]

President Trump exploits the paradox of Twitter. He uses it to circumvent the traditional channels of communication, enabling him to interface with the public in real time, but in doing so, his statements are seemingly impromptu, apparently lacking oversight and fact-checking. Often, Trump delivers information via Twitter before consulting with members of his cabinet or even Congress. A tweet in July 2017 unexpectedly announced a hard reversal on existing military policy: "[P]lease be advised that the United States Government will not accept or allow … Transgender individuals to serve in any capacity in the U.S. military."[69] But this tweet was sent from @realDonaldTrump, and not the official @POTUS Twitter handle. The improvisation of Trump's tweets presents a dilemma in the digital age; do all of the president's tweets count as official statements? According to the White House, tweets sent by the president, regardless of the handle used,

[67] Schwartz, Ian. 2017. Trump: 'I wouldn't be here if it wasn't for Twitter,' 'I have my own form of media.' *Real Clear Politics*, March 15. https://www.realclearpolitics.com/video/2017/03/15/trump_i_wouldnt_be_here_if_it_wasnt_for_twitter_i_have_my_own_form_of_media.html. Accessed 2 Feb 2018.

[68] Streitfeld, David. 2017. 'The Internet is broken': @ev is trying to salvage it. *The New York Times*, May 20. https://www.nytimes.com/2017/05/20/technology/evan-williams-medium-twitter-internet.html. Accessed 1 Feb 2018.

[69] Trump, Donald J. 2017. https://twitter.com/realDonaldTrump/status/890193981585444864?ref_src=twsrc%5Etfw&ref_url=http%3A%2F%2Fwjla.com%2Fnews%2Fnation-world%2Ftrump-tweets-transgender-individuals-cant-serve-in-us-military&tfw_site=abc7news. Accessed 2 Feb 2018.

are indeed official. This is problematic in some cases, such as when the president uses the world stage of Twitter to provoke foreign leaders. When North Korea's Supreme Leader, Kim Jong-un, who Trump refers to as "Little Rocket Man" on Twitter, warned that he has a nuclear button on his desk at all times, Trump tweeted: "Will someone from his depleted and food starved regime please inform him that I too have a Nuclear Button, but it is a much bigger & more powerful one than his, and my Button works!" This has initiated calls for Twitter to #BanTrump for fear that his reckless tweeting will lead us into a nuclear war. Despite the company enforcing strict guidelines that prohibit threatening others with violent or abusive behavior, Twitter has exempted the tweets of all elected world leaders from this policy. In a statement posted to its blog, Twitter justified its decision: "Blocking a world leader from Twitter or removing their controversial Tweets would hide important information people should be able to see and debate."[70] And although Twitter states that "No one person's account drives Twitter's growth, or influences these decisions," a research analyst at the stock brokerage firm, Monness, Crespi, Hardt & Co., Inc., estimates that the company would forfeit about $2 billion if Trump were to cease tweeting.[71]

Trump uses Twitter as a personal megaphone to shape the social zeitgeist. Perhaps it is our sharp political divisiveness, or the unpredictability of what Trump will say next, but many of us anxiously await the next presidential tweet to vehemently agree or disagree with it. It is significant to note that Twitter is Trump's preferred method of communication—he even has fired members of his administration by announcing it over Twitter instead of informing them personally. And, we are grappling with how to respond to the president's raw thoughts; there is considerable disagreement about the degree to which the media should cover Trump's tweets as *news* or as a form of streaming commentary. A 2018 article in *Politico Magazine* titled "Why Trump Tweets (And Why We Listen)" supposes that:

> [Twitter] is a technology perfectly suited to his need for attention and, more ominously, his recklessness. By blurring private and public discourse, Twitter allows Trump to turn locker-room talk, his favored idiom, into presidential speech. And it enables him to manhandle the public's attention, constantly yanking the media spotlight back on himself whenever it starts to wander.

[70] Twitter, Inc. 2018. World leaders on Twitter. https://blog.twitter.com/official/en_us/topics/company/2018/world-leaders-and-twitter.html. Accessed 4 Feb 2018.

[71] Bloomberg. 2017. What is Trump worth to Twitter? One analyst estimates $2 billion. *Fortune*, August 17. http://fortune.com/2017/08/17/trump-worth-to-twitter/. Accessed 2 Feb 2018.

Our social media platforms, and the smartphones on which we access them, provide us with instant news, which is capable of redirecting our attention at any given moment. But this abridged news that we consume in on-the-go bursts is more like a CliffsNotes study guide version of the news, allowing us to like and share the parts that we find agreeable, and filter out that with which we find disagreeable, all in the name of personalization. As articulated by Astra Taylor, in her book, *The People's Platform: Taking Back Power and Culture in the Digital Age*: "The reduction of news to whatever we happen to want to know in the moment is terrifying." Yet, this is precisely how we use our smartphones; the majority of Americans receive news and information primarily online, and more than half of smartphone users are notified of news through their smartphone notifications.[72] A 2017 study by the Pew Research Center in Journalism and Media found that Americans were equally likely to consume news in one of two ways: by clicking on a link via social media or by visiting the news source website directly. Regardless of the origination, readers were only able to recall the name of the news source about half of the time (56%). Remarkably, 10% of participants cited Facebook as the news source.[73] Astra Taylor adds:

> [E]ither the Internet has freed us from the stifling grip of the old, top-down mass media model, transforming consumers into producers and putting citizens on par with the powerful, or we have stumbled into a new trap, a social media hall of mirrors made up of personalized feeds, "filter bubbles," narcissistic chatter, and half-truths.

We are vulnerable when we allow ourselves to be guided by our devices, which can lead us to nebulous sources with mysterious authors and fraudulent information. But this is the new form of journalism that our technologies have helped to redefine.

[72] Lu, Kristine and Katerina Eva Matsa. 2016. More than half of smartphone users get news alerts, but few get them often. *Pew Research Center*. http://www.pewresearch.org/fact-tank/2016/09/08/more-than-half-of-smartphone-users-get-news-alerts-but-few-get-them-often/. Accessed 4 Feb 2018.

[73] Mitchell, Amy, Jeffrey Gottfried, Elisa Shearer and Kristine. 2017. How Americans encounter, recall, and act upon digital news. *Pew Research Center*. http://www.journalism.org/2017/02/09/how-americans-encounter-recall-and-act-upon-digital-news/. Accessed 2 Feb 2018.

Our smartphones have sired a freelance journalistic society, where everyone is armed with a photo/video camera and a microphone, making each of us a potential contributor to the news. Clay Shirky, an Associate Professor in the Carter Center of Journalism at NYU, describes this as the "shock of inclusion," where "the former audience is becoming increasingly intertwined with all aspects of news… as disseminators and syndicators and users of the news."[74] Jay Rosen is a Professor of Journalism at NYU and makes the argument that "The more people who participate in it the stronger the press will be."[75] He points to a 2009 experiment conducted by British newspaper *The Guardian*, which published more than 700,000 individual receipts claimed by Members of Parliament (MPs) and then invited readers to analyze the data in an effort to identify malfeasance and financial corruption of elected officials. The goal of the program was to evaluate each document individually and bookmark receipts that looked suspicious or that warranted further investigation. The program was only moderately successful in identifying corrupt political spending, but more importantly, it previewed how crowdsourcing might assist journalistic efforts.

Unlike the MP expense investigation, which was strategic, smartphones also have played integral roles in eyewitness journalism. In April 2015, six Baltimore Police officers were captured on a smartphone video forcefully arresting 25-year-old Freddie Gray and detaining him in a police van, where he would then suffer a severed spinal cord. Gray fell into a coma and died one week later. Kevin Moore, the man who recorded the incident from his smartphone, has since recorded more than 300 police interactions and has started a Baltimore branch of the WeCopwatch organization, a group "dedicated to the non-violent observation of the police."[76] In July 2016, a Minnesota man, Philando Castile, was shot and killed by a police officer during a routine traffic stop. His fiancé, Diamond Reynolds, live-streamed the incident on Facebook, which broadcast the final moments of Castile's life. There have been multiple instances of murder victims live-streaming their untimely deaths; Antonio Perkins was fatally shot while live-streaming a neighborhood party in Chicago, and Prentis

[74] Mitchell, Bill. 2010. Shirky: The shock of inclusion and new roles in the fabric of society. *Poynter*, October 19. https://www.poynter.org/news/shirky-shock-inclusion-and-new-roles-news-fabric-society. Accessed 31 Jan 2018.

[75] Rosen, Jay. 2011. What I think I know about journalism. *PressThink*, April 26. http://pressthink.org/2011/04/what-i-think-i-know-about-journalism/. Accessed 2 Jan 2018.

[76] WeCopwatch. 2018. http://wecopwatch.org/about/. Accessed 3 Mar 2018.

Robinson was murdered while live-streaming himself on a walk on the campus of Wingate University in North Carolina. Under Facebook's current policy, users are asked to report inappropriate content, which upon review, may be removed by the company. And in 2017, following the gruesome death of Robert Godwin by his murderer Steve Stephens, who shared the video on Facebook Live, Facebook added 3000 more moderators to review and remove content in an effort to prevent crimes from being live-streamed. In each of these cases, smartphones have turned bystanders into eyewitnesses, fundamentally changing the way that we observe, report, and share news.

In 2017, a 31-year-old Floridian man, Jamel Dunn, drowned in the middle of a pond after struggling and calling for help for nearly three minutes. A group of five teenagers witnessed the drowning, but instead of choosing to intervene, one of the teens recorded the tragic event on his smartphone, which also captured audio of the teens laughing and shouting obscenities at the distressed man. The video of the man's death was shared with friends on YouTube. Ultimately, the teens were not criminally charged, as there is no law that requires bystanders to render aid. I have to hope that if these teenagers had known the man was going to drown, better sense would have prevailed. But in that short span of three minutes, documenting the event became worth more than the intervention. I do wonder if the outcome would have been different if the smartphone had not been present. I'm not blaming the smartphone for this man's death, nor am I using it to excuse the teens' inaction. But, the *Tosh.0* culture of filming yourself doing stupid things might explain some variability. Robert Lustig, Professor of Pediatrics at the University of California San Francisco, makes the argument that:

> notifications from our phones are training our brains to be in a nearly constant state of stress and fear by establishing a stress-fear memory pathway. And such a state means that the prefrontal cortex, the part of our brains that normally deals with some of our highest-order cognitive functioning, goes completely haywire, and basically shuts down.[77]

[77] Brueck, Hilary. 2018. This is what your smartphone is doing to your brain—And it isn't good. *Business Insider*, March 10. http://www.businessinsider.com/what-your-smartphone-is-doing-to-your-brain-and-it-isnt-good-2018-3. Accessed 3 Apr 2018.

The result, Lustig believes, is that "You end up doing stupid things… And those stupid things tend to get you in trouble." This is a gross understatement for what happened in that Florida pond, but if we constantly view our world through a screen, then this inevitably will impact our decision-making; we might begin to treat others like film subjects rather than real people. According to Charles Seife, a Professor of Journalism at NYU, "We are altering our behavior toward one another because of the influence of the online world… In so doing, it's altering the way we interact with one another…"[78] As such, the ability to openly share newsworthy or graphic content to social platforms raises significant ethical questions about our roles and expectations within the mass journalism framework.

We are all journalists. If you carry a smartphone, then you are a potential newsgatherer, always on the scene and poised to capture and document events in real time. And every time that you like, reshare, or retweet a news story on social media, you are executing a mini-editorial decision to accredit that story. In doing so, we bypass the Code of Ethics that professional journalists are expected to honor. The Society of Professional Journalists (SPJ) bases this Code on four principles: (1) Seek Truth and Report It, (2) Minimize Harm, (3) Act Independently, and (4) Be Accountable and Transparent. Among these principles, the Code specifies explicit directives that journalists should follow, including, but not limited to, the following guidelines:

- Verify information before releasing it.
- Remember that neither speed nor format excuses inaccuracy.
- Gather, update and correct information throughout the life of a news story.
- Show compassion for those who may be affected by news coverage.

Now, think back to where and how the majority of Americans get their news: online, through social media and news websites. This is problematic because the promise of the digital age is immediacy, yet this is the enemy of good journalism. Twitter easily violates the first two guidelines, mostly because it is a speed-driven platform by design. Using eyewitness videos such as in the cases of fatal shootings can be emotionally powerful, but this violates the last two guidelines, as these videos are often graphic and provide only a snapshot of an event rather than the full context.

[78] Seife, Charles. 2014. *Virtual Unreality*. New York: Penguin Group.

Our new model of journalism, this News.0, challenges the traditional media architecture, presenting both great opportunity and great responsibility. As we continue to learn more about the extent to which Russia tampered with the 2016 presidential election in an effort to influence its outcome, we are reminded of the fragility of our online infrastructure, its susceptibility to fake news, and the rate at which it is spread. The kind of news that I describe above is far from fake; it is all too real. And it is evident that our increased exposure to our digital world is reshaping our identities and our roles in society—as consumers and producers, as citizens and journalists. Our technologies have the capacity to deeply change who we are.

References

Allen, Mike. 2017. Sean Parker unloads on Facebook: 'God only knows what it's doing to our children's brains.' *Axios*, November 9. Accessed November 12, 2017. https://www.axios.com/sean-parker-unloads-on-facebook-god-only-knows-what-its-doing-to-our-childrens-brains-1513306792-f855e7b4-4e99-4d60-8d51-2775559c2671.html.

Ayduk, Ozlem, Rodolfo Mendoza-Denton, Mischel Walter, G. Geraldine Downey, Philip K. Peake, and Monica Rodriguez. 2000. Regulating the interpersonal self: Strategic self-regulation for coping with rejection sensitivity. *Journal of Personality and Social Psychology* 79: 776–792.

Bennet, Jessica. 2014. Bubbles carry a lot of weight. *The New York Times*, August 29. Accessed November 12, 2017. https://www.nytimes.com/2014/08/31/fashion/texting-anxiety-caused-by-little-bubbles.html.

Bloomberg. 2017. What is Trump worth to Twitter? One analyst estimates $2 billion. *Fortune*, August 17. Accessed February 2, 2018. http://fortune.com/2017/08/17/trump-worth-to-twitter/.

Bosker, Bianca. 2016. The binge breaker. *The Atlantic*, November 2016. Accessed November 12, 2017. https://www.theatlantic.com/magazine/archive/2016/11/the-binge-breaker/501122/.

Boundless Mind. 2018. Accessed November 13, 2017. https://www.boundless.ai/about-us/.

Brueck, Hilary. 2018. This is what your smartphone is doing to your brain—And it isn't good. *Business Insider*, March 10. Accessed April 3, 2018. http://www.businessinsider.com/what-your-smartphone-is-doing-to-your-brain-and-it-isnt-good-2018-3.

Carr, Nicholas G. 2011. *The Shallows: What the Internet is Doing to Our Brains.* New York: W.W. Norton & Company.

CBS News. 2017. Norway's slow tv: Fascinating viewers for hours of days at a time. *CBS News*, May 7. Accessed December 12, 2017. https://www.cbsnews.com/news/norways-slow-tv-fascinating-viewers-for-hours-or-days-at-a-time/.

Chen, Chongyang, Kem Zhang, Xiang Gong, Sesia J. Zhao, Matthew K.O. Lee, and Liang Liang. 2017. Understanding compulsive smartphone use: An empirical test of a flow-based model. *International Journal of Information Management* 37: 438–454.

Chutel, Lynsey. 2017. Wole Soyinka is worried about the threat of fake news but things technology will still help us. *Quartz*, November 4. Accessed February 8, 2018. https://qz.com/1119907/wole-soyinka-is-embracing-technology-well-its-creative-potential-anyway/.

Constine, Josh. 2018. Facebook's U.S. user count declines as it prioritizes well-being. *TechCrunch*, January 31. Accessed February 4, 2018. https://techcrunch.com/2018/01/31/facebook-time-spent/.

Corkery, Michael. 2016. Goodbye, password. Banks opt to scan fingers and faces instead. *The New York Times*, June 21. Accessed November 10, 2017. https://www.nytimes.com/2016/06/22/business/dealbook/goodbye-password-banks-opt-to-scan-fingers-and-faces-instead.html?smprod=nytcore-iphone&smid=nytcore-iphone-share.

Dodge, Krystle. 2017. 25 fastest online Bachelor's degree programs. *Degree Query*, June 24. Accessed December 12, 2017. https://www.degreequery.com/fastest-online-bachelors-degree/.

Double Click. 2018. The need for mobile speed. How mobile latency impacts publisher revenue. Accessed January 12, 2018. https://www.doubleclickbygoogle.com/articles/mobile-speed-matters/.

ECPI University. 2018. ECPI University students go from zero to Bachelor's in 2.5 years (or less)! Accessed February 3, 2018. https://www.ecpi.edu/zero-to-bachelors.

Elhai, Jon D., Jason C. Levine, Robert D. Dvorak, and Brian J. Hall. 2017. Non-social features of smartphone use are most related to depression, anxiety, and problematic smartphone use. *Computers in Human Behavior* 69: 75–82.

Etherington, Darrell. 2017. People now watch 1 billion hours of YouTube per day. *TechCrunch*, February 28. Accessed November 12, 2017. https://techcrunch.com/2017/02/28/people-now-watch-1-billion-hours-of-youtube-per-day/.

Facebook. 2017. Always connected: How smartphones and social keep us engaged. Accessed November 1, 2017. https://www.nu.nl/files/IDC-Facebook%20Always%20Connected%20%281%29.pdf.

Farman, Jason. 2017. How buffer icons shape our sense of time and our practices of waiting. *Waiting for Word*, June 16. Accessed November 11, 2017. http://www.waitingforword.com/loading-how-buffer-icons-shape-our-sense-of-time-and-our-practices-of-waiting/.

———. 2017. The book. *Waiting for Word. Waiting for Word*, April 30. Accessed November 11, 2017. http://www.waitingforword.com/the-book/.

Flegenheimer, Matt. 2017. The year the news accelerated to Trump speed. *The New York Times*, December 29. Accessed February 2, 2018. https://www.nytimes.com/2017/12/29/us/politics/trump-news-overload.html.

Foundation for a Smoke-Free World. 2018. Accessed January 29, 2018. https://www.smokefreeworld.org/about-us.

Grynbaum, Michael M. 2017. Trump calls the news media the 'enemy of the American people.' *The New York Times*, February 17. Accessed April 4, 2018. https://www.nytimes.com/2017/02/17/business/trump-calls-the-news-media-the-enemy-of-the-people.html.

Ha, Young Wook, Jimin Kim, Christian Fernando Libaque-Saenz, Younghoon Chang, and Myeong Cheol Park. 2014. Use and gratifications of mobile SNSs: Facebook and KakaoTalk in Korea. *Telematics and Informatics* 32: 425–438.

Hamzelou, Jessica. 2016. $100 million project to make intelligence-boosting brain implant. *New Scientist*, October 20. Accessed December 12, 2017. https://www.newscientist.com/article/2109868-100-million-project-to-make-intelligence-boosting-brain-implant/.

Hunt, Julia. 2017. 'Fake news' named Collins Dictionary's official word of the year. *Independent*, November 2. Accessed February 4, 2018. http://www.independent.co.uk/news/uk/home-news/fake-news-word-of-the-year-2017-collins-dictionary-donald-trump-kellyanne-conway-antifa-corbynmania-a8032751.html.

John F. Kennedy Presidential Library and Museum. 2018. John F. Kennedy and the press. Accessed February 12, 2018. https://www.jfklibrary.org/JFK/JFK-in-History/John-F-Kennedy-and-the-Press.aspx.

Kernal. 2018. Accessed January 3, 2018. https://kernel.co/.

Kundera, Milan. 1995. *Slowness*. New York: HarperCollins Publishers.

Lu, Kristine, and Katerina Eva Matsa. 2016. More than half of smartphone users get news alerts, but few get them often. *Pew Research Center*. Accessed February 4, 2018. http://www.pewresearch.org/fact-tank/2016/09/08/more-than-half-of-smartphone-users-get-news-alerts-but-few-get-them-often/.

Mendonça, Pedro Xavier. 2014. Towards a material semiotics' rhetoric: Persuasion and mobile technologies. *Techne: Research in Philosophy & Technology* 18: 183–202.

MerchDope. 2018. YouTube statistics—2018. Accessed April 28, 2018. https://fortunelords.com/youtube-statistics/.

Mitchell, Amy, Jeffrey Gottfried, Elisa Shearer, and Kristine Lu. 2017. How Americans encounter, recall, and act upon digital news. *Pew Research Center*. Accessed February 2, 2018. http://www.journalism.org/2017/02/09/how-americans-encounter-recall-and-act-upon-digital-news/.

Mitchell, Bill. 2010. Shirky: The shock of inclusion and new roles in the fabric of society. *Poynter*, October 19. Accessed January 31, 2018. https://www.poynter.org/news/shirky-shock-inclusion-and-new-roles-news-fabric-society.

Nowlis, Stephen, Naomi Mandel, and Deborah Brown McCabe. 2004. The effect of a delay between choice and consumption on consumption enjoyment. *Journal of Consumer Research* 31: 502–510.

PC Mag. 2018. Technology imperative. Accessed February 2, 2018. https://www.pcmag.com/encyclopedia/term/64252/technology-imperative.

Philip Morris. 2018. Accessed January 29, 2018. https://www.pmi.com/faq-section/faq/why-do-you-want-to-replace-cigarettes.

Poundstone, William. 2017. *Head in the Cloud: Dispatches from a Post-fact World*. S.l., OneWorld Publications.

Reid, David. 2017. Supersonic flight promised by 2023 as Boom announces airline orders. *CNBC*, June 20. Accessed January 30, 2018. https://www.cnbc.com/2017/06/20/supersonic-flight-2023-as-boom-announces-airline-orders.html.

Richard, Michael G. 2012. How fast could you travel across the U.S. in the 1800s? *Mother Nature Network*, December 26. Accessed January 21, 2018. https://www.mnn.com/green-tech/transportation/stories/how-fast-could-you-travel-across-the-us-in-the-1800s.

Rosen, Jay. 2011. What I think I know about journalism. *PressThink*, April 26. Accessed January 2, 2018. http://pressthink.org/2011/04/what-i-think-i-know-about-journalism/.

Rosen, Jonathan. 2015. Does Milan Kundera still matter? *The Atlantic*, July/August 2015. Accessed February 2, 2018. https://www.theatlantic.com/magazine/archive/2015/07/does-milan-kundera-still-matter/395237/.

Schwartz, Ian. 2017. Trump: 'I wouldn't be here if it wasn't for Twitter,' 'I have my own form of media.' *Real Clear Politics*, March 15. Accessed February 2, 2018. https://www.realclearpolitics.com/video/2017/03/15/trump_i_wouldnt_be_here_if_it_wasnt_for_twitter_i_have_my_own_form_of_media.html.

Seife, Charles. 2014. *Virtual Unreality*. New York: Penguin Group.

Shieber, Jonathan. 2017. Meet the tech company that wants to make you even more addicted to your phone. *TechCrunch*, September 8. Accessed November 12, 2017. https://techcrunch.com/2017/09/08/meet-the-tech-company-that-wants-to-make-you-even-more-addicted-to-your-phone/.

Shoda, Yuichi, Walter Mischel, and Philip K. Peake. 1990. Predicting adolescent cognitive and self-regulatory competencies from preschool delay of gratification: Identifying diagnostic conditions. *Developmental Psychology* 26: 978–986.

Silverman, Craig. 2016. This analysis shows how fake election news stories outperformed real news on Facebook. *BuzzFeed News*, November 16. Accessed February 4, 2018. https://www.buzzfeed.com/craigsilverman/viral-fake-election-news-outperformed-real-news-on-facebook?utm_term=.lvrrv6YzJ#.nbExGbJAl.

Slow Food USA. 2018. The slow food manifesto. Accessed February 3, 2018. https://www.slowfoodusa.org/manifesto.

Slow Media. 2010. Accessed December 14, 2017. http://en.slow-media.net/manifesto.

Slow Shopping. 2018. Accessed December 14, 2017. http://www.slowshopping.org.uk/.

Smith, Aaron. 2015. U.S. smartphone use in 2015. *Pew Research Center*. Accessed November 1, 2017. http://www.pewinternet.org/2015/04/01/us-smartphone-use-in-2015/.

Smith, Aaron, and Monica Anderson. 2016. Online shopping and e-commerce. *Pew Research Center*. Accessed February 3, 2018. http://www.pewinternet.org/2016/12/19/online-shopping-and-e-commerce/.

Smith, Craig. 2018. Twitter mobile statistics and facts (February 2018). Accessed May 5, 2018. https://expandedramblings.com/index.php/twitter-mobile-statistics/.

Specter, Michael. 2015. Freedom from fries. *The New Yorker*, November 2. Accessed November 9, 2017. https://www.newyorker.com/magazine/2015/11/02/freedom-from-fries.

SpeedGolf USA. 2018. Accessed December 29, 2017. http://www.usaspeedgolf.com/.

———. 2018. Accessed December 29, 2017. http://www.usaspeedgolf.com/uschamps.

Streitfeld, David. 2017. 'The Internet is broken': @ev is trying to salvage it. *The New York Times*, May 20. Accessed February 1, 2018. https://www.nytimes.com/2017/05/20/technology/evan-williams-medium-twitter-internet.html.

Thomas, Lauren. 2018. Amazon grabbed 4 percent of all US retail sales in 2017, new study says. *CNBC*, January 3. Accessed January 5, 2018. https://www.cnbc.com/2018/01/03/amazon-grabbed-4-percent-of-all-us-retail-sales-in-2017-new-study.html.

Time Well Spent. 2018. Accessed April 1, 2018. http://www.timewellspent.io/.

Trump, Donald J. 2017. Accessed February 4, 2018. https://twitter.com/realdonaldtrump/status/918112884630093825?lang=en.

———. 2017. Accessed February 2, 2018. https://twitter.com/realDonaldTrump/status/890193981585444864?ref_src=twsrc%5Etfw&ref_url=http%3A%2F%2Fwjla.com%2Fnews%2Fnation-world%2Ftrump-tweets-transgender-individuals-cant-serve-in-us-military&tfw_site=abc7news.

Trump Twitter Archive. 2018. Accessed May 6, 2018. http://www.trumptwitterarchive.com/.

Turkle, Sherry. 2013. *Alone Together: Why We Expect More From Technology and Less From Each Other*. Cambridge, MA: Perseus.

Twitter, Inc. 2018. World leaders on Twitter. Accessed February 4, 2018. https://blog.twitter.com/official/en_us/topics/company/2018/world-leaders-and-twitter.html.

Vartabedian, Bryan. 2017. There is no bad technology, only bad technology habits. *33 Charts*, December 9. Accessed December 12, 2017. https://33charts.com/technology-habits/.

Verduyn, Philippe, David Seungjae Lee, Jiyoung Park, Holly Shablack, Ariana Orvell, Joseph Bayer, Oscar Ybarra, John Jonides, and Ethan Kross. 2015. Passive Facebook usage undermines affective well-being: Experimental and longitudinal evidence. *Journal of Experimental Psychology: General* 144: 480–488.

WeCopwatch. 2018. Accessed March 3, 2018. http://wecopwatch.org/about/.

Wilmer, Henry H., and Jason M. Chein. 2016. Mobile technology habits: Patterns of association among device usage, intertemporal preference, impulse control, and reward sensitivity. *Psychonomic Bulletin & Review* 23: 1607–1614.

Wilson, Mark. 2016. The UX secret that will ruin apps for you. *Fast Co Design*, July 6. Accessed November 11, 2017. https://www.fastcodesign.com/3061519/the-ux-secret-that-will-ruin-apps-for-you.

Winderman, Lea. 2014. Acing the marshmallow test. *American Psychological Association*, December 2014. Accessed February 2, 2018. http://www.apa.org/monitor/2014/12/marshmallow-test.aspx.

Xiaoqun, Zhang, and Louisa Ha. 2016. Mobile news consumption and political news interest: A time budget perspective. *Journal of Applied Journalism and Media Studies* 5: 277–295.

Zeitz, Joshua. 2017. Lessons from the fake news pandemic of 1942. *Politico*, March 12. Accessed February 4, 2018. https://www.politico.com/magazine/story/2017/03/lessons-from-the-fake-news-pandemic-of-1942-214898.

Zuckerberg, Mark. 2017. Accessed January 12, 2018. https://www.facebook.com/zuck/posts/10104146268321841.

CHAPTER 5

Outsourcing Memory

In February of 1958, Isaac Asimov, a science fiction writer, published a short story titled "The Feeling of Power" in the futuristic magazine, *If: Worlds of Science Fiction.*[1] The story considers a world dominated by computers and intelligent machines, which have replaced the need for human thought. The protagonist, a character named Myron Aub, is a "low-grade technician" in the military, and he has rediscovered how to perform basic mathematical functions such as multiplication—an intellectual ability that had been supplanted by an overdependence on computing technologies. Aub demonstrates a few multiplication problems for his superior officers who are skeptical of his "magic-making" and question the value of this "parlor trick." Aub answers that "this points the way towards liberation from the machine." In this dystopic scenario, technology has finally usurped humanity. Sixty years after Asimov's story was published, we continue to invest more of ourselves into our machines, cosigning our memories and offloading our personal knowledge externally onto our smartphones, treating them as portable hard drives, so that we might occupy our working memory for other, more important tasks. The more we relinquish to machines, the more we lose. Perhaps it is not a work of science fiction to suppose we might already have crossed the threshold where we have become cognitively dependent on our technologies.

[1] Asimov, Isaac. 1958. The feeling of power. *If: Worlds of Science Fiction* 8: 4–11.

A. J. Reid, *The Smartphone Paradox*,
https://doi.org/10.1007/978-3-319-94319-0_5

Abby Smith Rumsey, author of *When We Are No More: How Digital Memory Is Shaping Our Future*, argues that "from cuneiform to computer chip, each innovation in knowledge storage has increased our fitness as a species…free[ing] up space in our brain attics for new questions to ponder."[2] Her optimistic view of intellectual technologies operates from the premise that the human brain needs to declutter. But every few years, researchers discover that the brain's capacity is larger than previously thought. Paul Reber, Professor of Psychology at Northwestern University, estimates the capacity of the human brain to exceed 2.5 petabytes—or equivalent to the amount of content viewed on a television running 24 hours per day for 300 years. In other words, "We don't have to worry about running out of space in our lifetime."[3] The fear that our brains will reach its spatial limit drives the faulty assumption that we need devices to clear the cache. More important is that intellectual technologies are negatively impacting the processes by which we access information and the ways in which we generate meaningful relationships between individual pieces of information. And this, as it turns out, is the problem with treating our personal devices as added brain space.

A seminal 2011 study, "Google Effects on Memory: Cognitive Consequences of Having Information at our Fingertips," found that we are less likely to store and recall information if we believe it to be accessible later, and this is redefining the way our memory functions. In two experiments, the researchers instructed participants to remember 40 trivia statements. To do so, participants typed the trivia statements (such as, "An ostrich's eye is bigger than its brain") into a computer word processor. Half of the participants believed that the computer would save their typed responses, and the other half understood that their statements would be erased from the computer. In addition, half of the participants were asked to explicitly remember the trivia statements. Later, when the participants attempted a free recall of the information, the researchers observed a "direct forgetting" effect. Those who had believed their statements were saved to a computer were less likely to remember them on their own. Those participants who were told to explicitly remember the statements

[2] Rumsey, Abby Smith. 2016. *When We Are No More: How Digital Memory is Shaping Our Future*. New York: Bloomsbury Press.

[3] Reber, Paul. 2010. What is the memory capacity of the human brain? *Scientific American*, May 1. https://www.scientificamerican.com/article/what-is-the-memory-capacity/. Accessed 3 May 2018.

(as opposed to having them saved digitally) performed better on recall. Or, as the researchers explained: "Because search engines are continually available to us, we may often be in a state of not feeling we need to encode the information internally. When we need it, we will look it up." Our relationship with information and knowledge is fundamentally changing. Consequently, we are much more adept at remembering where information is stored rather than the actual information. The researchers in the study concluded that:

> When people expect information to remain continuously available (such as we expect with Internet access), they are more likely to remember where to find it than to remember the details of the item. One could argue that this is an adaptive use of memory—to include the computer and online search engines as an external memory system that can be accessed at will.[4]

However, there are conflicting views as to whether this "adaptive use of memory" is ultimately beneficial or harmful to our cognition. Rumsey welcomes the ways in which digital memory shapes our lives, saying, "We are adapting quite nimbly to having so much information at our fingertips." Digital memory, she believes, is just another benchmark in human evolution: "Outsourcing more and more knowledge to computers will be no better or worse for us personally and collectively than putting ink on paper." But we know now that there is inherent value to writing things down by hand that is not replicated in the digital environment. Aside from the benefits that basic literacy provides, handwriting actually strengthens our cognitive processes. Compared to typing, handwriting notes results in better recall transfer,[5] lengthier time of recall,[6] and activates the brain in different and more robust ways.[7] Indeed, writing actually improves the human condition.

[4] Sparrow, Betsy, Jenny Liu and Daniel M. Wegner. 2011. Google effects on memory: Cognitive consequences of having information at our fingertips. *Science* 333: 776–778.

[5] Mangen, A., L.G. Anda, G.H. Oxborough and K. Brønnick. 2015. Handwriting versus keyboard writing: Effect on word recall. *Journal of Writing Research* 7(2): 227–247.

[6] Bui, Dung C., Joel Myerson and Sandra Hale. 2013. Note-taking with computers: Exploring alternative strategies for improved recall. *Journal of Educational Psychology* 105: 299–309.

[7] James, Karin Harman and Laura E. Engelhardt. 2012. The effects of handwriting experience on functional brain development in pre-literate children. *Trends in Neuroscience and Education* 1: 32–42.

Perhaps there is a deeper connection between speed and memory. George A. Miller's 1956 seminal article, "The Magical Number Seven, Plus or Minus Two: Some Limits on Our Capacity for Processing Information," helped to establish the blueprint for better understanding our cognitive processes. Miller argued that our working memory, which he called the immediate memory, might function optimally when holding only 7 ± 2 bits of information at one time. But more recent research suggests that this magical number of items is closer to four,[8] or even as little as two.[9] Digital technologies typically speed up our processes; analog processes, such as handwriting and print reading, are more time-consuming and therefore necessarily more deliberate. French novelist Milan Kundera argues that "there is a secret bond between slowness and memory, between speed and forgetting." Technology writer Nicholas Carr takes this a step further, supposing that our memory should be preserved internally and that offloading our knowledge to devices weakens us: "When we outsource a memory to a machine, we also outsource a very important part of our intellect and even our identity." Carr then extrapolates this to mean: "Outsource memory, and culture withers." We might be becoming more adept at using external devices to search and retrieve our memories and information, all in the name of saving time and space, but in doing so, we are losing something far more important in exchange: ourselves.

What makes each of us a person is not well understood, and I am not going to attempt a deeply philosophical explanation here. (You can Google it instead.) However, I would argue that the baseline of our identity is comprised partially of a unique makeup of personal memories, experiences, and knowledge. A redistribution of these things onto our devices so that we might free up more of our working memory, so that we might continue to offload it again, is circular logic—an infinite loop of uploading and downloading. As I discuss later in this chapter, there is a significant difference between using a technology as an aid versus as a storage system, wherein the former is harmless and the latter is costly. We continue to infuse ourselves and our minds with technology without stopping to evaluate the consequences. Constant connection to our devices, and subse-

[8] Cowan, Nelson. 2001. The magical number 4 in short-term memory: A reconsideration of mental storage capacity. *Behavioral and Brain Sciences* 24: 87–114. https://doi.org/10.1017/S0140525X01003922.

[9] Gobet, Fernand and Gary Clarkson. 2010. Chunks in expert memory: Evidence for the magical number four … or is it two? *Memory* 12: 732–747.

quently to the Internet, creates an instinctive reaction to consult instead of think. Look up instead of ponder. And this is the underlying paradox of our smartphones; the greater the access to information, the lesser the understanding we possess of that information.

The Degeneration Generation

The calculator, as you know it, is dead. Last year, when I brought home a simple calculator for my daughter to use for checking her math homework, she declared that she'd rather continue using the app on her iPad. I quietly mourned all those poor schoolkids who will never learn that you can write "hello" upside down using only numbers on the TI-84 (0.1134 or 0.7734). This was a rite of passage for me and my friends in elementary school. (We later discovered other words, too.) Eventually, all modern schoolchildren who carry the moniker *digital native* will come to rely on the multifunctionality of their mobile devices for their calculator apps. And before long, they will just ask the device audibly: "What's 54 ÷ 12?" Inevitably, some of us will wonder whether or not it matters if the kids *actually have to type* the numbers on the keypad to arrive at their answer. Surely it would make no difference if they used the device's virtual assistant instead, *right?* Well, one thing is for sure: Asimov surely could not have foreseen a nine-year-old using a device that is one million times more powerful than all of NASA's computing power in 1969,[10] just to perform simple division.

Nicholas Carr's argument that new technologies weaken our identities and that "culture withers" sounds dangerously similar to Socrates's "elixir not of memory" alarmist posture. But there is something different about the technology-based arguments of the twenty-first century. Our knowledge often is contingent upon our Wi-Fi signal. We are not only experiencing an unprecedented increase in access to information and interaction with others; we are indulging in constant stimulation, which feeds an endless cycle of gratifications being sought and obtained. Over time, we come to rely on this digital-based personal assistant, instinctively reaching for our smartphones when we need to know the answer to something. Indeed, information acquisition is one of the most common gratifications obtained

[10] Puiu, Tibi. 2017. Your smartphone is millions of times more powerful than all of NASA's combined computing in 1969. *ZME Science*, September 10. https://www.zmescience.com/research/technology/smartphone-power-compared-to-apollo-432/. Accessed 29 Dec 2017.

from smartphone usage, but constantly using our devices to access information leads to a degeneration of our own cognitive processes, which consequently diminishes our ability to remember, comprehend, and understand.

M.C. Wittrock, an educational psychologist, wrote extensively on the idea that learning is a generative process, arguing that the focus of learning should be on "generative relations, rather than on storing information."[11] His argument was that unlike our digestive system, the neural system of the brain does not automatically transform inputs into outputs. That is, employing Google to look up the answer to a question does not necessarily result in the transfer of knowledge. A generative strategy could include summarizing or paraphrasing information, creating a visual map of information, or self-explaining that information—all ways to turn passive information consumption into active learning. By initiating these types of generative processes, our brains organize ideas and information into patterns of thought that are then further categorized into packages or units, called schema. The development of relationships between schemata is what fossilizes knowledge into our long-term memory; without the formation of connections between schemata, we resemble more of a well-trained parrot who mimics search engine page results than an intelligent person. Information is, according to computer philosophy writer Jaron Lanier, "alienated experience."[12] Schema formation requires context, something that is missing from shallow Internet searches. The Internet is a starry sky of individual bits of information, but knowledge is a meaningful constellation of relationships between them—that which the Internet alone cannot provide.

Building a library of transactive memories, as Rumsey advocates, is not entirely devoid of value. For example, I'm thankful that I no longer have to memorize the phone numbers of my contacts (despite the home phone numbers of my childhood friends being etched into my long-term memory), or that I have to recall how many cups are in a pint. In this sense, my smartphone acts as a memory aid. I can easily conjure my contact list or my Notes app that contains a list of my favorite recipes. Of course, there is no need to memorize the phone book or to remember specific recipes, for that matter. If the end goal is simply to prepare a delicious meal, it likely

[11] Wittrock, Merlin C. 1992. Generative learning processes of the brain. *Educational Psychologist* 27: 531–541.

[12] Lanier, Jaron. 2010. *You Are Not a Gadget: A Manifesto*. New York: Random House.

will not matter whether I follow the enumerated steps of a recipe or recall the steps from memory (assuming my recollection is accurate). But, talented chefs are able to ***improvise***, and this improvisation is made possible by understanding not only where and how to access individual recipes, but to interpret the relationship between recipes: what can be substituted, added, or left out. Experience plays an important role in developing expertise, but transactive memory robs us of that sophistication. Carr insists that "the Web provides a convenient and compelling supplement to personal memory, but when we start using [it] as a substitute for personal memory, bypassing the inner processes of consolidation, we risk emptying our minds of their riches."[13] Your smartphone is no more a reflection of your knowledge than your calculator is a statistics professor, or an online recipe is a Michelin-starred chef. Likewise, if I call someone and they pick up, what does it matter if I recalled the phone number or tapped the contact's icon on my iPhone? And what about those schoolchildren who ask their devices for mathematical solutions rather than type them into a keypad? In these instances, the truth is, it doesn't really matter. These tools are merely aids to memory. The benefit to modern technology is that we no longer have to store friends' phone numbers, or recipes, or even mathematical facts. But the underlying problem here is this basic argument is then extrapolated to scenarios that require a deeper synthesis of intellectual information, rather than just a basic delivery of facts. As design guru Don Norman says in his book, *The Design of Everyday Things*, "Even where the technology produces the answer, it is often buried in a list of potential answers, so we have to use our own knowledge—or the knowledge of our friends—to determine which of the potential items is the correct one." Technology produces information, not knowledge.

Earlier, in Chap. 2, I detailed my one-on-one conversation with Shonte, a 19-year-old undergraduate student. Throughout our discussion, she typified many of the same pro-technology views so commonly associated with her demographic: technology comes at a cost that is worthwhile. I challenged Shonte to consider the triangulation between her smartphone, information, and knowledge. Specifically, I asked her about whether or not retrieving information online leads to deeper understanding. Shonte reasoned, "Well, if I look up something like the capital of China again and again, eventually, I'll remember it." For Shonte, the

[13] Carr, Nicholas G. 2011. *The Shallows: What the Internet is Doing to Our Brains*. New York: W.W. Norton & Company.

medium of the content is irrelevant; the Internet is simply a much faster delivery system for accessing information, or as she puts it, "The whole world is at my fingertips." I explained that the Internet is a perfect tool for producing shallow information, or as Carr argues, "When we constrict our capacity for reasoning and recall or transfer those skills to a gadget, we sacrifice our ability to turn information into knowledge."[14] Like the calculator, there really is nothing wrong with using the Internet as an aid to memory, but a problem arises when we mistake collections of shallow points of information for a body of knowledge. I pushed back against Shonte's rationale by saying: "That is fine. But that is like a single data point for declarative knowledge—it's just one fact. But what if I then asked you a more abstract question about China's role in WWII? Or the effects of WWII on China's economy? Doesn't this require a deeper understanding of context and the relationships that exist between various data points of information?" Shonte replied:

> What do I know about China in WWII? Not much. But I could look it up. I feel like even if we have something that we can pull information from, what's the difference? I don't know if I'd be able to recall something just from reading it in a book either.

Indeed, there have been many media comparison studies that show no differences between the levels of comprehension as a function of medium; all things being equal, we comprehend just as much from a digital text as we do from a print-based text. However, that is not to say the two media are, in fact, equal. Because the physical makeup of digital and print reading is different, they produce significant differences in the *ways* that we read each format, and this can be problematic. Shonte is right in that her ability to recall is not entirely dependent on whether the information is displayed on a screen or on a printed page. But the roads traveled to arrive at those two points are quite different; our ways of reading print are unlike reading digital.

Naomi Baron is a Professor of Linguistics at American University in Washington, D.C. Her research centers on digital and print reading habits, and she has studied the effects of reading on screens. Her book, *Words*

[14] Carr, Nicholas G. 2017. How smartphones hijack our minds. *Wall Street Journal*, October 6. https://www.wsj.com/articles/how-smartphones-hijack-our-minds-1507307811. Accessed 4 May 2018.

Onscreen,[15] chronicles the trends in print and digital reading habits and makes an important argument; aside from the obvious differences in affordances, reading on a digital device such as a smartphone encourages lightweight, "one-off" reading, promoting speed but sacrificing comprehension and understanding. She argues that your smartphone is suitable for reading short or medium-length news articles and social media posts, but it is inadequate for close reading of texts and subsequent deeper understanding of complex topics. Baron distinguishes between "reading on the prowl," which includes skimming texts and scanning for information, and "continuous reading," which fosters deep reading. Smartphones and tablets support reading on the prowl because of the limited real estate of the screen and the heightened distractibility they afford. Consequently, our digital reading habits devastate our memory and, ultimately, our ability to acquire knowledge, otherwise known as cognition.

In Baron's own research, she has found that print reading (compared to digital reading) elicits greater motivation to read the text, a better memory recall of the content, and a higher likelihood of rereading. If our reading habits are primarily one-off and occur on-the-prowl, then we rely on snippets of information, often derived from headlines or skimming articles, which ultimately sacrifices context and perspective. Consider the news headline from January 5, 2018: "The U.S. Economy Added 2.1. Million Jobs in 2017." This certainly sounds like a bright spot for the Trump administration, and one that his press secretary has lauded, tweeting: "At least we can all agree the economy is better under President Trump."[16] But what the reader does not ascertain from that headline, or from that tweet, is that the month-to-month increase in employment actually began in 2011, under the Obama administration, and the job creation under Trump's first year as president is at its lowest level since 2010.[17,18] Comparatively, job growth under the Trump administration is

[15] Baron, Naomi. 2015. *Words Onscreen: The Fate of Reading in a Digital World*. New York: Oxford University Press.

[16] Sanders, Sarah. 2017. https://twitter.com/PressSec/status/939897264637652992. Accessed 12 Dec 2017.

[17] Jacobson, Louis. 2017. How strong has job growth been on Donald Trump's watch? *Politifact*, September 20. http://www.politifact.com/truth-o-meter/statements/2017/sep/20/donald-trump/how-strong-job-growth-been-trumps-watch/. Accessed 1 Dec 2017.

[18] Chinni, Dante. 2018. Bright spot for Trump in 2017, job creation faces new challenges. *NBC News*, January 7. https://www.nbcnews.com/politics/first-read/bright-spot-trump-2017-job-creation-faces-new-challenges-n835341. Accessed 2 Feb 2018.

less impressive when contextualized. To be sure, source bias plays an integral role in the way that we shape our views—especially when we skim news headlines, which is a behavior facilitated by our mobile devices. (The headline example above comes from *The Atlantic*, a left-leaning publication. Indeed, the more extreme the agenda of the publication, the more egregious examples of misleading headlines can be found.) In short, Baron argues that "Screens hasten us along. Print invites us to linger." In digital text, we take small hits of information. Print text is a more serious investment of our time and cognitive resources, which arguably is necessary for a contextualized understanding of the world around us.

I interviewed Dr. Baron for this book, and she offered valuable insight into the ways that our reading modalities shape our understanding of the content. To begin, the circumstances under which we are reading greatly influence both our performance and the outcome. The format in which you are reading this text (print or digital) might not be as significant as the conditions under which you are doing so (voluntarily or involuntarily). In Baron's words, "You can read anything you want, if you have a context for doing it." Reading an assigned text, as would be the case in most academic settings, versus reading for leisure are inherently different activities from the outset. Consequently, we cannot examine the effects of each modality solely as a product of its delivery system.

Under the right conditions, digital reading can be advantageous. Technology journalist Clive Thompson wrote the article "Reading *War and Peace* on my iPhone." In it, he chronicles his experiment to read Leo Tolstoy's masterpiece exclusively by way of his iPhone. Ultimately, Thompson found that this reading style was not only possible, but preferable. Most technology critics would discourage readers from tackling Tolstoy on the small screen; some would cite the physical side effects of reading a work of that length (according to Thompson's own calculations, it took him the equivalent of 27 hours of continuous reading time to complete *War and Peace*). Thompson even exploited one of the most disruptive features of digital text, the temptation to multitask: "I doubt I'd have gotten half of what I got out of *War and Peace* without Wikipedia ready at hand. It's hard to call that a distraction." However, he admits to increased social distraction, which was more difficult to overcome. He writes:

> I used to enjoy alerts; but with *War and Peace*, I shut them all down. I also had to turn off my *internal* alerts. This is harder to do, and more crucial. We typically assume that outside interruptions—digital beeps and boops—are chiefly what wreck our focus. But as science-of-attention researchers like Gloria Marks have found, the bigger problem is self-interruption. We're deeply social creatures. When we know that our pockets and purses contain full-on cocktail parties that are raging 24/7, we don't need beeps and buzzes from social networks to break our concentration. We break it ourselves, voluntarily, checking and rechecking Facebook the instant our mind wanders away from the plot of a novel.
>
> To focus on Tolstoy, I had to be much more "mindful." I had to start paying attention to my attention, to *notice* my own urges to peek at Twitter or email, so that I could decide to actively ignore them, instead of responding with a Pavolovian lunge for the app.

It's no doubt that talented readers like Clive Thompson can make this modality work. There is no denying that. But he is exceptional; the average digital reader is not voluntarily consuming Tolstoy. He or she is much more susceptible to social and internal distractions to which Thompson refers. Indeed, a major advantage of reading on a smartphone is convenience. As Thompson writes, "The downside of a phone is that it's a teensy portal into a book; the upside is it's always with you." But what about this? Are all environments suited for reading? Does reading on-the-prowl differ from reading under the deliberate condition to do so?

Learning theory suggests that environment is linked to the ways in which we acquire knowledge. The encoding specificity principle was first theorized by memory researchers Endel Tulving and Donald Thomson at the University of Toronto. Essentially, the principle states that the effectiveness of the ability to retrieve information is contingent upon the specific circumstances under which that information was first encoded. Reading on a mobile device guarantees a myriad of surroundings that are always changing: standing in line at the grocery store, at home on the couch, seated in a classroom, riding as a passenger in a car, to name a few. Similarly, situated cognition (sometimes referred to as situated learning) is a theory that describes learning as being situated within the coinciding activity during which it occurs.

> The activity in which knowledge is developed and deployed, it is now argued, is not separable from or ancillary to learning and cognition. Nor is it neutral. Rather, it is an integral part of what is learned. Situations might

> be said to co-produce knowledge through activity. Learning and cognition, it is now possible to argue, are fundamentally situated.[19]

The reading environment is an important influencer on what we get out of the text. We certainly understand this concept when it comes to our health; if we wish to regulate our consumption of something, such as junk food or alcohol, the first step is to modify our environment so as to prevent easy access to these things. Similarly, when we read, we must be cognizant of our purpose for reading, as well as how our surroundings might nurture or stifle our reading goals. The idea that environment and surrounds shape our ability to read and thing is well understood in education, particularly for developing early literacy skills. But as we grow older, we succumb to reading-on-the-prowl, both mentally and physically, in precarious and temporary situations mostly because we accept it as a trade-off for the ability to read anything anywhere, anytime. We negotiate with our technology in the name of convenience.

Just as I proclaimed "the calculator is dead" at the beginning of this subchapter, there have been many prognosticators that have said the same about the print book. Nicholas Negroponte, the founder of the Massachusetts Institute of Technology's Media Lab, proclaimed that the physical book would be dead in five years.[20] His prediction was made at a technology conference in 2010. Like many others before him, Negroponte cited the downfall of the film and music industries as the disastrous templates that print books inevitably face. But unlike watching film or listening to music, humans are not predisposed to reading; it is an unnatural act. Steven Pinker, a cognitive psychologist and linguist, says, "[We] are wired for sound, but print is an optional accessory that must be painstakingly bolted on."[21] Perhaps because reading must be learned, it is more sacrosanct than passive activities such as watching or listening, which come default and effortlessly. I'm confident that my prediction about the death of the calculator will fare better than Negroponte's ill-fated statement that

[19] Brown, John Seely, Allan Collins and Paul Duguid. 1989. Situated cognition and the culture of learning. *Educational Researcher* 18: 32–42.

[20] Siegler, M.G. 2010. Nicholas Negroponte: The physical book is dead in 5 years. *TechCrunch*, August 6. https://techcrunch.com/2010/08/06/physical-book-dead/?utm_source=TweetMeme&utm_medium=widget&utm_campaign=retweetbutton. Accessed 5 Feb 2018.

[21] McGuinness, Diane. 1997. *Why Our Children Can't Read, and What We Can Do About It*. New York: Free Press.

print would be dead by the year 2015. The calculator can be replaced easily by other digital tools; the printed word, however, cannot.

Sadly, the company Audible.com makes no distinction between reading a book and listening to a recording of someone reading a book. A recent commercial produced by the audiobook giant opens with a title screen that features a quote from *Business Insider*: "Successful people have one thing in common. They read." The article being referenced in the commercial asked nine successful people about their reading habits. Each one of them credited a heavy media diet of reading books as a direct contributor to their success, and they continue to read voraciously. From Oprah Winfrey to Mark Zuckerberg to Bill Gates, Elon Musk, Warren Buffet, and others, each claims to spend hours a day reading. The narrator in the commercial rhetorically asks, "How do they find the time? With Audible." But none of the successful people interviewed even mentioned audiobooks. They were talking about *reading*. Winfrey is shown holding up a Colson Whitehead novel; Gates is seen brandishing five of his favorite nonfiction titles. Each person recalls his or her relationship with print books and magazines. Not audiobooks. For Audible.com to make this leap from successful people read, therefore you should listen to books is a misleading and false conclusion. This is not to say that audiobooks themselves are devoid of value; indeed, it is more productive and entertaining to listen to an audiobook than not to. What is disconcerting is the suggestion that auditory processing of text is an acceptable substitute for print reading. Why read when you can listen? In fact, the commercial concludes with the puzzling tagline, "Listening is the new reading." Perhaps the prognosticators who warned about the death of print might have been more accurate if they had warned about the death of deep reading instead.

A 2016 Pew Research study found an uptick in the percentage of non-book readers in the United States, and they are predominantly lower-class, uneducated adults[22]—coincidentally, the same demographic that is least likely to own a smartphone. But it is not just that we are simply becoming a nation of nonreaders; it is that our reading tastes have shifted away from print and towards the digital, the abbreviated, and the convenient. Companies like Audible.com are only capitalizing on a digital culture of impulsivity and instant gratification that lacks patience with the printed

[22] Perrin, Andrew. 2018. Who doesn't read books in America? *Pew Research Center*. http://www.pewresearch.org/fact-tank/2016/11/23/who-doesnt-read-books-in-america/. Accessed 3 May 2018.

word, which requires time and focus: two adversaries of mobile devices. The President of the United States, who has been widely criticized for his "unusually light appetite for reading,"[23] even mistakes simplicity for efficiency in reading. In an interview with Axios, he stated, "I like bullets, or I like as little [text] as possible. I don't need, you know, 200-page reports on something that can be handled on a page."[24] There are some issues, such as foreign policy, that cannot (and should not) be distilled into a bulleted list, but rather deserve full attentiveness and time devoted to understanding its complexity. Some things are deserving of a novel, not a tweet.

Another example of our willingness to supplant deep print with shallow digital is the increasingly popular mobile app, The Skimm. Marketed specifically to 20–30-something female Millennials as a news app, The Skimm delivers bite-sized news content in audio format. According to the developers, "In less than 10 minutes, we'll give you the context you need to understand the biggest issues in the world. You'll know what happened, why it's important, and where we are now. All you have to do is listen."[25] Again, my grievance is not that news topics are reduced to audible bullet points, but that this likely satiates our desire to know and thus replaces the need to read further. The success of companies like Audible.com and apps like The Skimm points to a larger, more dangerous trend: that we view print as inconvenient and inefficient, and that the digital, audio solution provides us all that we need to know. Sure, it is technically possible for smartphone users to read entire novels on a screen, but it is more likely that digital text only encourages a degradation of the deep reading that print demands.

Smartphones are wonderfully useful shortcuts to the Internet, and they are perfectly suited for settling bets over trivial information, but we should not mistake them for representatives of our minds, nor should we use them as a substitute for print media. Rather than treating our smartphones as portable hard drives that we mindlessly summon for answers, we ought

[23] Fisher, Marc. 2016. Donald Trump doesn't read much. Being president probably wouldn't change that. *The Washington Post*, July 17. https://www.washingtonpost.com/politics/donald-trump-doesnt-read-much-being-president-probably-wouldnt-change-that/2016/07/17/d2ddf2bc-4932-11e6-90a8-fb84201e0645_story.html?utm_term=.cc87a435e496. Accessed 3 Feb 2018.

[24] Groulx, Robin. 2017. Reality bites: Trump's wake-up call. *AXIOS*, January 18. https://www.axios.com/reality-bites-trumps-wake-up-call-1513299979-3bd3a708-26be-4232-8faa-6970e65c6cf1.html. Accessed 3 Jan 2018.

[25] The Skimm. 2018. https://www.theskimm.com/app. Accessed 4 Feb 2018.

to reinvigorate the practice of slow and deliberate thought processes, such as those that originate from reading books and nuanced articles rather than tweets and Facebook memes, as well as engaging in meaningful discourse and intellectual debate rather than quipping each other in 280-character jabs. Our complicated relationship with digital reading might best be summed up by a Twitter user who goes by Sweatpants Cher (@House_Feminist), who tweeted in regard to Twitter's expansion of the maximum character limit from 140 to 280: "I secretly hope that twitter keeps extending the character limit as a social experiment, slowly conditioning our attention spans until we're able to read actual books again."[26]

Just Google It

Who Wants to Be a Millionaire was a popular television game show in the early 2000s, giving contestants the opportunity to win a top prize of one million dollars for answering a series of increasingly difficult trivia questions. *Millionaire*, as it became known, was a cultural juggernaut. Its blueprint was simple: the host sat face-to-face with the contestant and both were surrounded by a live studio audience on a round stage. The multiple-choice questions would start off basic (a $100 question once read: "Homeowners buy surge protectors to protect their possessions from unexpected surges of what?") and would get progressively more difficult (a $1,000,000 question once read: "Nephelococcygia is the practice of doing what?"). But there was some strategy involved with the game. If the contestant was unsure of the answer to a question, he or she could use three lifelines to help increase the chances of answering correctly. In the original version of the game, these lifelines included "50:50," which narrowed the multiple-choice answers down from four to two answers; "Ask the Audience," in which the audience members were polled on the question; and "Phone-A-Friend," in which the contestant was able to phone a contact presumably more expert on the topic and ask him or her for the correct answer or at least their best educated guess. This last lifeline was discontinued in 2010, after it became increasingly obvious that the person on the other end of the line was searching the Internet for the answer to the question rather than giving his or her guess on the trivia question. The common practice became to phone a friend, read the question quickly,

[26] Sweatpants Cher. 2018. https://twitter.com/House_Feminist/status/957109143650820097. Accessed 4 Feb 2018.

and hope that he or she could locate the answer online and relay the information back before time expired. The ruse was not well-disguised, as players on the other end of the line could be heard typing furiously. The rules of the game, of course, did not explicitly prohibit the strategy, and it became obvious that players did not view this for what it was: an unintentional loophole in the game's format and a clear misuse of resources. Yet, it is unclear whether contestants actually considered this method unethical or whether they truly did not make a distinction between *knowing* information and *accessing* information online. I suspect some did view it as outright cheating, or at least a gratuitous interpretation of the rule, but did it anyways. Still, I can't help but wonder if some contestants failed to see a difference. Regardless, the show was forced to rethink its format. The host at that time, Meredith Vieira, addressed the change in the gameplay by telling the studio audience:

> For the sake of the audience here [in the studio] and the audience at home, there has been a slight change in gameplay that I want to explain to you folks. On the board, we no longer have Phone-a-Friend as a lifeline. Now, I want to explain to you why. Technology has changed, as you know, over the years and we feel that it has compromised the integrity of that lifeline and the [original] intent, because often when a contestant calls somebody, a friend at home, who do they get? They get Mr. Internet, and we feel that it isn't fair that some people have access to a computer and some don't, because the game is really not about that; it's about what's inside somebody's head.[27]

In an attempt to explain why the game show would discontinue its Phone-a-Friend lifeline, Vieira deftly summarized the paradox of an entire generation, one in which the difference between "Mr. Internet" and "what's inside somebody's head" is greatly obscured. The producers of *Who Wants to Be a Millionaire* ultimately decided that having knowledge was more important than the ability to locate information, thus the modification in the format of the game. Michael Patrick Lynch argues that "Google-knowing," or relying on Google and other search engines for information-seeking, fortifies our transactive memory, but it does not improve our knowledge, and knowledge, according to Socrates, is "the only one good." In 2015, Google released internal data, which showed that more Google

[27]Wikipedia. 2018. Who wants to be a millionaire. https://en.wikipedia.org/wiki/Who_Wants_to_Be_a_Millionaire_(U.S._game_show)#Lifelines. Accessed 4 Feb 2018.

searches take place on mobile devices than on desktops.[28] (I realize that I'm referring exclusively to Google here, and that this is not entirely representative of all Internet searches, but Google is ranked as the most used search engine worldwide, dwarfing even its nearest competitor, Baidu.[29]) Our smartphones are wonderful retrieval devices, but they are not our teachers. They fetch information so that we might be momentarily enlightened, but they ultimately rob us of the generative processes that are instrumental to forming a key building block of ourselves, and by extension, our culture.

Internet search engines such as Google quicken our access to information and immediately gratify our curiosity by compiling an overwhelming number of websites in response to any question posed, but consulting Google is not an exercise in knowledge acquisition. It is at best, a means to an end. For instance, I often tell my writing students that Wikipedia is an ideal place to begin their research if they lack a basic understanding of the topic. (They are usually shocked to hear this after experiencing years of teachers villainizing the site as an unreliable and nonacademic tool.) But the Internet can be highly fickle. Search results and answers are not always one and the same. Let's try a quick exercise. Try Googling a low-level trivia question such as "What is the capital of Nicaragua?" This will yield a results page that correctly identifies Managua and provides an abundance of declarative knowledge related to the capital city (127,000,000 page results, to be specific). This fundamental question about the capital of Nicaragua requires a basic semantic understanding of the words *capital* and *Nicaragua*. (No worries, though, if the user incorrectly used *capitol* instead of *capital*, or misspelled Nicaragua, Google can infer what you meant and yields the same search results.) Further, one would have to possess the knowledge of both the concept that Nicaragua is a country and the rule that countries have capitals. Consequently, search results are dependent upon the search keywords that we input, and the keywords that we select to use in our search are rooted in our preexisting understanding of that topic. (Hopefully, you can start to see a problem here.) For example, when the phrase "Is the Earth flat?" is Googled, the first result is a 2016 article published in *Popular Science* titled "10 Easy Ways You Can Tell for Yourself that the Earth is Not

[28] Google. 2015. Building for the next moment. https://adwords.googleblog.com/2015/05/building-for-next-moment.html. Accessed 12 Feb 2018.

[29] Internet Live Stats. 2018. Google search statistics. http://www.internetlivestats.com/google-search-statistics/. Accessed 12 Feb 2018.

Flat."[30] But when that phrase is presented as "Flat Earth," the first three search results point to Wiki sites dedicated to explaining the beliefs of flat-Earthers, and the fourth result provides a link to The Flat Earth Society, a biased source to say the least. And we know that the top-ranked search results are the most often-clicked and regarded as being the most credible.[31] The problem arises when a search engine is used to find quick answers to complex issues. Researchers at the Welten Institute Research Centre for Learning, Teaching, and Technology in the Netherlands studied the search behavior patterns of adolescents, finding that:

> When searching for rather straight-forward facts, formulating search queries and the shallow evaluation of search results is not a problem (e.g., searching for the height of the Eiffel tower). However, when people search for information about more complex issues, such as the causes of climate change, search queries can be formulated in different ways, resulting in a diversity of information.[32]

We have anointed the omniscient search engine to be the purveyor of information, but Google is not wise. Search engines are merely algorithmic responses to our chosen keywords, which in turn are the product of our preexisting knowledge and biases.

As an experiment, put this book down, grab your smartphone, and begin typing a common phrase into the Google search engine and see how that phrase is populated in the search box. Try phrases like *how do I*, or *who is the*. You'll see that Google acts like a friend who tries to finish your sentences for you, suggesting popular searches that begin with the same phrase. This feature, known as Google Autocomplete, offers insight into the perverse ways that Internet users interact with search engines. Tamar Yehoshua is the Vice President of Product Management at Google, as well as the leader for the Mobile Search Team. In a 2016 blog post, Yehoshua explains how autocomplete is populated:

[30] Schottlender, Moriel. 2016. 10 easy ways you can tell for yourself that the Earth is not flat. *Popular Science*, January 26. https://www.popsci.com/10-ways-you-can-prove-earth-is-round. Accessed 12 Feb 2018.

[31] Unkel, Julian and Alexander Haas. 2017. The effects of credibility cues on the selection of search engine results. *Journal of the Association for Information Science and Technology* 68: 1850–1862.

[32] Walhout, Jaap, Paola Oomen, Halszka Jarodzka and Saskia Brand-Gruwel. 2017. Effects of task complexity on online search behavior of adolescents. *Journal of the Association for Information Science and Technology* 68: 1449–1461.

> Autocomplete isn't an exact science, and the output of the prediction algorithms changes frequently. Predictions are produced based on a number of factors including the popularity and freshness of search terms. Given that search activity varies, the terms that appears in Autocomplete for you may change over time… It's also important to keep in mind that Autocomplete predictions aren't search results and don't limit what you can search for. It's a shortcut for those who are interested.[33]

There is even an online *Family Feud*-style game titled Google Feud[34] that asks you to guess how Google Autocomplete will finish phrases such as *is it wrong to be*, *can I still buy*, and *do fish*. The player gets three attempts to guess any of the top ten answers that appear in the results list, which is ordered by frequency of actual Google searches. Some automatic phrases are absurdly comical, such as the top answer to *is it bad to … sleep with socks on*. Other Autocomplete-generated phrases are upsetting. The top fill-in phrase for *is it wrong to be* is *gay*, and the second most frequented search phrase for *is it wrong to* is *sleep with your sister*. Still further, Google's auto-suggestions for search queries can reflect racist and misogynistic undertones; the phrase *is Obama* is met with the top auto-filled response, *Kenyan*, and searching the phrase *things a woman should* generates the following expressions, by order of popularity:

> … *know*
> … *do to keep her man*
> … *never say to a man*
> … *ask for in a divorce*

This is the non-neutrality of technology. Autocomplete is a complex algorithmic reflection of the top Internet searches with matching phrasing, location-based user data, and Internet browsing history all influencing the suggested phrases, but it certainly can take on a more rhetorical significance. And Autocomplete is not unique to Google; all of the major search engines use their own formula to populate search queries for their users. The Autocomplete awareness reached fever pitch during the 2016 presidential race, when researchers questioned whether or not search engines accounted for a variation in voter perception of candidates. One study

[33] Yehoshua, Tamar. 2016. Google search autocomplete. *Google*, June 10. https://blog.google/products/search/google-search-autocomplete/?m=1. Accessed 25 Jan 2018.

[34] Google Feud. 2018. http://www.googlefeud.com/. Accessed 24 Jan 2018.

found that search rankings could potentially have shifted candidate preferences of undecided voters by a margin of 20% or higher.[35] Yehoshua defends the search engine feature, saying that "the autocomplete algorithm is designed to avoid completing a search for a person's name with terms that are offensive or disparaging." Still, it is not too difficult to find an example that nullifies this official statement. This is a classic example of the non-neutrality of technology at work. Google denies any deliberate tampering or persuasion of search engine results, and no one has uncovered any evidence to suggest otherwise. Autocomplete is the product of code, not malicious employees with hidden agendas. Yet, behind every line of code, and behind every search query, there is a flawed human, susceptible to misinformation.

But this is a book about smartphones, not just search engines or the Internet. The significance here is that smartphones operate as the conduit to Internet, placing it within our grasp at any moment's notice. Smartphones mainline the Internet into our conversations, our interactions, our lives, making it virtually inescapable. And the way in which we articulate our search queries not only says a lot about us, but it also informs the way in which search results are presented. Smartphone-based intelligent assistants (IAs) such as Siri, Alexa, and Cortana are gaining steam; the Pew Research Center reports that nearly half of Americans use an IA, primarily on their smartphones. The most commonly cited reasons for using an IA is its hands-free convenience and because "it's fun."[36] The IA has only expedited our impetuous search habits by allowing us to bypass the keyboard and make audible demands of our devices. Voice recognition lowers the barrier to search online; Apple users have the entirety of the Internet at their beck and call just by uttering, "Hey Siri." If we can argue that the Internet is not wise, we can extend this to mean that these digital-based personal assistants are even less wise, only facilitating our use of the unwise Web. Yet we treat conversation with our devices the same way a curious child interacts with his or her parent, authentically exchanging questions for answers. Still, in some ways, because IAs sound human, it is

[35] Epstein, Robert and Ronald E. Robertson. 2015. The search engine manipulation effect (SEME) and its possible impact on the outcomes of elections. *Proceedings of the National Academy of Sciences of the United States of America* 112: E4512–E4521.

[36] Olmstead, Kenneth. 2017. Nearly half of Americans use digital voice assistants, mostly on their smartphones. *Pew Research Center*. http://www.pewresearch.org/fact-tank/2017/12/12/nearly-half-of-americans-use-digital-voice-assistants-mostly-on-their-smartphones/. Accessed 24 Jan 2018.

difficult to see that our online search efforts may not provide conclusive answers, rather a mirror of our preexisting views, which may be flawed.

The topic of vaccinations is a controversial one, unless you ask the experts. Then, the answer is clear: vaccinations safely and effectively stem the spread of disease. But in recent years, outspoken celebrities and politicians have suggested that vaccination might be linked to autism, prompting waves of new parents to question whether they should vaccinate their children, despite the Centers for Disease Control and Prevention (CDC),[37] the Food and Drug Administration (FDA),[38] and the American Academy of Pediatrics (AAP),[39] all taking the position that there is no causation between vaccines and autism. If the Internet has taught us anything, it is that there is a vastly expanding repository of information that is becoming harder to sift through, evaluate, and trust. Consider the following exercise with an IA.

Me: Siri, should I get my child vaccinated?
Siri: I can't answer that, Alan.

It seems that Siri does not want to weigh in on this crucial question, even though the responsible answer is "Yes." But I am not deterred. I rephrase my question as this:

Me: Siri, are vaccinations good?

This time, the results include a list of five websites, led by one titled "Five Important Reasons to Vaccinate Your Child"[40] from www.vaccines.gov, followed by four other articles that appear to be from credible and authentic sources. Below these articles, though, a Twitter widget presents a collection of tweets from random, unverified users, whose text matches the

[37] Center for Disease Control and Prevention. 2018. Autism spectrum disorder. https://www.cdc.gov/ncbddd/autism/topics.html. Accessed 13 Jan 2018.

[38] U.S. Food & Drug Administration. 2018. Thimerosal and vaccines. https://www.fda.gov/BiologicsBloodVaccines/SafetyAvailability/VaccineSafety/ucm096228.htm. Accessed 13 Jan 2018.

[39] American Academy of Pediatrics. 2010. Thimerosal in vaccines not linked to autism. https://www.aap.org/en-us/about-the-aap/aap-press-room/Pages/Thimerosal-In-Vaccines-Not-Linked-to-Autism.aspx. Accessed 13 Jan 2018.

[40] U.S. Department of Health and Human Services. 2018. Five important reasons to vaccinate your child. https://www.vaccines.gov/more_info/features/five-important-reasons-to-vaccinate-your-child.html. Accessed 14 Jan 2018.

keywords *vaccinations, are*, and *good*. This is disconcerting because these unqualified views are unsolicited, yet they are presented millimeters apart from factual, research-based information from medical sites. This false illusion of equivalency only highlights the limitations of an algorithmic-driven IA with a human voice with which we relate. Again, I rephrase the question:

Me: Siri, are vaccinations bad?

Surprisingly, this returns a list of different websites originating from dubious sources, including an article titled, "Six Reasons to Say NO to Vaccination."[41] This time, the Twitter widget provides a list of tweets containing the keywords *vaccinations, are*, and *bad*. Naturally, these tweets are unqualified opines.

This exercise illustrates an important point beyond just that intelligent assistants aren't quite that intelligent. Rather, this example shows how complicated, loaded, or controversial questions deserve more thoughtful responses than what a search engine can provide. Further, the Internet-fueled answers we receive to our questions are heavily influenced by the ways in which we search the very same Internet, which is influenced by our preexisting beliefs and views. In some ways, we are only reaffirming ourselves and the answers we'd like to hear (consider the subtle difference between "Is there a God?" and "Is there no God?"). This is ironic given our willingness to resign ourselves to the wisdom of the Web. But the Internet only transmits bits of information, not knowledge, and by extension, not wisdom. And our smartphones are only vehicles for accessing that information on impulse. In his book, *Building a Bridge to the Eighteenth Century: How the Past Can Improve Our Future*, Neil Postman recognizes that:

> The problem addressed in the nineteenth century was how to get more information to more people, faster, and in more diverse forms. For 150 years, humanity has worked with stunning ingenuity to solve this problem. The good news is that we have. The bad news is that, in solving it, we have created another problem, never before experienced: information glut, information as garbage, information divorced from purpose and even meaning.[42]

[41] The Healthy Home Economist. 2018. Six reasons to say No to vaccination. https://www.thehealthyhomeeconomist.com/six-reasons-to-say-no-to-vaccination/. Accessed 14 Jan 2018.

[42] Postman, Neil. 1999. *Building a Bridge to the Eighteenth Century: How the Past Can Improve Our Future*. New York: Random House, Inc.

Smartphones move information, in many cases, dumb information. Traditional news sources that were once held to higher editorial standards have been replaced, or at least diluted by, the fleeting news headlines and information bursts that fuel the Internet in perpetuity. For many, the phrase *Did you read [insert name of article here] in the [insert name of print newspaper here]?* is interchangeable with *Did you see what [insert name here] said on [insert name of social media platform here]?* This is problematic because, as Postman points out, the Internet is not a "'truth' medium; it is an information medium." The stalwarts of the Internet are not truth-seekers, nor are they editors with any sort of culpability. The Internet is a sprawling canvas shaded by truth, benefiting most from clicks and views instead of nuance and understanding, and smartphones are the perfect vehicle to complement the Internet model of brevity and convenience.

Are We Dumb?

In March 2005, I moved from Columbus, OH to Wilmington, NC to attend graduate school. Admittedly, geography played a large role in this decision; I was tired of the relentless Ohio winters, and I wanted to live by the sea. Somehow, I managed to convince my then-girlfriend (and future wife) to leave her wonderful teaching job, move south, and rent a dilapidated house with me just a few miles from the beach. I remember sitting at a local diner drinking coffee while thumbing through the classifieds in the local newspaper, *The Star News*, looking for decent-paying hourly jobs. (Sadly, the diner, Whitey's, has since been bulldozed and replaced with a Walgreens.) I came across an ad that read, "Want to Work on the Water?" and my ocean-loving mindset got the better of me once again. The job was in marine construction: building residential piers, floating docks, walkways, and bulkheads. I was a newly minted graduate student armed with a B.A. in English and had never built anything useful in my entire life, nor had I ever step foot on a residential pier before, and I certainly couldn't have explained what a bulkhead was for (I think I even referred to the arsenic-laden round posts that support the pier's frame as *pylons* instead of *pilings*—a common mispronunciation—for several weeks, until I was corrected). It turned out that the jobsite usually did include an ocean view, but the ad neglected to mention the hard labor that often would obscure this ideal setting: spending entire days behind a compound miter saw, routing deck boards for 12-hour shifts, humping lumber hundreds of yards to the end of the pier, trudging through marshlands to do work on the underbelly of the structure, and on and on. Consequently, the small company had a high turnover rate, something not uncommon in the construction industry, but I usually worked with the same crew of hardworking and misguided carpenters: an 18-year-old high school dropout, a 50-something ex-musician, and an ex-convict probably in his early 40s (we never actually discussed the details of how he earned the ex-convict status). I viewed the work as being difficult but rewarding. Almost sadistically Zen-like. Looking back, this mentality may have come easier for me because I knew that eventually I would leave the job site, unlike my brothers-in-carpentry who understandably had a tepid view of their careers.

After several years of this informal apprenticeship, I slowly acquired the knowledge and skills required for pier craftsmanship. Over time, I learned intricacies such as how the permitting process worked with the Coastal Area Management Act (CAMA), how to calculate high and low mean tides, how to design a blueprint, how to diagnose boat lift problems, and more. Even after I had finished my Master's degree, I continued working on piers, eventually branching off and starting my own business: Salty Dog Pier Co. Unexpectedly, I had become an expert in marine construction. In his book, *The Death of Expertise*, Tom Nichols, a self-described "public intellectual,"[43] points out that we readily acknowledge the expert abilities of *technicians*, people who possess certain and often tangible skill-sets such as doctors and classical pianists, yet we too easily dismiss those with cerebral expertise. No one hears Beethoven's 32 Piano Sonatas and thinks, "I could play that," unless he or she is classically trained on the piano, but everyone thinks himself or herself to be well-informed of politics, religion, and other areas of conversation not suitable for Thanksgiving dinners. We recognize that some endeavors, particularly those of technicians, require extensive training and experience, in other words, *expertise*. And although building a pier is not as critical as performing a surgery, it is best left to a technician rather than a novice. But the Internet has become the great equalizer; YouTube yields 289,000 results for "how to build a pier" and 3.6 million videos for "how to perform surgery." The danger here, according to Nichols, is that the Internet conflates "knowing things" with "understanding them":

[43] Nichols, Tom. 2017. *The Death of Expertise*. New York: Oxford University Press.

> Accessing the Internet can actually make people dumber than if they had never engaged a subject at all. The very act of searching for information makes people think they've learned something, when in fact they're more likely to be immersed in yet more data they do not understand. This happens because after enough time surfing, people no longer can distinguish between things that may have flashed before their eyes and things they actually *know*[44]

Let me be clear. It is not that searching the Internet makes us dumb, but our online behaviors might well already be a manifestation of our intelligence. In the previous section, I argue that the Internet can be a reflection of ourselves: our prior knowledge, our preconceptions, our biases. And it is because of this that the Internet often can only amplify, not install, our intelligence and our dumbness. Indeed, there is good information to be found online; this book might not have been possible without online journals, academic databases, and the information highway. But years of experience have taught me how to identify, evaluate, critique, and synthesize information. These are not innate qualities of all Internet users; this is a new set of digital literacies that must be learned. The problem with the Internet as a medium is that it is a tool, not a teacher, yet we fail to differentiate between the two.

Therefore, dumbness cannot be a function of information; any of us can summon information by way of a search engine. Instead, I define dumbness as the disparity between what we think we know and what we actually know. The problem we are facing in this Information Age, however, is that we often mistake the two. The Internet has democratized information, but in doing so, we confuse *perceived knowing* with *actual knowing*. The psychological explanation for this is called the Dunning-Kruger effect, wherein there is a failure to recognize one's level of competence on a given subject.[45] Image 5.1 illustrates the researchers' observations that those who are most confident tend to be either the least or most knowledgeable in that specific area.

As the researchers point out, though, "Competence begets calibration." That is, with increased competence comes the ability to gauge understanding more accurately. In the field of teaching and learning, this

[44] Nichols, Tom. 2017. *The Death of Expertise*. New York: Oxford University Press.

[45] Kruger, Justin and David Dunning. 1999. Unskilled and unaware of it: How difficulties in recognizing one's own incompetence lead to inflated self-assessments. *Journal of Personality and Social Psychology* 77: 1121–1134. https://doi.org/10.1037/0022-3514.77.6.1121.

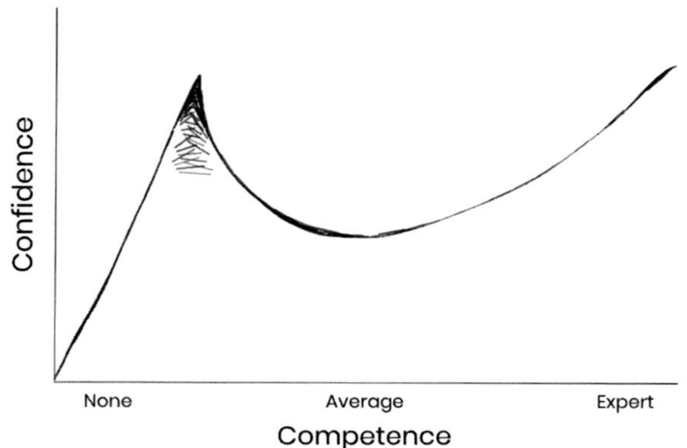

Image 5.1 The Dunning-Kruger effect shows how confidence and competence intersect. Source: Author

can be explained in terms of a learner's level of calibration, or the "degree to which judgments or performance accurately reflect actual performance."[46] Measuring calibration is simple and typically takes place in two ways: prediction (asking the learner to predict a score on a comprehension test) and postdiction (asking the learner to gauge how well he or she did on a completed comprehension test). Similar to what the researchers Dunning and Kruger observed in their experiments, studies on calibration consistently show that the overconfident tend to be the lowest-performing and the least calibrated.[47] Certainly confidence does not indicate competence, and in fact, this is better described as an inverse relationship between the two.

[46] Bol, Linda, Douglas J. Hacker, Patrick O'Shea and Dwight Allen. 2005. The influence of overt practice, achievement level, and explanatory style on calibration accuracy and performance. *The Journal of Experimental Education* 73: 269–290. https://doi.org/10.3200/JEXE.73.4.269-290.

[47] Bol, Linda, Rose Riggs, Douglas J. Hacker, Daniel L. Dickerson and John A. Nunnery. 2010. The calibration accuracy of middle school students in math classes. *Journal of Research in Education* 21: 81–96; Glenberg, Arthur M. and William Epstein. 1985. Calibration of comprehension. *Journal of Experimental Psychology: Learning, Memory, and Cognition* 11: 702–718. https://doi.org/10.1037//0278-7393.11.1-4.702; Glenberg, Arthur M., Thomas Sanocki, William Epstein and Craig Morris. 1987. Enhancing calibration of comprehension. *Journal of Experimental Psychology: General* 116: 119–136.

The Internet simultaneously delivers us to information *and* misinformation in the world, resulting in an obfuscated boundary between fact and fiction. Consequently, reading on the Internet requires a judicious degree of skepticism. A gross side effect of democratizing information is that it favors the confident and masks expertise; if you can say something with conviction, it is more likely to be believed by others. And as the Dunning-Kruger effect observes, those who possess the most confidence on a topic are those groups who are the most and the least knowledgeable about that topic.

In December 2017, Twitter users were presented with an exemplary case study of this phenomenon when a conversation thread about the existence of the Megalodon went viral. Before I describe the conversation, I shall provide you with some context. I am not a marine biologist, nor do I have any background in the marine sciences. For these matters, I defer to the experts, and among that group, it is scientific consensus that the prehistoric ocean-dweller has been extinct for millions of years. That said, the infamous Twitter exchange began when a user, The Unexplained (@Unexplained), posted an infographic depicting the size comparisons between modern and extinct animals, listing the Megalodon among those that are extinct. Another Twitter user, who identifies as Kori Baumer, raised objection to the infographic prompting multiple experts to join the conversation. The following thread ensued verbatim on Twitter:

Kori Baumer	Megalodon is not extinct that's already been proven
Doug Sloan	LOL! By whom, when and how??
Kori Baumer	You're joking right
Doug Sloan	No. Where's your proof that Carcharodon Megalodon exists today?
Kori Baumer	Megalodon yes it was off a island swimming around
Doug Sloan	Please provide definitive proof that a fish that is currently carbon dated to have appeared about 23 million yrs ago is still around today. Off some island. Swimming around.
Kori Baumer	I don't have a picture
Doug Sloan	You don't have a picture because Carcharodon megalodon no longer exists. Is it impossible that they exist? No. But its highly improbable and there is no definitive proof.

Kori Baumer	I don't just keep pictures like that but yes he is still out there
Doug Sloan	You cant prove it because definitive proof simply doesn't exist. Whales have expanded 10×'s in size over millions of yrs. Theyre slow & lumbering. There's no way whales grow that big with Megalodons swimming around as the apex predator. They would've evolved differently.
Kori Baumer	SMH right
Doug Sloan	Exactly. But if you doubt me check with expert marine bio sources like: @NOAA @WhySharks Matter @JohnRMoffitt @MarBiolNews
Dr. David Shiffman	Megalodon is extinct. There is absolutely no doubt about this. There is absolutely no evidence otherwise, other than obviously fake photos and videos.
Craig McClain, Ph.D.	To reiterate again @WhySharksMatter absolutely no evidence exist that Megalodon is still alive. Megalodon is definitively extinct.
Kori Baumer	And I suppose that you believe that prehistoric creatures have no existence at all on this Earth whatsoever when there's a third or most of the ocean hasn't been discovered yet
Craig McClain, Ph.D.	I know because of fossils that many creatures one dwelled in the oceans and on land. Many of them, like Megalodon, went extinct.
Kori Baumer	Most of those creatures they find are some extinct but most of them that they believe that are extinct actually aren't because they actually have found them now if you believe that the Megalodon is extinct because there's no government proof then that should tell you a reason.
Craig McClain, Ph.D.	I really wanted to have a conversation with you about why you believe this and provide evidence otherwise. I am afraid now that the conversation is veering toward a "massive government conspiracy to cover up Megalodon's existence" I must leave this conversation.

Kori Baumer	I don't trust people on to giving them proof because of the government because I know the government watches this stuff also I believe that you should sit here and do some research I've done my research now it's your turn to do your research
Craig McClain, Ph.D.	You are literally having a conversation right now with two of world's leading researchers on large animals and sharks. We have dedicated our lives to this.
Kori Baumer	Well I'm not wrong
Craig McClain, Ph.D.	It matters when someone has expertise. I don't take my car to be fixed to a baker. I don't call a mechanic to put a fire out at my house. I don't ask a dentist to make me a cake. I don't ask a firefighter to fix my teeth. We rely on people training with education and experience.

The tragic conversation begins with Baumer decrying the legitimacy of the infographic, citing photographic evidence that the Megalodon still exists today. Seemingly, Baumer does not have any professional expertise in this area. Another Twitter user identifying as Doug Sloan (@DougSloan) responded, but he also presumably lacks a background in marine science; his Twitter profile states that he is a "Political Analyst, Democratic Strategist, Chair of DC NAACP Political Action Committee & DC Native." Sloan, however, is quick to invoke actual experts by mentioning four different Twitter handles, one of whom responds. @WhySharksMatter is the handle for Dr. David Shiffman: a Postdoctoral Research Fellow at Simon Fraser University, where he researches the feeding behaviors and ecology of sharks. He underscores the view that the "Megalodon is extinct." The conversation also attracts the attention of Dr. Craig McClain, who is the Executive Director for the Louisiana University Marine Consortium. According to his online CV, McClain has conducted oceanographic research for 20 years and published over 50 papers in the area. Dr. McClain spearheads the conversation with Baumer, attempting to provide an educational context to the debate over whether or not the Megalodon still exists, but to no avail. Baumer insists on her correctness, leaving the experts and others on Twitter speechless.

The conversation appeared as a Moment on Twitter, ensuring hundreds of thousands of users would read the exchange. Moments, which Twitter describes as "curated stories showcasing the very best of what's happening on Twitter," stitch together individual tweets and replies to present a bigger story. This one was titled "Is the Megalodon extinct? One Twitter user speaks to two world experts." Kori Baumer received a barrage of public shaming and backlash as a result of the public conversation. The tweets have since been deleted by Baumer, and it is nearly impossible to uncover the original conversation in its entirety. I reached out to Kori Baumer, Dr. McClain, and Dr. Shiffman for comment in hopes of better understanding their takeaways from the conversation. In their email responses, both Dr. McClain and Dr. Shiffman declined to discuss the experience further. McClain replied: "I feel a little uncomfortable about this. The vitriol that consume many to attack someone for their ignorance was off putting at best. In the end, being calm, rationale, and polite won. I had a great conversation with her outside of Twitter." Shiffman responded, "I think I'd prefer to not talk about this, it feels like 'punching down.'" I did, however, get the chance to speak at length with Baumer, though she was very guarded and would only speak via DM in Twitter.

It took a bit of convincing before Kori actually believed that I genuinely wanted to speak to her about the experience and not to troll her, like so many had done previously. She informed me that she had been the victim of cyberbullying "by like four thousand people" as a result of the conversation and the subsequent Twitter Moment that went viral. I asked Kori about how she thought the whole Megalodon conversation went, and she replied, "people think I'm freaking crazy." I inquired about the conversation that Kori had with Dr. McClain offline, after the Twitter conversation. She admitted that "he was very kind, but he doesn't believe that Megalodons still exist like I do." Clearly, Kori's views on the Megalodon have not evolved, despite McClain's tutoring efforts. As the conversation progressed, I asked Kori whether or not she felt that the Internet makes us smarter. Her response was not an uncommon one: "I'm not sure the internet makes us smarter it's not always the internet that we find information on. sometimes it's books."

In a similar vein, *The Wall Street Journal* article, "Does the Internet Make You Smarter?," authored by Clay Shirky, advocates for the Internet as a networked tool of enlightenment. He says, "This issue isn't whether there's lots of dumb stuff online—there is, just as there is lots of dumb stuff in bookstores." Both Kori and Clay make a valid point here. Not all books are high-minded. But this argument overlooks an important logistical detail: smartphones deliver that dumb information directly to our pockets, whereas there is a greater barrier to entry to reading dumb books. What used to require effort to find dumb information in a bookstore is now effortless; bad information can be delivered directly to us, often unsolicited, and we are compelled to look at it. The smartphone has simultaneously networked us with the most brilliant minds in the world, and it has eroded the buffer between us and dumbness. Still, Shirky views this trade-off optimistically:

> We are living through a similar explosion of publishing capability today, where digital media link over a billion people into the same network. This linking together in turn lets us tap our cognitive surplus, the trillion hours a year of free time the educated population of the planet has to spend doing things they care about. In the 20th century, the bulk of that time was spent watching television, but our cognitive surplus is so enormous that diverting even a tiny fraction of time from consumption to participation can create enormous positive effects.[48]

The cognitive surplus that Shirky writes about romanticizes our Internet behaviors. His logic is similar to that of Moore's Law, which I discussed in Chap. 2. Simply having more of something does not mean that it becomes positively activated by default. Or, as Steven Pinker explains, "Sheer processing power is not a pixie dust that magically solves all your problems." Just as the increasing number of transistors in a circuit can never result in a technological singularity, a surplus of good information on the Internet does not automatically ensure its application. A catalyst is needed. In the context of the Internet, that catalyst is self-driven; we must be able to distinguish fact from opinion, fiction from nonfiction. And as it turns out, many of us are not well-calibrated.

The Twitter exchange about Megalodons is a microcosm for the Internet and the types of online interactions it facilitates. Perhaps it is that we use the Internet to reaffirm our existing belief structures rather than seeking to fact-check our views. So, by its nature, does the Internet make us dumb? No—not hardly. "Dumb" is not the appropriate word choice here. Instead, the Internet exposes our intelligence (or lack thereof) and

[48] Shirky, Clay. 2010. Does the internet make you smarter? *Wall Street Journal*, June 4. https://www.wsj.com/articles/SB10001424052748704025304575284973472694334. Accessed 3 Feb 2018.

magnifies our weaknesses; this makes us vulnerable to others online. Dangerously, the Internet can make us feel like we are experts, which only bolsters our confidence and intensifies our perspectives. I'm fascinated by the Megalodon conversation thread. Not because it was humiliating for Kori but because it perfectly models the transformation of human knowledge that is currently underway. If we are all professors online, who are the learners? Perhaps this sentiment is best summarized in my conversation with Kori, when she concluded, "I don't know how everybody else feels, but I'm sticking to what I know."

References

American Academy of Pediatrics. 2010. Thimerosal in vaccines not linked to autism. Accessed January 13, 2018. https://www.aap.org/en-us/about-the-aap/aap-press-room/Pages/Thimerosal-In-Vaccines-Not-Linked-to-Autism.aspx.

Asimov, Isaac. 1958. The feeling of power. *If: Worlds of Science Fiction* 8: 4–11.

Baron, Naomi. 2015. *Words Onscreen: The Fate of Reading in a Digital World*. New York: Oxford University Press.

Bol, Linda, Douglas J. Hacker, Patrick O'Shea, and Dwight Allen. 2005. The influence of overt practice, achievement level, and explanatory style on calibration accuracy and performance. *The Journal of Experimental Education* 73: 269–290. https://doi.org/10.3200/JEXE.73.4.269-290.

Bol, Linda, Rose Riggs, Douglas J. Hacker, Daniel L. Dickerson, and John A. Nunnery. 2010. The calibration accuracy of middle school students in math classes. *Journal of Research in Education* 21: 81–96.

Brown, John Seely, Allan Collins, and Paul Duguid. 1989. Situated cognition and the culture of learning. *Educational Researcher* 18: 32–42.

Bui, Dung C., Joel Myerson, and Sandra Hale. 2013. Note-taking with computers: Exploring alternative strategies for improved recall. *Journal of Educational Psychology* 105: 299–309.

Carr, Nicholas G. 2011. *The Shallows: What the Internet is Doing to Our Brains*. New York: W.W. Norton & Company.

———. 2017. How smartphones hijack our minds. *Wall Street Journal*, October 6. Accessed May 4, 2018. https://www.wsj.com/articles/how-smartphones-hijack-our-minds-1507307811.

Center for Disease Control and Prevention. 2018. Autism spectrum disorder. Accessed January 13, 2018. https://www.cdc.gov/ncbddd/autism/topics.html.

Chinni, Dante. 2018. Bright spot for Trump in 2017, job creation faces new challenges. *NBC News*, January 7. Accessed February 2, 2018. https://www.

nbcnews.com/politics/first-read/bright-spot-trump-2017-job-creation-faces-new-challenges-n835341.

Cowan, Nelson. 2001. The magical number 4 in short-term memory: A reconsideration of mental storage capacity. *Behavioral and Brain Sciences* 24: 87–114. https://doi.org/10.1017/S0140525X01003922.

Epstein, Robert, and Ronald E. Robertson. 2015. The search engine manipulation effect (SEME) and its possible impact on the outcomes of elections. *Proceedings of the National Academy of Sciences of the United States of America* 112: E4512–E4521.

Fisher, Marc. 2016. Donald Trump doesn't read much. Being president probably wouldn't change that. *The Washington Post*, July 17. Accessed February 3, 2018. https://www.washingtonpost.com/politics/donald-trump-doesnt-read-much-being-president-probably-wouldnt-change-that/2016/07/17/d2ddf2bc-4932-11e6-90a8-fb84201e0645_story.html?utm_term=.cc87a435e496.

Glenberg, Arthur M., and William Epstein. 1985. Calibration of comprehension. *Journal of Experimental Psychology: Learning, Memory, and Cognition* 11: 702–718. https://doi.org/10.1037//0278-7393.11.1-4.702.

Glenberg, Arthur M., Thomas Sanocki, William Epstein, and Craig Morris. 1987. Enhancing calibration of comprehension. *Journal of Experimental Psychology: General* 116: 119–136.

Gobet, Fernand, and Gary Clarkson. 2010. Chunks in expert memory: Evidence for the magical number four … or is it two? *Memory* 12: 732–747.

Google. 2015. Building for the next moment. Accessed February 12, 2018. https://adwords.googleblog.com/2015/05/building-for-next-moment.html.

Google Feud. 2018. Accessed January 24, 2018. http://www.googlefeud.com/.

Groulx, Robin. 2017. Reality bites: Trump's wake-up call. *AXIOS*, January 18. Accessed January 3, 2018. https://www.axios.com/reality-bites-trumps-wake-up-call-1513299979-3bd3a708-26be-4232-8faa-6970e65c6cf1.html.

Internet Live Stats. 2018. Google search statistics. Accessed February 12, 2018. http://www.internetlivestats.com/google-search-statistics/.

Jacobson, Louis. 2017. How strong has job growth been on Donald Trump's watch? *Politifact*, September 20. Accessed December 1, 2017. http://www.politifact.com/truth-o-meter/statements/2017/sep/20/donald-trump/how-strong-job-growth-been-trumps-watch/.

James, Karin Harman, and Laura E. Engelhardt. 2012. The effects of handwriting experience on functional brain development in pre-literate children. *Trends in Neuroscience and Education* 1: 32–42.

Kruger, Justin, and David Dunning. 1999. Unskilled and unaware of it: How difficulties in recognizing one's own incompetence lead to inflated self-assessments. *Journal of Personality and Social Psychology* 77: 1121–1134. https://doi.org/10.1037/0022-3514.77.6.1121.

Lanier, Jaron. 2010. *You Are Not a Gadget: A Manifesto*. New York: Random House.

Mangen, A., L.G. Anda, G.H. Oxborough, and K. Brønnick. 2015. Handwriting versus keyboard writing: Effect on word recall. *Journal of Writing Research* 7 (2): 227–247.

McGuinness, Diane. 1997. *Why Our Children Can't Read, and What We Can Do About It*. New York: Free Press.

Nichols, Tom. 2017. *The Death of Expertise*. New York: Oxford University Press.

Olmstead, Kenneth. 2017. Nearly half of Americans use digital voice assistants, mostly on their smartphones. *Pew Research Center*. Accessed January 24, 2018. http://www.pewresearch.org/fact-tank/2017/12/12/nearly-half-of-americans-use-digital-voice-assistants-mostly-on-their-smartphones/.

Perrin, Andrew. 2018. Who doesn't read books in America? *Pew Research Center*. Accessed May 3, 2018. http://www.pewresearch.org/fact-tank/2016/11/23/who-doesnt-read-books-in-america/.

Postman, Neil. 1999. *Building a Bridge to the Eighteenth Century: How the Past Can Improve Our Future*. New York: Random House, Inc.

Puiu, Tibi. 2017. Your smartphone is millions of times more powerful than all of NASA's combined computing in 1969. *ZME Science*, September 10. Accessed December 29, 2017. https://www.zmescience.com/research/technology/smartphone-power-compared-to-apollo-432/.

Reber, Paul. 2010. What is the memory capacity of the human brain? *Scientific American*, May 1. Accessed May 3, 2018. https://www.scientificamerican.com/article/what-is-the-memory-capacity/.

Rumsey, Abby Smith. 2016. *When We are No More: How Digital Memory is Shaping Our Future*. New York: Bloomsbury Press.

Sanders, Sarah. 2017. Accessed December 12, 2017. https://twitter.com/PressSec/status/939897264637652992.

Schottlender, Moriel. 2016. 10 easy ways you can tell for yourself that the Earth is not flat. *Popular Science*, January 26. Accessed February 12, 2018. https://www.popsci.com/10-ways-you-can-prove-earth-is-round.

Shirky, Clay. 2010. Does the internet make you smarter? *Wall Street Journal*, June 4. Accessed February 3, 2018. https://www.wsj.com/articles/SB10001424052748704025304575284973472694334.

Siegler, M.G. 2010. Nicholas Negroponte: The physical book is dead in 5 years. *TechCrunch*, August 6. Accessed February 5, 2018. https://techcrunch.com/2010/08/06/physical-book-dead/?utm_source=TweetMeme&utm_medium=widget&utm_campaign=retweetbutton.

Sparrow, Betsy, Jenny Liu, and Daniel M. Wegner. 2011. Google effects on memory: Cognitive consequences of having information at our fingertips. *Science* 333: 776–778.

Sweatpants Cher. 2018. Accessed February 4, 2018. https://twitter.com/House_Feminist/status/957109143650820097.

The Healthy Home Economist. 2018. Six reasons to say NO to vaccination. Accessed January 14, 2018. https://www.thehealthyhomeeconomist.com/six-reasons-to-say-no-to-vaccination/.

The Skimm. 2018. Accessed February 4, 2018. https://www.theskimm.com/app.

Unkel, Julian, and Alexander Haas. 2017. The effects of credibility cues on the selection of search engine results. *Journal of the Association for Information Science and Technology* 68: 1850–1862.

U.S. Department of Health and Human Services. 2018. Five important reasons to vaccinate your child. Accessed January 14, 2018. https://www.vaccines.gov/more_info/features/five-important-reasons-to-vaccinate-your-child.html.

U.S. Food & Drug Administration. 2018. Thimerosal and vaccines. Accessed January 13, 2018. https://www.fda.gov/BiologicsBloodVaccines/SafetyAvailability/VaccineSafety/ucm096228.htm.

Walhout, Jaap, Paola Oomen, Halszka Jarodzka, and Saskia Brand-Gruwel. 2017. Effects of task complexity on online search behavior of adolescents. *Journal of the Association for Information Science and Technology* 68: 1449–1461.

Wikipedia. 2018. Who wants to be a millionaire. Accessed February 4, 2018. https://en.wikipedia.org/wiki/Who_Wants_to_Be_a_Millionaire_(U.S._game_show)#Lifelines.

Wittrock, Merlin C. 1992. Generative learning processes of the brain. *Educational Psychologist* 27: 531–541.

Yehoshua, Tamar. 2016. Google search autocomplete. *Google*, June 10. Accessed January 25, 2018. https://blog.google/products/search/google-search-autocomplete/?m=1.

CHAPTER 6

Digital Socialites

In October 2004, I was a senior at The Ohio State University. That same month, there was a buzz on campus about a new website that had just been made available to OSU students: Facebook. Originally, the social networking site was called TheFacebook.com, and it grouped its users by order of university, requiring them to register with their institution-provided email addresses. Despite having participated in online chat rooms and AOL Instant Messenger in the late 1990s, I consider Facebook to be my first authentic experience with social media. Perhaps this is because Facebook radically changed the way I perceived and used social media. And it was Facebook that ultimately forced me to reconsider my technological habits. From its inception in a Harvard dorm room, no one could have predicted that this network would be the most popular social network ever, trafficking more than two billion active monthly users. In my research for this book, I came across a November 2004 issue of The Ohio State University's campus newspaper, *The Lantern*, which featured an article titled "Web Site Network 'Pokes' Strangers." The author of the article, Shaheen Samavati, had set out to ask students what they thought about the new site. In her reporting, she wrote:

> Amanda Rhodes has added a new step to her laptop routine. The sophomore in finance checks her e-mail and instant messages, but those tasks are no longer her top priority. Now she checks TheFacebook.com to see if classmates she found online accepted her friend invitations. Since the college social-networking site opened itself up to Ohio State on Oct. 10, its popularity has steadily increased.

A. J. Reid, *The Smartphone Paradox*,
https://doi.org/10.1007/978-3-319-94319-0_6

> …
> Despite its widespread popularity, Facebook still has its skeptics. "I don't really understand the interest in Facebook," said Andrew Perry, a sophomore in international business. He said a lot of his friends used it, but he has never been interested in things like Web logs or other Internet material outside of e-mail and music. Kevin Bliss, a junior in accounting, registered on The Facebook to see what it was about and was unimpressed. "Facebook is annoying," Bliss said. "It's a waste of time."[1]

Ironically, I found Kevin Bliss on Facebook; he now has more than 600 friends and actively posts. He declined to comment on whether his view towards Facebook has changed, but I suspect he still thinks it is annoying and a waste of time, if only inevitable. The magnetism of Facebook has attracted more than two billion users worldwide, and users average a total of 41 minutes on the site each day. The Facebook mobile app is a staple in the pantheon of social media apps, and there are more than one billion mobile users daily, with mobile ads accounting for 88% of Facebook's advertising revenue in 2016.[2] Facebook is ubiquitous, especially with its primary demographic, 25–34-year-olds. Perhaps it is not a coincidence that this demographic would have been experiencing the most formative social years of their lives when the networking site emerged. Facebook's first president, Sean Parker, reminisced in an interview with Axios:

> When Facebook was getting going, I had these people who would come up to me and they would say, 'I'm not on social media.' And I would say, 'OK. You know, you will be.' And then they would say, 'No, no, no. I value my real-life interactions. I value the moment. I value presence. I value intimacy.' And I would say, … 'We'll get you eventually.'[3]

To me, Facebook served much more of a social purpose when it was more exclusive; in its beginning days, it forced me to make new connections

[1] Samavati, Shaheen. 2004. Web site network 'pokes' strangers. *The Lantern*, November 7. https://www.thelantern.com/2004/11/web-site-network-pokes-strangers/. Accessed 14 Jan 2018.

[2] Zephoria. 2018. The top 20 valuable Facebook statistics. https://zephoria.com/top-15-valuable-facebook-statistics/. Accessed 20 April 2018.

[3] Allen, Mike. 2017. Sean Parker unloads on Facebook: 'God only knows what it's doing to our children's brains.' *Axios*, November 9. https://www.axios.com/sean-parker-unloads-on-facebook-god-only-knows-what-its-doing-to-our-childrens-brains-1513306792-f855e7b4-4e99-4d60-8d51-2775559c2671.html. Accessed 12 Nov 2017.

with fellow OSU constituents who I might not have known otherwise. But as Facebook became more inclusive, I found myself using it to maintain existing relationships with close family and friends, rather than forging new relationships. And in most cases, Facebook functioned as a substitute for actual conversation or interaction. In 2017, I deactivated my Facebook account—not to make some grandiose statement about social media, or because I was paranoid about Facebook's data mining techniques, but because I didn't like what it was doing to me. My wife and I would have daily conversations about what someone else had shared online: "Did you know the Tremonts had another baby? You have to see the pictures. He's so cute." These glimpses into others' lives satiated our social connectedness; we knew just enough about what was going on, but the actual interaction with that person rarely extended beyond a like or a superfluous comment. It felt voyeuristic, not social. The final straw came during the 2016 presidential election, which damaged a lot of personal relationships for me. For me, Facebook had become toxic, and I was finally done with it. Now, I maintain an Instagram account where I share pictures of my loved ones, and a Twitter account where I can connect with others and follow news stories. I write letters and make phone calls to friends. It is much more satisfactory.

We are social beings by nature. Not surprisingly, then, social connectedness is one of the most primary gratifications sought from our smartphones. Our devices have become portals into digital social clubs; indeed, four of the top five most downloaded apps of all time are social media-based. However, some argue that our online sociability only superficially improves our connection with others. Sherry Turkle, MIT Professor, raises poignant questions about the differences between connection and conversation and whether or not we substitute the latter with the former. In the article "The Flight From Conversation," featured in *The New York Times*, Turkle makes the case that we let technology control our relationships: "In the silence of connection, people are comforted by being in touch with a lot of people—carefully kept at bay. We can't get enough of one another if we can use technology to keep one another at distances we can control: not too close, not too far, just right. I think of it as a Goldilocks effect."[4] When we text, email, post on social media, we are cautiously test-

[4] Turkle, Sherry. 2012. The flight from conversation. *The New York Times*, April 21. http://www.nytimes.com/2012/04/22/opinion/sunday/the-flight-from-conversation.html. Accessed 4 April 2018.

ing the waters in our relationships, protecting the vulnerabilities that exist in face-to-face conversation. The smartphone provides the perfect buffer between analog and digital worlds, giving us the option to put down the device when we choose analog interaction and pick it up again when we choose the digital. Turkle's main argument is that online connection should not supersede real-world interaction, for in doing so, we lose deeper contact with ourselves and with others. When she appeared on the late-night comedy show, *The Colbert Report*, host Stephen Colbert challenged her on the notion that technology creates distance rather than togetherness. He asked, "Even if I get information from you in little sips, doesn't that add up to a gulp? Aren't I eventually knowing more about you?" Turkle rebuked that idea:

> We are tempted to think that our little "sips" of online connection add up to a big gulp of real conversation. But they don't. E-mail, Twitter, Facebook, all of these have their places—in politics, commerce, romance and friendship. But no matter how valuable, they do not substitute for conversation. Connecting in sips may work for gathering discrete bits of information or for saying, "I am thinking about you." Or even for saying, "I love you." But connecting in sips doesn't work as well when it comes to understanding and knowing one another.

Keith Hampton, a Professor at Rutgers University, vehemently disagrees with Turkle. He argues that "the small sips that come from the steady contact of social media can add up to a big gulp of information about the activities, interests and opinions of the people we connect with. They communicate mutual awareness and closeness along with information that we wouldn't otherwise receive." Like many others, Hampton sees technology as enhancing our sociability, making our relationships "more persistent and pervasive" instead of shallow and fleeting.

Whether or not you believe our technologies make us more or less sociable, one thing is undeniable: the steady opportunity for "sips" of online communication encourages a culture of incessant smartphone-checking and interaction. Indeed, researchers have shown that those who use social media on their smartphones are more likely to develop compulsive or even addictive tendencies.[5] In *Reclaiming Conversation:*

[5] Jeong, Se-Hoon, Hyoung Kim, Jung-Yoon Yum and Yoori Hwang. 2016. What type of content are smartphone users addicted to?: SNS vs. games. *Computers and Human Behavior* 54: 10–17.

The Power of Talk in a Digital Age, Turkle says of mobile technology, "[It] is here to stay, along with all the wonders it brings. Yet it is time for us to consider how it may get in the way of other things we hold dear—and how once we recognize this, we can take action. *We can both redesign technology and change how we bring it into our lives.*"[6] Recent research shows distressing signs that our obsessive relationship with technology is unhealthy. Like a bass to a shiny lure, we are easily enticed by our smartphones, which offer escape from the everyday monotony of school, work, and family. We have come to expect and depend on the constant stream of the digital content that lies just beyond our fingertips. Smartphones compete with and outrival our comparatively trifling lives, as they are capable of the on-demand gratification of our most basic social needs.

On Being Nowhere

Smartphones can transport us out of nearly any undesirable situation. A doctor's office waiting room, a public bus, an extra-long line at the grocery, a lecture hall. If we don't like where we are at any given moment, we can reach for our smartphones and dip into a more pleasant virtual experience. There are no more sanctuaries—perhaps literally—as a 2013 survey found that one in five American churchgoers access their phones during church service. Smartphones have become our personal rescuers, providing a safe harbor to which we can retreat when we find ourselves in social discomfort or are simply bored with our surroundings.

Sometimes, we deliberately use our devices to send an overt message to others. For instance, if you take a stroll on any college campus, you are guaranteed to see throngs of students traversing campus grounds in between classes scrolling through their smartphones to indulge in a small kernel of interaction before they reach their next destination. If it is a three-minute walk to our next class, we instinctively reach for the smartphone. Three minutes is plenty of time to check in with social media, respond to a text, and listen to a song. Anything but simply walk. Consequently, earbuds and headphones have become a universally understood language for social repulsion, signifying to others: do-not-disturb. In fact, many of us are probably guilty of faking our device usage, listening to nothing, but finding respite in their personal asylum from others. A 2015

[6] Turkle, Sherry. 2015. *Reclaiming Conversation: The Power of Talk in a Digital Age*. New York: Penguin Press.

article in *The New York Times* chronicled this trend of phantom engagement with mobile devices, declaring "When we wear headphones, it is a signal to everyone that we're shut off, unavailable and, much like napping adults, absolutely not to be bothered."[7] In fact, I wrote the majority of this book in public spaces—libraries, coffee shops, bookstores—and at the beginning of each writing session, I would don earbuds with nothing playing. Ironically, the very objects that plague us with overstimulation might also provide us with a digital safe haven for a quiet retreat.

Although we think of our smartphones as an entry point into our digital existences, we must consider how repeatedly checking out of the physical world also might destabilize relationships with those around us. Indeed, the mere presence of a smartphone has been shown to stymie the overall quality of in-person interactions. Researchers in a 2016 study asked participants to engage in one-on-one face-to-face conversations in one of two experimental groups. The first group was prompted with a casual conversation topic, and the second with a more meaningful topic. But the researchers were not interested in the content of the participants' conversations; instead, they observed their behavioral cues from a distance and then asked participants to rate the quality of the conversation. The researchers saw something peculiar. In short, the participants who sat down at the table and placed their smartphones in front of them (roughly a third of the participants did this) had less-fulfilling and lower-quality conversations. It seemed that the presence of the smartphone, even when lying dormant, had rendered an effect on the other person. The researchers concluded:

> [M]obile phones hold symbolic meaning in advanced technological societies. Even when they are not in active use or buzzing, beeping, ringing, or flashing, they are representative of people's wider social network and a portal to an immense compendium of information. In their presence, people have the constant urge to seek out information, check for communication, and direct their thoughts to other people and worlds[8]

[7] Mannering, Lindsay. 2015. Now playing in your headphones: Nothing. *The New York Times*, December 22. https://www.nytimes.com/2015/12/24/fashion/headphones-now-playing-nothing.html?mcubz=3. Accessed 4 Mar 2018.

[8] Misra, Shalini, Lulu Cheng, Jamie Genevie and Miao Yuan. 2014. The iPhone effect: The quality of in-person social interactions in the presence of mobile devices. *Environment and Behavior* 1–24. https://doi.org/10.1177/0013916514539755.

This phenomenon was dubbed the "iPhone effect." Brandishing your smartphone subtly suggests to others that you are available for conversation, yet open to interruption. Maralee McKee, who is a self-proclaimed "Modern Manners and Etiquette Expert" ranks this as the 5th most annoying techno-habit, advising that during one-on-one or small group conversations "It's savvy and gracious to keep your phone off the table and off your lap."[9] The aura that surrounds the smartphone is that it invites distraction, and this is often too hard to resist.

The rude practice of engaging with your smartphone while in the company of others has become so common that it has a name: "phubbing" (***ph***one + sn***ubbing***). The term was coined in 2012 when an Australian marketing firm released the documentary *A Word is Born* as a promotional tool to mark the sixth edition of Australia's national dictionary, the *Macquarie Dictionary*.[10] The film captures the official proceedings of the Macquarie word council, making it the first time that the birth of a word has been documented. Though the word usage is still somewhat obscure, we all can relate to what it means. Chances are, you have been phubbed by someone at one time or another, and you are likely guilty of having phubbed someone on more than one occasion. Phubbing seems to be dependent on the formality of the situation and the level of comfortability that we have with the phubee. We hopefully wouldn't engage with our smartphones under formal conditions, such as while standing in front of a judge or while in a job interview, but we find it much easier to do so when we perceive the situation to be informal or when the power dynamic shifts in our favor. Researchers from the Hankamer School of Business at Baylor University found that when bosses engage in smartphone use in front of their employees (a practice deemed bPhubbing, or, boss phubbing), supervisory trust is undermined, and employee engagement is negatively affected.[11] When stakes are high, we subconsciously keep the phone hidden away, and this alone suggests that phubbing is not an entirely inconsequential behavior.

[9] McKee, Maralee. 2018. The 7 most annoying cell phone habits and how to avoid them. *Manners Mentor*. https://www.mannersmentor.com/only-at-work/how-to-avoid-the-seven-most-common-cell-phone-sins. Accessed 29 Mar 2018.

[10] McCann Worldgroup. 2013. Introducing 'phubbing.' https://www.prnewswire.com/news-releases/introducing-phubbing-227230861.html. Accessed 13 Mar 2018.

[11] Roberts, James A., Ben H. Williams and Meredith E. David. 2017. Put down your phone and listen to me: How boss phubbing undermines the psychological conditions necessary for employee engagement. *Computers in Human Behavior* 75: 206–217.

It is probably safe to assume that, to varying degrees, phubbing occurs in almost all romantic relationships where one or both partners own a smartphone. This type of phubbing, known as pPhubbing (partner phubbing), is the incessant checking or engagement with a smartphone while in the presence of a significant other, and it likely erodes the quality of that relationship. A 2016 survey by Deloitte found that more than a third of respondents have had disagreements with their partners due to mobile phone usage. pPhubbing marginalizes both people, leaving them in a state of relationship purgatory: neither here nor there. Turkle describes this as residing in a "forever elsewhere." And, as pPhubbing creates a "barrier to meaningful conversation," it also can be the source of relationship jealousy.[12] Perhaps it is not surprising, then, that Facebook is cited as a contributing factor to one-third of all divorce cases. Studies repeatedly affirm that couples with frequent instances of pPhubbing report lower levels of relationship satisfaction and personal well-being.[13] In one particular study, researchers from the University of North Carolina Wilmington examined 170 participants involved in exclusive romantic relationships where both partners owned a smartphone. The qualitative measures suggested that increased smartphone dependency was associated with less relational certainty, or the degree of confidence in the relationship. However, the researchers reported that: "[T]he actual time spent with smartphones does not directly affect relationships; rather, it is the psychological sense of needing the device that is negatively linked to relationship attitudes and satisfaction."[14] Another study describes pPhubbing as a type of "technoference," in which technology interferes with couple interactions, sending an "implicit message" that the person values his or her device over his or her partner.[15] It is becoming clear that the

[12] Krasnova, Hanna, Olga Abramova, Isabelle Notter and Annika Baumann. 2016. Why phubbing is toxic for your relationship: Understanding the role of smartphone jealousy among Generation Y users. *Research Papers* 109. https://aisel.aisnet.org/ecis2016_rp/109.

[13] Roberts, James A. and Meredith E. David. 2016. My life has become a major distraction from my cell phone: Partner phubbing and relationship satisfaction among romantic partners. *Computers in Human Behavior* 54: 134–141.

[14] Lapierre, Matthew A. and Meleah N. Lewis. 2016. Should it stay or should it go now? Smartphones and relational health. *Psychology of Popular Media Culture*. https://doi.org/10.1037/ppm0000119.

[15] McDaniel, Brandon T. and Sarah M. Coyne. 2016. 'Technoference': The interference of technology in couple relationships and implications for women's personal and relational well-being. *Psychology of Popular Media Culture* 5: 85–98. https://doi.org/10.1037/ppm0000065.

smartphone is directly responsible for breeding relationship conflicts, as it steals our attention away from and deprioritizes those around us.

Our capacity for attention is finite; in order to avoid information and sensory overload, we selectively process some information at the expense of other information in our surrounding environments.[16] In fact, we might even think of our cognitive architecture as a type of human bandwidth, or the amount of information that we can process at one time. Information processing requires a tandem effort between our cognitive processes of attention and working memory. And while the relationship between the two processes is not fully understood, it is undeniable that they are both limited resources. There is considerable disagreement upon the quantification of these processes; some have suggested that the length of our attention spans is decreasing, and limitations on our working memory have been estimated to be anywhere from as few as two or as many as nine bits of information at once. When we engage with our smartphone, regardless of our reason for doing so, we are allocating a fraction of our information processing ability towards the device and away from our surroundings. The dedication of our cognitive resources depends on how we use our smartphone; social use, such as scrolling through Instagram photos, is less taxing than process use, such as reading or composing text, which draws more from our cognitive reserve. Nevertheless, our devices effectively compete for our attention, and as Nicholas Carr warns, "We cede control over our attention at our own peril." Dividing our attention, or what most people harmlessly refer to as *multitasking*, compromises our situational awareness, pulling us out of the present and putting us into a nowhere state of cognitive impairment.

The smartphone champions multitasking. Each time we consult a smartphone, we are engaging with it in three distinct ways: visually, manually, and cognitively. We visually attend to the content on the screen, manually hold and manipulate the device, and invest cognitive resources into processing the information. And under certain circumstances where our psychomotor and cognitive skills are already in use, such as while driving or crossing a busy intersection, this can be catastrophic. The Division of Motor Vehicles (DMV) cites that the leading cause of death in teens is texting and driving, and the Governors Highway Safety Association (GHSA) reports a significant uptick in pedestrian traffic fatalities, citing "distraction due to growing use of smartphone technology" as a contrib-

[16] Pashler, Harold. 1998. *The Psychology of Attention*. Cambridge, MA: The MIT Press.

uting factor.[17,18] Multitasking is a dangerous affordance of the smartphone because when our attention is fragmented, performance suffers; numerous studies have shown multitasking to worsen cognitive control and efficiency.[19,20,21] Even after we disengage, we sometimes continue to find ourselves under the spell of our devices. Sophie Leroy popularized the term *attention residue* in her 2009 paper titled "Why Is It So Hard To Do My Work? The Challenge of Attention Residue When Switching Between Work Tasks." She describes the phenomenon as "the persistence of cognitive activity about a Task A even though one stopped working on Task A and currently performs a Task B."[22] We might experience attention residue even after putting down our phone and moving on to something else. Our thoughts might bleed into the next task, handicapping our attentional resources and impacting our overall wherewithal. Unlike our smartphones, which are built to execute multiple tasks simultaneously, our human brains lag behind when we attempt to multitask.

Smartphones make us especially vulnerable to multitasking behaviors, particularly because they facilitate impulsivity and sensation-seeking: two key personality traits that have been identified in frequent multitaskers.[23] And just as researchers have identified social interaction gratification as a top reason for smartphone usage, in general, this is also a central motive for smartphone multitasking.[24] When we multitask with our devices, it

[17] Division of Motor Vehicles. 2018. Texting and driving. https://www.dmv.org/distracted-driving/texting-and-driving.php. Accessed 24 Mar 2018.

[18] Governors Highway Safety Association. 2017. Pedestrian traffic by state. https://www.ghsa.org/resources/spotlight-peds17. Accessed 24 Mar 2018.

[19] Junco, Reynol and Shelia R. Cotton. 2011. Perceived academic effects of instant message use. *Computers & Education* 56: 370–378.

[20] Clayson, Dennis E. and Debra A. Haley. 2012. An introduction to multitasking and texting: Prevalence and impact on grades and GPA in Marketing classes. *Journal of Marketing Education* 35: 26–40.

[21] Loh Kep Kee and Ryota Kanai. 2014. Higher media multi-tasking activity is associated with smaller gray-matter density in the anterior cingulate cortex. *PLoS One* 9: e106698.

[22] Leroy, Sophie. 2009. Why is it so hard to do my work? The challenge of attention residue when switching between work tasks. *Organizational Behavior and Human Decision Processes* 109: 168–181.

[23] Sanbonmatsu, David M., David L. Strayer, Nathan Medeiros-Ward and Jason M. Watson. 2013. Who multi-tasks and why? Multi-tasking ability, perceived multi-tasking ability, impulsivity, and sensation seeking. *PLoS One* 8: e54402. https://doi.org/10.1371/journal.pone.0054402.

[24] Hwang, Yoori, HyoungJee Kim and Se-Hoon Jeong. 2014. Why do media users multitask?: Motives for general, medium-specific, and content-specific types of multitasking. *Computers in Human Behavior* 36: 542–548.

often leads us down a familiar path to social media, where bottomless news feeds and infinite clickholes hold our attention hostage. Consequently, we exist in a state of being nowhere—physically anchored to but cognitively divorced from our surroundings. Not fully here nor there. And while in this state, our very perception of reality can become distorted.

A 2018 study published in the *Journal of Psychiatry Research* found that heavy social media users might experience distorted perceptions of time, that is, users who demonstrate addictive behaviors towards social media have an elongated perception of time in between sessions of social media use. One of the authors of the study, Ofir Turel, explains that this is a quality often exhibited in other addict types:

> '[A]ddicted' video gamers perceive their [gaming] sessions to be shorter than they actually are; heavy smokers think that the between-cigarettes time interval is longer than it actually is; and obese people perceive that the between-meals time intervals are longer than they actually are.[25]

When we are engaged in a task or activity that we find enjoyable, such as skimming social media feeds, time "flies by." Conversely, performing dreaded tasks seemingly slow down the passage of time. Researchers Shan Xu and Prabu David posit that "Although the finding that time passes quickly when engaged in a more entertaining activity than a less entertaining activity is predictable, the perceived passage of time when the two activities were combined offers a plausible, functional explanation for multitasking."[26] A conceivable rationale for socially driven multitasking is that it helps to mitigate a boring situation by speeding up the passage of time. You probably are more likely to conjure your smartphone during an academic lecture than while watching a movie in a theater (depending on the movie, of course). But researchers argue that experiencing a distorted perception of time while mobile multitasking with social media might be an important marker of addiction.

Our devices are the doors to our pixelated realities, where time becomes relative. When we are engrossed in the screen, we alienate those physically

[25] Technology.org. 2018. People with a heightened risk for social media addiction have a distorted perception of time. https://www.technology.org/2018/01/16/people-with-a-heightened-risk-for-social-media-addiction-have-a-distorted-perception-of-time/. Accessed 16 Mar 2018.

[26] Xu, Shan and Prabu David. 2018. Distortions in time perceptions during task switching. *Computers in Human Behavior* 80: 362–369.

around us—sometimes on purpose and sometimes by mistake. Perhaps what makes the smartphone enticing is that it can offer us something that the natural world does not: control. In our phones, we get to control the things we see, the people with whom we interact, the ways in which we are entertained. But in the natural world, we do not possess this level of governance. As a result, we find ourselves trying to simultaneously coexist in the natural and in the digital, using our devices are pick-me-ups when the real world is substandard. This leaves us inattentive and partially present. The irony is that when we are in both worlds, we are in neither, and sometimes, our digital relationships come at the expense of our analog ones, decreasing the quality of in-person interactions and jilting partners for social media posts. In one of my favorite films, *Inception*, the characters have mastered the art of lucid dreaming—a term coined in 1913 by Dutch psychiatrist Frederik van Eeden, who described a dream where he had "a full recollection of [his] day-life, and could act voluntarily."[27] In lucid dreams, the dreamer controls the narrative of the dream and becomes self-actualized while his sleeping body lies dormant. Similarly, our phones generate a type of lucidity on demand, in which we enter a dream-like state of alternative reality, becoming mentally abstracted and physically departed.

Oversharing

In November 2014, Bob Dylan stepped onto the stage at Kimmel Center for the Performing Arts in Philadelphia, PA, to an audience of one. The man, Fredrik Wikingsson, was participating in a Swedish film series *Experiment Ensam* (*Experiment Alone*), which places individuals alone into social scenarios in an attempt to understand whether togetherness and sharing make certain experiences more enjoyable. In this episode, Bob Dylan and his band would perform an entire concert for Wikingsson as he sat alone in a vast theater. Despite having seen Dylan in concert 20 times previously, the man was visibly overcome with emotion, coming close to weeping at times. During the set, the superfan appeared to be extremely uncomfortable, not knowing exactly how to behave. Arbitrarily seated six rows back from the stage, he was unsure whether to clap after each song or to slink back into his chair and avoid the uncomfortable awkwardness that filled the empty music hall between tracks. At the conclusion of the

[27] van Eeden, Frederik. 1913. A study of dreams. *Proceedings of the Society for Psychical Research* 26.

final song, Dylan walked off stage. Wikingsson stood up, hurled a "Thank you very much" towards the musicians, turned, and slowly walked out of the theater. The experiment had ended just like that. Two weeks after the concert, Wikingsson was interviewed about the experience. He was asked specifically whether he felt the concert would have been more enjoyable if it had been shared with others. He replied:

> I'm both grateful and happy that I was the only one there. In the moment, it wouldn't have been as intense with other people there. But once I stepped out of the theater, all confused and dizzy, it could have been more intense if I had someone to share it with. In that way, I'm torn about the experience. It was incredibly intense then and there, but after the fact and forever after, I miss having someone to share it with.[28]

Wikingsson's experience illustrates the basic human inclination to share and to participate with others. Because sharing experiences is integral to relationship forming, it is no wonder that social integration is one of the most common uses for our smartphones. Indeed, these mobile devices simplify our ability to maintain personal and professional relationships with others by giving us an outlet for sharing anything almost immediately. When we share our experiences with others on social media, we paraphrase our real-world experiences in the form of digital vignettes for others to comment and like. We can broadcast our thoughts and actions to anyone, effectively creating an instant sense of community. And, we can reach into our pockets and share in our friends' lives, if only voyeuristically. In doing so, we often find ourselves experiencing our lives through the prism of the screen, in an effort to document every lived experience as a shared one.

Perhaps there is no better example of this than 13-year-old Ryan McKenna. Now known on social media as the "Super Bowl Selfie Kid," the Massachusetts teen gained Internet fame after apparently phubbing a major pop star during one of the most watched television events of the year. Justin Timberlake gave a lively performance during the Super Bowl LII halftime show, which garnered more than 100 million viewers worldwide. For his final song, Timberlake waded through the audience, dancing and singing the words to "Can't Stop the Feeling." Television cameras

[28] Kreps, Daniel. 2014. Watch Bob Dylan perform private concert for one lucky superfan. *Rolling Stone*, December 13. https://www.rollingstone.com/music/videos/watch-bob-dylan-perform-private-concert-one-lucky-superfan-20141213. Accessed 14 Mar 2018.

captured the moment when the pop star sidled up to McKenna while the teen fumbled with his phone. During the waning seconds of the song, Timberlake posed for a selfie with the teen, who later explained that the reason he was phubbing the pop star was because he had been recording the action with video and was trying to switch into camera mode to take a photo. But even after taking the selfie, an international television audience watched as the cameras showed Timberlake energizing everyone in the audience but the teen, who had retreated back into his device. Watching that painfully awkward interaction play out on national television, which spanned only seconds, the dichotomy between the real and the digital could not have been more evident.

McKenna was only exhibiting normal behavior in the smartphone era. And it's not just the spectator who has become documentarian; often, the subjects being celebrated also document and share their experience from the perspective of their devices. At the opening ceremonies of the Olympics, you can watch as groups of athletes enter the stadium, most of whom are holding up their smartphones to record the momentous occasion. Spectatorship has become our favorite sport. This has given way to products like Ubiquiti's FrontRow device, which is a two-inch round-shaped livestreaming camera that you wear as a necklace, and the Narrative Clip, an even smaller livestreaming camera intended to be clipped to an article of clothing. Both products claim to alleviate the problem of viewing life through a screen by cataloguing your entire existence, hands-free, instead. Although wearable livestreaming cameras have not caught on fully, they likely will have a place in our culture of capture. A 2015 article in *The Guardian* refers to the excessive habit of documenting and sharing events as "Pics or it didn't happen" and calls this the "populist mantra of the social networking age."[29] Usually, the phrase is a rebuttal to a text message or an online post, questioning the credibility of the author's statement. For example: "I climbed Mt. Kilimanjaro!"—Pics or it didn't happen. Sometimes, however, this protocol can cross the line into oversharing; the aforementioned Justin Timberlake violated Tennessee state law when he uploaded a selfie to Instagram of himself voting inside a polling station. Timberlake's selfie has since been removed from Instagram, but Tennessee law has been revised to allow photography inside a voting

[29] Silverman, Jacob. 2015. 'Pics or it didn't happen'—The mantra of the Instagram era. *The Guardian*, February 26. https://www.theguardian.com/news/2015/feb/26/pics-or-it-didnt-happen-mantra-instagram-era-facebook-twitter. Accessed 14 Mar 2018.

booth. In 2016, Music producer DJ Khaled was criticized for livestreaming the entire birth of his son via Snapchat. He began filming with his smartphone once his fiancée's water broke and ended transmission when his son was delivered successfully. The criticism was not that he overshared, but that he documented and publicized a traditionally intimate process.

Artists Arvida Byström and Molly Soda published a 300-page book, titled *Pics or It Didn't Happen: Images Banned from Instagram*, which features images that have been removed from Instagram because they violate community standards. Most of these images focus on nonsexually suggestive nude selfies, menstruation photos, and other subjects that challenge the thorny relationship that exists between society's conservative views of the human body, feminism, and censorship. According to Soda, "As women, we grow up learning to be critical of our own bodies, as well as other women's bodies—there is a great sense of shame … a nude photograph immediately becomes pornographic even if that is not the intent." Byström and Soda brilliantly reveal the hypocrisy of the digital socialite; our online selves are not, in fact, our actual selves.

In her text, *Seeing Ourselves Through Technology*, author Jill Walker Rettberg argues that when we share status updates, images, and videos online, we are not modeling the same type of social behaviors that we do in real life. Rather, our social media accounts advertise a composite of who we actually are and how we wish to be perceived by others—a digital self-representation. We share content not only for others to see, but also for ourselves to feel validated. Walker adds:

> When we share photos of our children or a new home or a night out with friends our target audience is not just our friends, but also ourselves. Social media is about communication with others, but we should be equally aware of how we use social media to reflect upon ourselves.

Socialization, when experienced through the interface of technology, reduces a person to his or her timeline. And as a result, "we encounter other people in social media as *texts*" rather than as a "as a living, breathing human being."[30] The Pew Research Center reports that the average number of Facebook friends is 338,[31] but a theoretical limitation known as

[30] Rettberg, Jill W. 2014. *Seeing Ourselves Through Technology: How We Use Selfies, Blogs and Wearable Devices to See and Shape Ourselves*. New York: Palgrave Macmillan.

[31] Smith, Aaron. 2014. What people like and dislike about Facebook. *Pew Research Center*. http://www.pewresearch.org/fact-tank/2014/02/03/6-new-facts-about-facebook/. Accessed 13 Mar 2018.

Dunbar's Number contends that, on average, we can realistically sustain only five intimate friends, 15 close friends, 50 good friends, and a maximum of 150 friends in the general sense of the word. This discrepancy between our online Rolodex and our limited ability to maintain friendships suggests that social media becomes less about sociability with others and more about our self-expression aimed at others.

In 2012, Harvard researchers used neuroimaging techniques to demonstrate the cognitive effects of sharing. Since 80% of social media posts consist of "announcements about one's own immediate experiences,"[32] the authors rationalized that our online sharing habits must be intrinsically valuable. Participants underwent functional magnetic resonance imaging (fMRI) scans, which revealed that when we self-disclose information to others, we experience a powerful reward on par with the types of pleasure responses we receive from food and sex. More specifically, the results found that intrinsic reward was derived from two types of sharing: "introspecting about the self and communicating information to other people." Using a small financial incentive to determine the worth of sharing, participants demonstrated consistently that they were willing to waive additional monies in order to disclose more about themselves. According to the researchers, "[P]articipants were willing to forgo money to introspect about the self, and even more money when they were able to disclose the results of such introspection to another person." In short, we value self-disclosure highly, and social media platforms provide an outlet for sharing. In an ironic twist of fate, however, social media becomes more about me than you.

Social media platforms, like the smartphones on which we launch them, are not neutral. Although they can be used responsibly to foster online relationships and build social capital, there is compelling evidence that an unhealthy level of engagement with social media negatively affects overall well-being,[33] mental health,[34] and self-esteem[35] and can promote seden-

[32] Tamir, Dina I. and Jason P. Mitchell. 2012. Disclosing information about the self is intrinsically rewarding. *Proceedings of the National Academy of Sciences* 109: 8038–8043.

[33] Shakya, Holly and Nicholas A. Christakis. 2016. Association of Facebook use with compromised well-being: A longitudinal study. *American Journal of Epidemiology* 185: 203–211.

[34] Morrison Catriona and Helen Gore. 2010. The relationship between excessive Internet use and depression: A questionnaire-based study of 1319 young people and adults. *Psychopathology* 43: 121–126.

[35] Feinstein Brian, Rachel Hershenberg, Vickie Bhatia, Jessica Latack, Nathalie Meuwly and Joanne Davila. 2013. Negative social comparison on Facebook and depressive symptoms: Rumination as a mechanism. *Psychology of Popular Media Culture* 2: 161–170.

tary living and Internet addiction. Much of the research on social media utilizes social comparison theory, which asserts that we establish our own sense of worth through a constant loop of self-evaluation based on what we see from others. Social media did not invent social comparison; the popular idiom "Keeping up with the Joneses" originated as the title of a 1913 comic strip in which the McGinis family struggled to match the standard of living set by their neighbors, the Jones family. Since there have been social circles, there has been social comparison, but our social media have escalated the number of social comparisons we make, greatly impacting our psychological well-being. But it is unfair to demonize social media altogether; like smartphones, the technology exacerbates, not causes, the underlying emotions of the user. A 2018 study of Facebook users illustrates this non-neutrality of social media, citing that the effects of social media on psychological well-being are dependent upon the orientation of the user, either boosting optimism and inspiration or having the opposite effect, increasing pessimism and depression.[36]

Companies like Facebook are aware of the impact that social media have on our mental health, and as a result, they are beginning to take steps to channel more positive interactivity online. For instance, polling apps like tbh, Polly, Brighten, and Friendo have risen in popularity, especially with teens. The mobile app tbh, which is online shorthand for "to be honest," prompts users with a complimentary phrase such as "Hotter than the sun" and "Always nice to talk to" and asks him or her to identify one of four friends who most closely matches the statement. The respondents are anonymous, but users receive notifications when they are picked. The result is a feel-good moment. Facebook acquired the app in late 2017, signaling an important shift in how we view the role of social media in society. Perhaps one day the novelty effect of social media will have worn off, and our culture of sharing will have evolved into a culture of purposeful sharing instead. Or, as one developer from tbh said, "While the last decade of the Internet has been focused on open communication, the next milestone will be around meeting people's emotional needs."[37]

[36] Park, Sun Young and Young Min Baek. 2018. Two faces of social comparison on Facebook: The interplay between social comparison orientation, emotions, and psychological well-being. *Computers in Human Behavior* 79: 83–93.

[37] Shaban, Hamza. 2017. What is TBH? Facebook's newly acquired anonymous teen compliment app? *The Washington Post*, October 1. https://www.washingtonpost.com/news/the-switch/wp/2017/10/17/tbh-facebooks-new-anonymous-teen-compliment-app-explained/?utm_term=.a61a862c1433. Accessed 1 Nov 2018.

In 2013, Facebook teamed with researchers from Princeton University to conduct a large-scale study of 689,000 unsuspecting Facebook users. The controversial study, which published its findings in the Proceedings of the National Academy of Sciences of the United States of America (PNAS), sought to determine the extent to which users' emotions could be transferred to other users by manipulating exposure to positive or negative emotional content in users' news feeds. This process, known as emotional contagion, occurs when "people transfer positive and negative moods and emotions to others."[38] Indeed, the researchers found that the emotions expressed by friends on Facebook affect our emotional states; summarily, the study concluded that the positivity or negativity of emotions that we view on Facebook breeds the equivalent emotion in our own Facebook activity, spreading an emotional contagion. Seeing a fewer number of positive emotional content in our news feed reduces the frequency of positive emotional content that we post. And vice-versa. Facebook regrettably proved not only that we are impressionable of others on social media, but also that our emotions can be shaped by algorithms and news feeds. We are emotionally malleable. A few years after this study, Facebook would publicly apologize for a leaked document that allegedly showed advertisers how it could provide emotional insights on its users, specifically targeting teens who felt "defeated," "overwhelmed," "anxious," "stupid," "useless," and a host of other emotional keywords that might be exploited by online advertising.[39]

Being constantly exposed to social media means we experience more emotions—of our own and of others. Oversharers, those who post to social media frequently, receive constant doses of positive and negative feedback that can become overwhelming. Author Don Norman, author of *Emotional Design: Why We Love (or Hate) Everyday Things*, explains that "Emotion and cognition are tightly intertwined." And much like we are prone to cognitive overload, which strangles our ability to think, emotional overload might also cause us to atrophy at the cognitive and emotional level. Emotional overload, or what is also referred to as emotional overwhelm, occurs when we are inundated with emotions and is a byproduct of heavy

[38] Kramer, Adam D.I., Jamie E. Guillory and Jeffrey T. Hancock. 2014. Emotional contagion through social networks. *Proceedings of the National Academy of Sciences* 111: 8788–8790.

[39] Levin, Sam. 2017. Facebook told advertisers it can identify teens feeling 'insecure' and 'worthless.' *The Guardian*, May 1. https://www.theguardian.com/technology/2017/may/01/facebook-advertising-data-insecure-teens. 2 May 2018.

social media use. According to Norman, residing in a highly positive emotional state can be conducive to creative endeavors, but it lacks in the ability to concentrate. This person might appear unfocused and disengaged. A highly negative emotional state yields intense focus but to a fault. This person might seem intent and narrow-minded. Norman adds, "The extremes of both states, however, can be dangerous." As is the case with smartphone usage, a moderate level of interaction on social media likely will not have a discernable impact. But an unhealthy fixation on our devices to satiate our social desires is a dangerous gamble, as social media apps can behave like a Trojan horse for habitual, compulsive, and even addictive smartphone use.

Social media apps present an incalculable risk to youth, who are already in their formative stages of developing self-image. Though we hear often about the Millennial generation (estimated by most demographers to include those born between the years 1980 and 1995), there is growing concern over Generation Z—those born between 1996 and 2010, and "the first generation to be raised in the era of smartphones."[40] The inherent risk is that this generation, once described in *The New York Times* as the "antidote"[41] to Millennials, has not existed without social media. Their perception of the world and of relationship building is seen entirely through the prism of social media and sharing. Generation Z embodies oversharing because of the insatiable need to fulfill the social media vacuum, fueling the temporary outrage machine until the next thing comes along. An article in *Scientific American* cites the work of author Winifred Gallagher, saying that:

> [O]ur human brain is biologically primed for novelty, which, in turn, has helped us to survive cataclysmic environmental change. Unfortunately, this hardwired thirst can be overwhelming in the information age, in which every hyperlink, tweet, text, e-mail and Instagram photograph can be an opportunity to experience something new.[42]

[40] Williams, Alex. 2015. Move over, Millennials, here comes Generation Z. *The New York Times*, September 18. https://www.nytimes.com/2015/09/20/fashion/move-over-millennials-here-comes-generation-z.html. Accessed 4 May 2018.

[41] Williams, Alex. 2015. Move over, Millennials, here comes Generation Z. *The New York Times*, September 18. https://www.nytimes.com/2015/09/20/fashion/move-over-millennials-here-comes-generation-z.html. Accessed 4 May 2018.

[42] Kardaras, Nicholas. 2016. Generation Z: Online and at risk? *Scientific American*, September 1. https://www.scientificamerican.com/article/generation-z-online-and-at-risk/. Accessed 1 May 2018.

It has been argued, then, that Generation Z (sometimes described as iGen) is "on the brink of the worst mental-health crisis in decades."[43] Recent statistics on teen depression, unhappiness, loneliness, and even suicide rates suggest at least a correlation between smartphone use and mental health, though it might also be true that social media worsens teens by amplifying their preexisting mental health problems. Like our smartphones, social media inflame and accelerate our psychological, social, and emotional selves—therefore, we must choose how we use it, not let it use us.

#Slacktivism

On August 11, 2017, in Charlottesville, VA, thousands of protesters clashed at the site of a confederate monument. A group named Unite the Right had scheduled a rally to oppose the removal of a statue of Robert E. Lee in a public park. The fringe group attracted members from various factions including the alt-right, neo-Nazis, white supremacists, and white nationalists. A substantially larger number of anti-protesters, including members of the far-left group Antifa, faced off against the members of the far-right movement, resulting in widespread violent confrontations throughout the downtown and surrounding areas. Prior to its scheduled start time, the rally was declared unlawful by law enforcement, effectively fragmenting the large, cantankerous crowd into different parts of downtown Charlottesville, making it even more unmanageable. Protestors and anti-protestors remained connected through smartphones and social media to regroup in real time and to pop-up elsewhere around the city, sidestepping law enforcement. The tension reached crescendo when a 20-year-old man drove through a crowd of anti-protesters, injuring more than a dozen and killing a 32-year-old woman named Heather Heyer. In subsequent days, the hashtag #Charlottesville dominated the social media landscape, and Heyer became digitally memorialized as #HeatherHeyer. Charlottesville was a divining rod for political divisiveness and fringe politics, which was emboldened by President Trump's improvised remarks in a press conference that there was "blame on both sides" and that there were "some very fine people on both sides." Former-President Barack Obama weighed in on Twitter, quoting Nelson Mandela: "No one is born hating another

[43] Twenge, Jean. 2017. Have smartphones destroyed a generation? *The Atlantic*, September 2017. https://www.theatlantic.com/magazine/archive/2017/09/has-the-smartphone-destroyed-a-generation/534198/. Accessed 2 May 2018.

person because of the color of his skin or his background or his religion…" The tweet received 4.6 million likes, making it the most liked tweet of all time.[44] But slowly, the virality of these hashtags tapered off, and we collectively moved on to other issues. Just in the span of time that I have been writing this book, social media have used hashtags to express their support for victims of mass shootings (#MSDstrong, #VegasStrong, #Texas ChurchMassacre), sexual assault (#MeToo), hurricanes (#Irma, #Harvey, #Maria), and domestic terror attacks (#ManhattanAttack).

Hashtags have become an obligatory statement on current events. We use them to express outrage, publicize our empathy, and raise awareness. But rhetorically, punctuating an online post with the hashtag du jour is a form of self-disclosure to others that you are either in support of or opposed against something, thereby staking your position on the matter. British journalist James Bartholomew describes hashtag activism as a type of "virtue-signaling"[45]—or, the way in which we "camouflage" our own egotism by making proclamations online. According to Bartholomew, tweeting a statement such as "I hate 4 × 4s!" actually translates to "[I] care about the environment." For most, sharing #Charlottesville and #HeatherHeyer on social media not only signaled digital empathy, it implied an alignment with the central position of the anti-protestors who were in Charlottesville, Virginia, who were there to oversee the removal of a confederate monument. Hashtags are dog whistles for our belief systems—digital billboards that advertise our social and political views. Circulating the hashtags #MarchforOurLives, #MarchForScience, and #WomensMarch both acknowledge the event and insinuate an endorsement of its mission. Sharing the hashtag #Enough on social media has become popular in the aftermath of a school shooting, but this not only implies that you have had enough of gun violence, it suggests an outlook that is sympathetic to gun reform, an especially politicized and polarizing issue. Often, hashtags contain multiple layers of meaning, which when unpacked, represent your core values. In essence, you are your hashtag.

[44] Schwarz, Hunter. 2017. Obama's Charlottesville tweet is most liked in Twitter history. *CNN*, August 16. http://www.cnn.com/2017/08/15/politics/obamas-charlottesville-tweet/index.html. Accessed 3 May 2018.

[45] Bartholomew, James. 2015. The awful rise of 'virtue signalling.' *The Spectator*, April 18. https://www.spectator.co.uk/2015/04/hating-the-daily-mail-is-a-substitute-for-doing-good/. Accessed 2 May 2018.

Hashtag activism is a derivative of the larger social media complex in that it reveals more about ourselves than the cause we are representing. Remember #Kony2012? The hashtag permeated Facebook, Twitter, and Instagram as part of an online campaign to raise awareness of the Ugandan guerrilla group leader, Joseph Kony, who committed egregious acts of violence using child soldiers. Similarly, in 2014, the hashtag #BringBackOurGirls received more than 1.5 billion impressions on Twitter, after a jihadist terrorist group in Nigeria kidnapped roughly 300 school girls. Yet, aside from bringing these despicable figures into our social consciousness, there was little that social media users could affect from half a world away. None of us could search Ugandan or Nigerian jungles for Kony or for missing schoolchildren, but we could share articles, memes, and hashtags on our social networks. Raising awareness is valuable, but it is sometimes the full extent of our involvement.

It is because of this willingness to propagate hashtags coupled with an inability to create observable results that social media users have been criticized for their "slacktivism," or the argument that social media participation acts as a substitute for direct involvement. Tagging posts with a popular hashtag and updating profile pictures to show support of a cause self-discloses your position to others, but it does not necessarily equate to action. A study of 306 Millennials found that online activism fulfills "interpersonal utility/social interaction gratifications of expression, belonging and participation."[46] The danger of hashtag activism, or slacktivism, is that it might just satiate the need to be heard or to take a stand without much effort. A 2017 study in *Information, Communication & Society* found that sharing a social cause video on Facebook increases the likelihood of volunteerism but warns that "online social action satisfies youths' moral and psychological needs for engagement, thereby excusing them from participating in traditional offline forms of engagement."[47] For some, composing a tweetstorm about the #WomensMarch was just as good as being there in person, but true activism requires sacrifice.

[46] Dookhoo, Sasha R. 2015. How millennials engage in social media activism: A uses and gratifications approach. http://etd.fcla.edu/CF/CFE0005941/SDookhoo_Thesis_Final_Submission.pdf. Accessed 2 May 2018.

[47] Lane, Daniel S. and Sonya Dal Cin. 2018. Sharing beyond Slacktivism: The effect of socially observable prosocial media sharing on subsequent offline helping behavior. *Information, Communication & Society* 21: 1523–1540.

In 2013, the *Journal of Consumer Research* published the article "The Nature of Slacktivism: How the Social Observability of an Initial Act of Token Support Affects Subsequent Prosocial Action," in which researchers categorized activism through social media as either *token support* or *meaningful support*. Liking a Facebook page, sharing a meme, or posting a hashtag requires little effort and entails no significant sacrifice, and thus it is token. Meaningful support is defined by a tangible contribution, such as a monetary or time-based donation. The researchers found that the act of being seen providing token support derails motivation to contribute any further meaningful support. Internet users who made public gestures of token support, which did not include substantial or tangible contributions, were less likely to respond to a subsequent call for meaningful support (either monetary or time-based). An argument can be made that the initial token support that is so easily spread on social media platforms, whether it is using a trendy hashtag or posting hollow expressions, primarily makes us feel better about ourselves.

It stands to reason, then, that social media encourage us to be more cathartic than activist. In many ways, social media have become the new town square, where we act as judge, jury, and executioner. Social media fulfill our need to feel heard without the prerequisite of having someone there to hear us. In his book, *So You've Been Publicly Shamed*, author Jon Ronson chronicles several stories where Internet shaming has cost individuals their livelihoods, their reputations, and their relationships. He says, "We are defining the boundaries of normality by tearing apart the people outside it."[48] Indeed, piling on others via social media forms a comradery, a sense of rightness. It's plausible that we feel a compulsion to comment, post, or share something on social media each time there is breaking news, in order to feel connected to others. Sometimes, we turn to social media to be comforted. In an article in *The Telegraph* titled "Why Do We All Feel Compelled to Tweet After a Tragedy?," author Jamie Bartlett contemplates:

> [S]ocial media is based on the (correct) assumption that we social creatures want to publicly share our thoughts with others, and enjoy the feeling of gratification if it evokes a response. It's part of the design: how many Likes do you have? How many views? How many retweets? The subject matter is irrelevant. What matters is to say something, and to have others respond.[49]

[48] Ronson, Jon. 2015. *So You've Been Publicly Shamed*. New York: Riverhead Books.

[49] Bartlett, Jamie. 2015. Why do we feel compelled to tweet after a tragedy? *The Telegraph*, January 14. http://www.telegraph.co.uk/technology/twitter/11341683/Why-do-we-all-feel-compelled-to-tweet-after-a-tragedy.html. Accessed 27 Feb 2018.

Anthony Jeselnik is an edgy comedian who delivers his dark content with deadpan. His material pushes the sensitivities and tests the political correctness of his audiences; Jeselnik revels in making jokes about uncomfortable subjects that are usually regarded as off-limits for comedy: national tragedies, the death of loved ones, pedophilia, domestic abuse. In an NPR interview, titled "Anthony Jeselnik: The Dark Prince of Comedy," host Ophira Eisenberg describes the comedian's style as "highly intelligent, shocking one-liners."[50] Jeselnik's brand of comedy is almost masochistic. His goal is to "find things you shouldn't make a joke about, and find a way to make a joke." In his standup special, *Thoughts and Prayers*, the Dark Prince brags that he is the only comedian willing to make jokes about national tragedies on the day that they happen. Jeselnik argues that this practice is innocuous because he is not humiliating the victims of those tragedies; instead, he is weaponizing humor to combat sadness. He defends his insensitivity saying it is no worse than the flood of empty gestures posted to social media in the wake of tragedy:

> [P]eople see something horrible happen in the world, and they run to the Internet. They run to their social media … and they all write down the exact same thing: 'My thoughts and prayers.' Do you know what that's worth? Fucking nothing. Less than nothing. You're not giving your time, your money, or even your compassion. All you were doing is saying, 'Don't forget about me today.'

In a break from his rapid-fire quips, Jeselnik seems to be holding up a mirror to his audience to make a sobering point; the paradox of social media is that platforms of connectedness and social behavior often are used to bolster our own image. To be seen doing rather than simply doing. Or, as Jeselnik describes it, "a wedding photographer who only takes selfies."

Some philanthropic efforts have managed to exploit our selfish giving. Charity Miles is an example of a "socially-driven, for-profit company" that capitalizes on the charitable reciprocity that we have come to expect. The company partners with more than 40 not-for-profit charities and makes a financial donation every time the user tracks a human-centered activity like biking, walking, and running while using the smartphone app. Bikers earn 10 cents per mile for their charity, and walkers and runners earn 25 cents

[50] Eisenberg, Ophira. 2014. Anthony Jeselnik: The dark prince of comedy. *Ask Me Another*, April 14. https://www.npr.org/2014/08/14/340113255/anthony-jeselnik-the-dark-prince-of-comedy. Accessed 13 May 2018.

per mile. As of 2018, Charity Miles has generated more than $2.5 million in donations, and it strongly encourages its donors to share their achievements across social media. Similarly, the ALS Association benefitted substantially from the #IceBucketChallenge, a viral challenge in which people shared videos of themselves dumping ice-cold water over their heads and then nominating others on social media to do the same or else donate money to the cause. Many participated in the challenge without actually donating money, suggesting that virtue-signaling played a role, but in the end, the event raised more than $115 million. Philanthropy works well when publicized, and our devices have given us more ways to contribute.

Online giving is growing steadily; a quarter of donors make their contributions via a mobile device.[51] Micro-donation apps like Tinbox, Pledgeling, One Today, and Donate a Photo let users donate $1 per day to a charity of their choosing, often in exchange for personal information. Smartphone apps Charity Tap and FreeRice gamify charitable giving; in Charity Tap, players tap an empty rice bowl until it is filled, and FreeRice is a trivia-style game that donates ten grains of rice for each question answered correctly. In this new form of digital altruism, the donated money comes from corporate sponsorship crowdfunding, rather than from the users. Last, the Mobile Giving Foundation (MGF) has partnered with wireless providers to create a Mobile Giving Channel, "a single channel available to wireless subscribers of all US wireless carriers by which users can instantaneously respond to charitable solicitations by a text message."[52] Mobile giving, often referred to as text-to-donate, is done by texting a KEYWORD to a SHORTCODE that is tied to a specific organization and cause. The amount of the donation is deducted from that month's wireless bill and is tax-deductible. This trend of online and mobile giving shows us that slacktivism might not be an indictment on the connected culture; it might be an even more productive form of postmodern activism.

Smartphones have played an integral role in social movements, becoming essential tools of protest. Bijan Stephen writes in an article on Wired.com, "Any large social movement is shaped by the technology available to it and tailors its goals, tactics, and rhetoric to the media of its time."[53] The

[51] NP Source. 2018. The ultimate list of online giving statistics. https://nonprofitssource.com/online-giving-statistics/. Accessed 14 Apr 2018.

[52] Mobile Giving Foundation. 2018. For donors. http://www.mobilegiving.org/donors/. Accessed 28 Mar 2018.

[53] Stephen, Bijan. 2015. Get up, stand up. *Wired*, November 2015. https://www.wired.com/2015/10/how-black-lives-matter-uses-social-media-to-fight-the-power/. Accessed 1 May 2018.

smartphone is capable of shining a spotlight on injustice and then broadcasting that to the entire world. Just as the printing press, the radio, the television, and the Internet articulated mass communication efforts, so too does the smartphone, but faster. The Black Lives Matter movement is prime example of how postmodern activism works. Following the acquittal of George Zimmerman, who fatally shot a young black teen in Florida, Oakland-native Alicia Garza posted a message to Facebook that read: "Black people. I love you. I love us. Our lives matter, Black Lives Matter." Patrisse Cullors then shared the post along with the hashtag #BlackLivesMatter. Together with Opal Tometi, the three women formed the Black Lives Matter activist movement: "an ideological and political intervention in a world where Black lives are systematically and intentionally targeted for demise."[54] The movement has used social media effectively to recruit social activists and orchestrate protests around the country, helping to bring issues of racial inequity to the forefront of society's conscience. Judy Lubin, a sociologist and political analyst, has said that smartphones make protest more accessible.[55] And according to Bijan Stephen, smartphones and social media have "helped make today's struggle feel both different from and continuous with the civil rights era. All the terror and greatness we associate with that moment is right in front of our faces, as near to us as our screens."[56]

But just as our technologies can facilitate social progress, they also can be used to organize evil. The events of Charlottesville showed us that fringe groups like Unite the Right, neo-Nazis, and white supremacists also use these tools to connect and strategize. As Zeynep Tufekci points out in his book, *Twitter and Tear Gas: The Power and Fragility of Networked Protest*:

> And those tools shape the course of events and social movements in often unpredictable ways. The contradictory and sometimes counterintuitive dynamics unleashed by the emergence of the printing press demonstrate all

[54] Black Lives Matter. 2018. Herstory. https://blacklivesmatter.com/about/herstory/. Accessed 1 Feb 2018.

[55] Adams, Kimberly. 2016. Smartphones play crucial role for Black Lives Matter. *Marketplace*, July 11. https://www.marketplace.org/2016/07/11/wealth-poverty/smartphones-play-crucial-role-black-lives-matter. Accessed 1 Feb 2018.

[56] Stephen, Bijan. 2015. Get up, stand up. *Wired*, November 2015. https://www.wired.com/2015/10/how-black-lives-matter-uses-social-media-to-fight-the-power/. Accessed 1 Feb 2018.

too clearly that there is little that is straightforward about the implications of a revolutionary communications technology. And when it comes to understanding the strengths, weaknesses, challenges, opportunities, and future of networked movements, we have likely just begun to see what it may all mean.[57]

Social media are a delivery vehicle for all types of information, and in this sense, they appear to be neutral. But upon further contemplation, social media and the devices on which we access them are far from neutral; they inherently drive connection and accelerate movements—good and evil—and they have a residual influence on our views. By default, they transform all of us into slacktivists to some degree. Indeed, Biz Stone, founder of Twitter, argued in a 2010 article in *The Atlantic* that social media strengthens activism, rather than dampens it, calling Twitter a "viable agent of change."[58]

Slacktivism, a hallmark of the smartphone era, consists of more than just hashtags and retweets. It is a modern adaptation of civic engagement in which we are all enlisted. Raising awareness is not a substitute for activism, but it can be a catalyst, and this is more beneficial than a society that remains disconnected, disparate, and willfully unaware.

References

Adams, Kimberly. 2016. Smartphones play crucial role for Black Lives Matter. *Marketplace*, July 11. Accessed February 1, 2018. https://www.marketplace.org/2016/07/11/wealth-poverty/smartphones-play-crucial-role-black-lives-matter.

Allen, Mike. 2017. Sean Parker unloads on Facebook: 'God only knows what it's doing to our children's brains.' *Axios*, November 9. Accessed November 12, 2017. https://www.axios.com/sean-parker-unloads-on-facebook-god-only-knows-what-its-doing-to-our-childrens-brains-1513306792-f855e7b4-4e99-4d60-8d51-2775559c2671.html.

Bartholomew, James. 2015. The awful rise of 'virtue signalling.' *The Spectator*, April 18. Accessed May 2, 2018. https://www.spectator.co.uk/2015/04/hating-the-daily-mail-is-a-substitute-for-doing-good/.

[57] Tufekci, Zeynep. 2017. *Twitter and Tear Gas: The Power and Fragility of Networked Protest*. New Haven, CT: Yale University Press.

[58] Stone, Biz. 2010. Exclusive: Biz Stone on Twitter and activism. *The Atlantic*, October 19. https://www.theatlantic.com/technology/archive/2010/10/exclusive-biz-stone-on-twitter-and-activism/64772/. Accessed 1 May 2018.

Bartlett, Jamie. 2015. Why do we feel compelled to tweet after a tragedy? *The Telegraph*, January 14. Accessed February 27, 2018. http://www.telegraph.co.uk/technology/twitter/11341683/Why-do-we-all-feel-compelled-to-tweet-after-a-tragedy.html.

Black Lives Matter. 2018. Herstory. Accessed February 1, 2018. https://blacklivesmatter.com/about/herstory/.

Clayson, Dennis E., and Debra A. Haley. 2012. An introduction to multitasking and texting: Prevalence and impact on grades and GPA in Marketing classes. *Journal of Marketing Education* 35: 26–40.

Division of Motor Vehicles. 2018. Texting and driving. Accessed March 24, 2018. https://www.dmv.org/distracted-driving/texting-and-driving.php.

Dookhoo, Sasha R. 2015. How millennials engage in social media activism: A uses and gratifications approach. Accessed May 2, 2018. http://etd.fcla.edu/CF/CFE0005941/SDookhoo_Thesis_Final_Submission.pdf.

Eisenberg, Ophira. 2014. Anthony Jeselnik: The dark prince of comedy. *Ask Me Another*, April 14. Accessed May 13, 2018. https://www.npr.org/2014/08/14/340113255/anthony-jeselnik-the-dark-prince-of-comedy.

Feinstein, Brian, Rachel Hershenberg, Vickie Bhatia, Jessica Latack, Nathalie Meuwly, and Joanne Davila. 2013. Negative social comparison on Facebook and depressive symptoms: Rumination as a mechanism. *Psychology of Popular Media Culture* 2: 161–170.

Governors Highway Safety Association. 2017. Pedestrian traffic by state. Accessed March 24, 2018. https://www.ghsa.org/resources/spotlight-peds17.

Hwang, Yoori, HyoungJee Kim, and Se-Hoon Jeong. 2014. Why do media users multitask?: Motives for general, medium-specific, and content-specific types of multitasking. *Computers in Human Behavior* 36: 542–548.

Jeong, Se-Hoon, Hyoung Kim, Jung-Yoon Yum, and Yoori Hwang. 2016. What type of content are smartphone users addicted to?: SNS vs. games. *Computers and Human Behavior* 54: 10–17.

Junco, Reynol, and Shelia R. Cotton. 2011. Perceived academic effects of instant message use. *Computers & Education* 56: 370–378.

Kardaras, Nicholas. 2016. Generation Z: Online and at risk? *Scientific American*, September 1. Accessed May 1, 2018. https://www.scientificamerican.com/article/generation-z-online-and-at-risk/.

Kramer, Adam D.I., Jamie E. Guillory, and Jeffrey T. Hancock. 2014. Emotional contagion through social networks. *Proceedings of the National Academy of Sciences* 111: 8788–8790.

Krasnova, Hanna, Olga Abramova, Isabelle Notter, and Annika Baumann. 2016. Why phubbing is toxic for your relationship: Understanding the role of smartphone jealousy among Generation Y users. *Research Papers* 109. https://aisel.aisnet.org/ecis2016_rp/109.

Kreps, Daniel. 2014. Watch Bob Dylan perform private concert for one lucky superfan. *Rolling Stone*, December 13. Accessed March 14, 2018. https://www.rollingstone.com/music/videos/watch-bob-dylan-perform-private-concert-one-lucky-superfan-20141213.

Lane, Daniel S., and Sonya Dal Cin. 2018. Sharing beyond Slacktivism: The effect of socially observable prosocial media sharing on subsequent offline helping behavior. *Information, Communication & Society* 21: 1523–1540.

Lapierre, Matthew A., and Meleah N. Lewis. 2016. Should it stay or should it go now? Smartphones and relational health. *Psychology of Popular Media Culture*. https://doi.org/10.1037/ppm0000119.

Leroy, Sophie. 2009. Why is it so hard to do my work? The challenge of attention residue when switching between work tasks. *Organizational Behavior and Human Decision Processes* 109: 168–181.

Levin, Sam. 2017. Facebook told advertisers it can identify teens feeling 'insecure' and 'worthless.' *The Guardian*, May 1. Accessed May 2, 2018. https://www.theguardian.com/technology/2017/may/01/facebook-advertising-data-insecure-teens.

Loh, Kep Kee, and Ryota Kanai. 2014. Higher media multi-tasking activity is associated with smaller gray-matter density in the anterior cingulate cortex. *PLoS One* 9: e106698.

Mannering, Lindsay. 2015. Now playing in your headphones: Nothing. *The New York Times*, December 22. Accessed March 4, 2018. https://www.nytimes.com/2015/12/24/fashion/headphones-now-playing-nothing.html?mcubz=3.

McCann Worldgroup. 2013. Introducing 'phubbing.' Accessed March 13, 2018. https://www.prnewswire.com/news-releases/introducing-phubbing-227230861.html.

McDaniel, Brandon T., and Sarah M. Coyne. 2016. 'Technoference': The interference of technology in couple relationships and implications for women's personal and relational well-being. *Psychology of Popular Media Culture* 5: 85–98. https://doi.org/10.1037/ppm0000065.

McKee, Maralee. 2018. The 7 most annoying cell phone habits and how to avoid them. *Manners Mentor*. Accessed March 29, 2018. https://www.mannersmentor.com/only-at-work/how-to-avoid-the-seven-most-common-cell-phone-sins.

Misra, Shalini, Lulu Cheng, Jamie Genevie, and Miao Yuan. 2014. The iPhone effect: The quality of in-person social interactions in the presence of mobile devices. *Environment and Behavior*: 1–24. https://doi.org/10.1177/0013916514539755.

Mobile Giving Foundation. 2018. For donors. Accessed March 28, 2018. http://www.mobilegiving.org/donors/.

Morrison, Catriona, and Helen Gore. 2010. The relationship between excessive Internet use and depression: A questionnaire-based study of 1,319 young people and adults. *Psychopathology* 43: 121–126.

NP Source. 2018. The ultimate list of online giving statistics. Accessed April 14, 2018. https://nonprofitssource.com/online-giving-statistics/.

Park, Sun Young, and Young Min Baek. 2018. Two faces of social comparison on Facebook: The interplay between social comparison orientation, emotions, and psychological well-being. *Computers in Human Behavior* 79: 83–93.

Pashler, Harold. 1998. *The Psychology of Attention*. Cambridge, MA: The MIT Press.

Rettberg, Jill W. 2014. *Seeing Ourselves through Technology: How We Use Selfies, Blogs and Wearable Devices to See and Shape Ourselves*. New York: Palgrave Macmillan.

Roberts, James A., and Meredith E. David. 2016. My life has become a major distraction from my cell phone: Partner phubbing and relationship satisfaction among romantic partners. *Computers in Human Behavior* 54: 134–141.

Roberts, James A., Ben H. Williams, and Meredith E. David. 2017. Put down your phone and listen to me: How boss phubbing undermines the psychological conditions necessary for employee engagement. *Computers in Human Behavior* 75: 206–217.

Ronson, Jon. 2015. *So You've Been Publicly Shamed*. New York: Riverhead Books.

Samavati, Shaheen. 2004. Web site network 'pokes' strangers. *The Lantern*, November 7. Accessed January 14, 2018. https://www.thelantern.com/2004/11/web-site-network-pokes-strangers/.

Sanbonmatsu, David M., David L. Strayer, Nathan Medeiros-Ward, and Jason M. Watson. 2013. Who multi-tasks and why? Multi-tasking ability, perceived multi-tasking ability, impulsivity, and sensation seeking. *PLoS One* 8: e54402. https://doi.org/10.1371/journal.pone.0054402.

Schwarz, Hunter. 2017. Obama's Charlottesville tweet is most liked in Twitter history. *CNN*, August 16. Accessed May 3, 2018. http://www.cnn.com/2017/08/15/politics/obamas-charlottesville-tweet/index.html.

Shaban, Hamza. 2017. What is TBH? Facebook's newly acquired anonymous teen compliment app? *The Washington Post*, October 1. Accessed November 1, 2018. https://www.washingtonpost.com/news/the-switch/wp/2017/10/17/tbh-facebooks-new-anonymous-teen-compliment-app-explained/?utm_term=.a61a862c1433.

Shakya, Holly, and Nicholas A. Christakis. 2016. Association of Facebook use with compromised well-being: A longitudinal study. *American Journal of Epidemiology* 185: 203–211.

Silverman, Jacob. 2015. 'Pics or it didn't happen'—The mantra of the Instagram era. *The Guardian*, February 26. Accessed March 14, 2018. https://www.theguardian.com/news/2015/feb/26/pics-or-it-didnt-happen-mantra-instagram-era-facebook-twitter.

Smith, Aaron. 2014. What people like and dislike about Facebook. *Pew Research Center*. Accessed March 13, 2018. http://www.pewresearch.org/fact-tank/2014/02/03/6-new-facts-about-facebook/.

Stephen, Bijan. 2015. Get up, stand up. *Wired*, November 2015. Accessed May 1, 2018. https://www.wired.com/2015/10/how-black-lives-matter-uses-social-media-to-fight-the-power/.

Stone, Biz. 2010. Exclusive: Biz Stone on Twitter and activism. *The Atlantic*, October 19. Accessed May 1, 2018. https://www.theatlantic.com/technology/archive/2010/10/exclusive-biz-stone-on-twitter-and-activism/64772/.

Tamir, Dina I., and Jason P. Mitchell. 2012. Disclosing information about the self is intrinsically rewarding. *Proceedings of the National Academy of Sciences* 109: 8038–8043.

Technology.org. 2018. People with a heightened risk for social media addiction have a distorted perception of time. Accessed March 16, 2018. https://www.technology.org/2018/01/16/people-with-a-heightened-risk-for-social-media-addiction-have-a-distorted-perception-of-time/.

Tufekci, Zeynep. 2017. *Twitter and Tear Gas: The Power and Fragility of Networked Protest*. New Haven, CT: Yale University Press.

Turkle, Sherry. 2012. The flight from conversation. *The New York Times*, April 21. Accessed April 4, 2018. http://www.nytimes.com/2012/04/22/opinion/sunday/the-flight-from-conversation.html.

———. 2015. *Reclaiming Conversation: The Power of Talk in a Digital Age*. New York: Penguin Press.

Twenge, Jean. 2017. Have smartphones destroyed a generation? *The Atlantic*, September. Accessed May 2, 2018. https://www.theatlantic.com/magazine/archive/2017/09/has-the-smartphone-destroyed-a-generation/534198/.

van Eeden, Frederik. 1913. A study of dreams. *Proceedings of the Society for Psychical Research* 26: 431–461.

Williams, Alex. 2015. Move over, Millennials, here comes Generation Z. *The New York Times*, September 18. Accessed May 4, 2018. https://www.nytimes.com/2015/09/20/fashion/move-over-millennials-here-comes-generation-z.html.

Xu, Shan, and Prabu David. 2018. Distortions in time perceptions during task switching. *Computers in Human Behavior* 80: 362–369.

Zephoria. 2018. The top 20 valuable Facebook statistics. Accessed April 20, 2018. https://zephoria.com/top-15-valuable-facebook-statistics/.

CHAPTER 7

Going Dark

On the morning of October 16, 2014, former FBI Director, James Comey, delivered a prescient speech in a public discussion forum held at the Brookings Institution in Washington, D.C., titled: "Going Dark: Are Technology, Privacy, and Public Safety on a Collision Course?"[1] Comey was advocating for a closer partnership between government agencies and private companies, to assist law enforcement and national security officials in criminal investigations. His argument was to update and expand the Communications Assistance for Law Enforcement Act (CALEA), which is the existing law that mandates telecommunication providers to build infrastructure into their networks to assist law enforcement agencies to intercept information for criminal investigation purposes. This raised significant questions surrounding the privacy of users' online data and how that is situated within national security efforts. Comey further articulated his plea, arguing that:

> technology has forever changed the world we live in. We're online, in one way or another, all day long. Our phones and computers have become reflections of our personalities, our interests, and our identities. They hold much that is important to us… Unfortunately, the law hasn't kept pace with technology, and this disconnect has created a significant public safety problem. We call it 'Going Dark.'

[1] FBI. 2014. Going dark: Are technology, privacy, and public safety on a collision course? https://www.fbi.gov/news/speeches/going-dark-are-technology-privacy-and-public-safety-on-a-collision-course. Accessed 12 Apr 2018.

A. J. Reid, *The Smartphone Paradox*,
https://doi.org/10.1007/978-3-319-94319-0_7

Specifically, Comey was warning that tech-savvy criminals use smartphone encryption as a refuge from law enforcement, and that technology companies are somewhat complicit by not providing local, state, and government agencies with backdoor access. Comey also pointed out that "many iPhones and other Apple devices will be encrypted by default," rendering even the tech companies unable to access the information stored on an individual's phone. Retrieving encrypted data from a criminal's phone would the equivalent of "a safe that can't be cracked."

And then, just over one year later, on December 2, 2015, two violent extremists carried out a mass shooting and bombing attempt in San Bernardino, California that killed 14 and seriously injured 22 others. Law enforcement obtained an iPhone 5c that belonged to one of the extremists, which presumably contained sensitive information that could help contextualize the shooting and possibly even thwart a similar attack. But as Comey had forewarned, the four-digit passcode-protected iPhone would be inaccessible without the cooperation of Apple. The FBI claims that it can unlock a locked smartphone in under 26 minutes, but after ten incorrect attempts, a security feature wipes the device clean and erases all data. A backup security feature increases the amount of time permitted between attempts.[2] So, while the FBI could unlock the device, it would do so at the expense of the stored information—defeating the purpose of the investigation.

A standoff between the FBI and Apple ensued, sparking national debate over the constitutionality of law enforcement agencies' rights to data mine personal devices and the ethical responsibilities of tech companies to provide the access. The FBI requested that the tech company build a backdoor to the iPhone. In an open letter to customers, Apple CEO Tim Cook said the following: "Specifically, the FBI wants us to make a new version of the iPhone operating system, circumventing several important security features, and install it on an iPhone recovered during the investigation."[3] Apple complied with the investigation but ultimately refused to build the security-evasive operating system, citing that once a backdoor had been

[2] Nakashima, Ellen. 2016. FBI paid professional hackers one-time fee to crack San Bernardino iPhone. *The Washington Post*, April 12. https://www.washingtonpost.com/world/national-security/fbi-paid-professional-hackers-one-time-fee-to-crack-san-bernardino-iphone/2016/04/12/5397814a-00de-11e6-9d36-33d198ea26c5_story.html?utm_term=.4e0beae065d7. Accessed 12 Mar 2018.

[3] Apple. 2016. A message to our customers. https://www.apple.com/customer-letter/. Accessed 4 Mar 2018.

created, it would open up the possibility for any law-abiding citizen's phone to be breached. The government agency responded forcefully by invoking the All Writs Act of 1789, which authorizes the "issue [of] all writs necessary or appropriate in aid of their respective jurisdictions and agreeable to the usages and principles of law."[4] The move was heralded by some as a creative use of an unprecedented law, and others viewed it as a blatant overreach of the arm of the law. The FBI would eventually withdraw its request of Apple, having reportedly paid $900,000 to a third party to unlock the iPhone instead. The contents of the phone remain classified.

The San Bernardino case brought the growing issue of "going dark" to heightened public attention. As personal technologies such as devices, apps, and cloud-based computing become more encrypted, law enforcement agencies struggle more with surveillance and intelligence-gathering efforts. In a plea for interagency relationships between the public and private sectors, Deputy Attorney General Rod Rosenstein said in a 2017 speech: "The truth is that 'going dark' threatens to disable law enforcement and enable criminals and terrorists to operate with impunity," noting that thousands of devices are being stored by the Department of Justice and remain "impervious to search warrants."[5] As we continue to allow our devices to underwrite our lives in more personal ways, we retreat further into the darkness, expecting cybersecurity but compromising privacy.

Privacy and Surveillance

We are living in an unprecedented time in history. The Internet has given us greater access to more information than ever before, as well as the ability to connect with more people than was previously possible. Marshall McLuhan identified this concept in 1964 as the "global village"—a metaphorical description of how technology and electronic media shrink the natural world, "extend[ing] our central nervous system itself in a global

[4] Legal Information Institute. 2018. 28 U.S. Code § 1651—Writs. https://www.law.cornell.edu/uscode/text/28/1651. Accessed 20 Mar 2018.

[5] U.S. Department of Justice. 2017. Deputy Attorney General Rod J. Rosenstein delivers remarks on encryption at the United States Naval Academy. https://www.justice.gov/opa/speech/deputy-attorney-general-rod-j-rosenstein-delivers-remarks-encryption-united-states-naval. Accessed 21 Mar 2018.

embrace, abolishing both space and time as far as our planet is concerned."[6] But all this connectivity comes at a cost. In exchange for the free flow of information and unbridled networking, we negotiate a slice of ourselves. This subchapter addresses both privacy and surveillance, conflating the two concepts to an extent, but recognizing that each informs the other. It's important to understand first the concept of privacy, and then the ways in which our devices compromise privacy through surveillance.

Definitions of privacy fluctuate between contexts and by country. The term privacy is not explicitly articulated in the U.S. Constitution, nor in federal or state law. However, the Bill of Rights establishes a "zone of privacy" which is interpreted to include various privacies such as beliefs (Amendment I), the home (Amendment III), person and possessions (Amendment IV), and vague protection against disparagement by others (Amendment IX). The earliest argument for protecting individuals' privacies appears in 1890, when the *Harvard Law Review* published an article titled, "The Right to Privacy" by Samuel Warren and Louis Brandeis. The article was a pushback against the recent technological developments of instant photography and audio recording devices, their growing ubiquity, and the increasing threat to personal privacy. The authors state:

> The intensity and complexity of life, attendant upon advancing civilization, have rendered necessary some retreat from the world, and man, under the refining influence of culture, has become more sensitive to publicity, so that solitude and privacy have become more essential to the individual; but modern enterprise and invention have, through invasions upon his privacy, subjected him to mental pain and distress, far greater than could be inflicted by mere bodily injury.[7]

Indeed, the emergence of personal devices brings with it unwanted sensitivity to publicity. Warren and Brandeis were particularly concerned about unconsented surveillance and the potential for defamation that it created. Later, when Brandeis became a Supreme Court Justice, he articulated a definition of privacy in Olmstead v. United States (1928): "the right to be let alone—the most comprehensive of rights and the right most valued by civilized men." Privacy, it seems reasonable to conclude, is not a privilege but a right of individuals.

[6] McLuhan, Marshall. 1964. *Understanding Media: Extensions of Man*. New York: McGraw-Hill.

[7] Warren, Samuel and Louis Brandeis. 1890. The right to privacy. *Harvard Law Review* 4: 5.

In the age of devices, we are vulnerable to an invasion of our privacy in two major ways. First, our own likeness becomes more easily compromised when the majority of people are carrying in their pockets a smartphone, which also serves as a photo, video, and audio recording device. An article in *The Atlantic* asks, "How Many Photographs of You Are Out There in the World?" The author, Rose Eveleth, ultimately concludes that there is no way to tell. On any given day, we might upload our own photos to social media, appear accidentally in the background of someone else's photo, and be recorded by security cameras, closed-circuit TV systems, red-light cameras, and satellite imagery, depending on where you live. The proliferation of recording devices coupled with the popularity of social media outlets translates to an estimated 1.8 billion images uploaded to the Internet each day.[8] Second, our devices are gateways into our personal data; researchers from Princeton University and the University of California, Berkeley report that seven out of ten apps on our smartphones are not only collecting and archiving personal data that is derived from our usage but also sharing it with a third party, unbeknownst to users. Each time we unlock our smartphone, we advertise sensitive information including personal conversations over text, email, and messaging apps, phone call history and contacts, location data and history, web browsing activity, and any photos and videos stored on your device or in the cloud.

Legislation on digital privacy has not yet caught up with communications technology. The Electronic Communications Privacy Act (ECPA) was authored in 1986 and is cited often to protect the privacy of Internet users. The Act makes it unlawful for anyone, including law enforcement, to disclose the contents of electronic communication. Though the language in the act is referring to the 1986 definition of computing, it has been used more recently to include smartphone activity under the generic term "electronic communication." Digital Due Process is a "diverse coalition of privacy advocates" supported by organizations like the American Civil Liberties Union (ACLU) and the American Legislative Exchange Council (ALEC) and private companies like Apple, Microsoft, Amazon, and Google. Its overarching goal is to

[8] Eveleth, Rose. 2015. How many photographs of you are out there in the world? *The Atlantic*, November 2. https://www.theatlantic.com/technology/archive/2015/11/how-many-photographs-of-you-are-out-there-in-the-world/413389/. Accessed 13 Feb 2018.

> simplify, clarify, and unify the ECPA standards, providing stronger privacy protections for communications and associated data in response to changes in technology and new services and usage patterns, while preserving the legal tools necessary for government agencies to enforce the laws, respond to emergency circumstances and protect the public.[9]

And clarification is urgently needed. In 2014, the Supreme Court heard arguments in the landmark case, *Riley v. California*, which found the warrantless search of the contents of a smartphone is unconstitutional. The case opinion reads: "The police generally may not, without a warrant, search digital information on a cell phone seized from an individual who has been arrested."[10] This was a victory for digital privacy advocates but a blow to law enforcement agencies. Yet there is a loophole; if a smartphone user unlocks his or her phone using biometric data, meaning fingerprint touch or face ID, police are legally authorized to require the user to unlock the phone. A 2014 precedent set by a Virginia circuit court judge found that the biometric data used in phone unlocking is no different from the fingerprinting and mugshot photos collected during routine booking procedure. Then, in late 2017, the Supreme Court heard another significant case related to digital privacy. *Carpenter v. United States*, on which the Supreme Court is still deliberating at the time of this writing, questions whether or not the government may lawfully seize and search location data generated by a smartphone without first seeking a warrant. The rationale for this argument, which some see as a clear violation of the Fourth Amendment, is that smartphone users divulge their data voluntarily because they choose to use a smartphone. But smartphones have become part of our society's communication infrastructure, making their use necessary, not voluntary.

We are caught in what might be described as a "privacy paradox"—the contradiction that privacy is a main concern for Internet users, yet we willingly and recklessly trade our privacy for small returns. A 2013 study found that Internet users were willing to trade in their personally identifiable information for as little as € 7, or the price of a Big Mac.[11] This is not necessarily indicative of our sensitive information apathy as much as

[9] Digital Due Process. 2018. https://digitaldueprocess.org/. Accessed 13 Feb 2018.

[10] Riley v. California. 2013. https://www.supremecourt.gov/opinions/13pdf/13-132_8l9c.pdf. Accessed 18 Feb 2018.

[11] Carrascal, Juan Pablo, Christopher Riederer, Vijay Erramilli, Mauro Cherubini and Rodrigo de Oliveira. 2011. Your browsing behavior for a Big Mac: Economics of personal

it is suggestive that we are captives of our own devices. In Milan Kundera's novel, *Slowness*, which I discussed earlier in Chap. 4, a character named Vincent offers up his soliloquy on the privacy that we forfeit by living in a modern society:

> Dear sir, we cannot choose the era we are born into. And we all of us live under the gaze of the cameras. This is part of the human condition from now on. Even when we fight a war, we're fighting it under the eye of the camera. And when we want to protest against anything, we can't make ourselves heard without cameras. We are all dancers, as you say. I would even say: either we're dancers or we're deserters.

Vincent goes on to say that every generation, at every point throughout the history of time, struggles with *modernity*. With new technology come new sets of problems, reservations, optimism, proponents, and opponents. For many smartphone users, compromising personal information for technology use is not acceptable, but it's simply the cost of doing business. Sometimes, we willingly betray our own privacy for convenience. At Three Squares Market, a tech company in Wisconsin, company employees were given the option to have a radio-frequency identification (RFID) device injected into their hands for the purposes of entering the building and paying for cafeteria food without having to swipe an ID card.[12] Shockingly, the majority of the employees voluntarily opted into the experiment, making Three Squares Market the first American company to offer such invasive technology. But when it comes to surveillance, we often do not have the luxury of choice.

Our smartphones can double as highly sophisticated tracking devices. In fact, we might even have found this to be a useful function at times; the Find My iPhone or Find My Device feature is standard on iOS and Android devices and can help locate a misplaced smartphone. So, it should not have come as a shock to most people when a document released by WikiLeaks alleged that the Central Intelligence Agency (CIA) effectively uses smartphones to surveil persons of interest. In their data dump from March 2017, WikiLeaks released more than 8000 documents that were extracted from the CIA's Center for Cyber Intelligence. The classified documents

information online. In *Proceedings of the 22nd International Conference on World Wide Web* 189–200.

[12] Astor, Maggie. 2017. Microchip implants for employees? One company says yes. *The New York Times*, July 25. https://www.nytimes.com/2017/07/25/technology/microchips-wisconsin-company-employees.html. Accessed 4 Mar 2018.

seemed to confirm a special CIA unit called the Mobile Devices Branch, which uses specialized malware to infiltrate users' smartphones and retrieve data before it is encrypted. According to WikiLeaks, "Infected phones can be instructed to send the CIA the user's geolocation, audio and text communications as well as covertly activate the phone's camera and microphone."[13] This government overreach seems scarily Orwellian, but in reality, it is highly unlikely that your data is being monitored closely by the CIA. The total number of working smartphones is estimated to be around 200 million in the United States alone. Instead, government agencies monitor sensitive keywords used in communication transmissions; in 2012, the Department of Homeland Security acknowledged that it monitors Facebook, primarily, for 374 keywords, specifically.[14]

Consumers have expressed strong demand for surveillance products. Wireless camera systems, video doorbells, and video baby monitors all provide us a sense of security, but any time we use our wireless Internet to stream surveillance video, we are opening a door to voyeurism. A Moscow-based website, insecam.org, is an online collection of more than 73,000 IP live streaming cameras. The site, which allows users to upload links to camera feeds, was found hosting private footage from Wi-Fi-enabled baby monitors and home security cameras that are not password-protected. The FAQ page of the website states that they will remove camera feeds upon request, "But remember that your camera still will be available to all internet users… The only solution to make your camera private is to set up a password!"[15] Some surveillance tools extend beyond the home. Tile is a Bluetooth-powered 1.5″ × 1.5″ location-tracking device and retails for around $25. According to their website, the "Tile app connects you to the world's largest lost-and-found community, where friends and strangers work together to find everything that matters."[16] If you have ever misplaced your car keys or wallet, this product sounds like a modern-age necessity. But what about using the Tile to track others and their belongings? What about the ex-boyfriend who sticks the tracking device on his ex-girlfriend's car? Tile, Inc. dismisses scenarios like this one, citing a major shortcoming of the product; the maximum range is only 200′. But as the technology

[13] Wikileaks. 2017. https://wikileaks.org/ciav7p1/. Accessed 5 Apr 2018.

[14] U.S. Department of Homeland Security. 2011. https://epic.org/foia/epic-v-dhs-media-monitoring/Analyst-Desktop-Binder-REDACTED.pdf. Accessed 4 Mar 2018.

[15] Insecam. 2018. http://www.insecam.org/en/faq/. Accessed 4 Mar 2018.

[16] Tile. 2018. https://www.thetileapp.com/en-us/products/mate. Accessed 4 Mar 2018.

improves, so will surveillance products like these, and we will be forced to decide whether the benefits outweigh the drawbacks.

There are measures that can be taken to reduce your digital vulnerability. On personal devices, encrypted messaging apps like WhatsApp, Telegram, and Silence offer a private messaging alternative to the default texting app on smartphones. Privacy browsers like Epic, Brave, and Tor remove website tracking cookies and reroute searches and online activity through proxied servers. Any technologies that stream video over wireless Internet should be password-protected. In addition to safeguarding our devices, there are growing efforts to create awareness for Internet users on how our data is being used and by whom. The Haystack Project is an initiative started by academics that maps the relationships between apps and third-party tracking services in an interactive web online in order to help users "identify privacy leaks."[17] And, a new industry of identity monitoring services like Experian and LifeLock offers dark web scans and identity protection for monthly subscription fees, sparking a profitable market that has been estimated to be worth $3 billion.[18] It turns out that people will pay for peace of mind. But as we continue to make more of our everyday things smarter, we are generating more opportunities for a breach of personal privacies.

The term Internet of Things, or IoT, refers to the infrastructure of physical devices that are connected to a vast network of everyday things and users. Many IoT consumer products strive to make our homes more intelligent; features like thermostats, door locks, garage doors, kitchen appliances, lighting, outlets, washers and dryers, robot vacuums, and irrigation systems have all been smartened with software. And the IoT continues to creep into nearly every aspect of our lives. In 2017, there was an estimated 8.4 billion connected devices worldwide, an increase of 31% from the year prior, and 500 billion devices are expected to be connected by the year 2030.[19,20] We have embraced voice-controlled digital assistants

[17] ICS Haystack Panopticon. 2016. https://www.haystack.mobi/panopticon/. Accessed 5 Mar 2018.

[18] Weisman, Steve. 2017. Is identity theft protection worth it? *USA Today*, April 22. https://www.usatoday.com/story/money/columnist/2017/04/22/identity-theft-protection-worth/100554362/. Accessed 4 Mar 2018.

[19] Gartner. 2017. Gartner says 8.4 billion connected 'things' will be in use in 2017, up 31 percent from 2016. February 7. https://www.gartner.com/newsroom/id/3598917. Accessed 5 Mar 2018.

[20] Cisco. 2016. Internet of things. https://www.cisco.com/c/dam/en/us/products/collateral/se/internet-of-things/at-a-glance-c45-731471.pdf. Accessed 6 Mar 2018.

like Amazon Echo, Google Home, and the Apple Homepod to help manage hands-free requests of our devices. But because these devices are activated by a command phrase—"Alexa," "OK Google," or "Hey Siri"—they must always be listening, waiting to be summoned, and hearing everything that is being said in their presence. Depending on the device, this data is stored differently. For instance, Amazon's Alex stores past queries in its app settings. You can view all of your previous Google Home activity by visiting myactivity.google.com. As far as we know, these companies do not store the voice data that devices hear peripherally. As far as we know. As we technologize our every move, we leave a trail of data, generating big data and even bigger opportunity for intrusion.

The Technoself

There are some things in life that are enjoyed best without the help of digital technology. For me, that thing is surfing. When I am not working or spending time with my family, you can probably find me floating on my shortboard somewhere off the coast of North Carolina. I revel in the 85° bath-like water temperatures in the summers and tolerate the 41° frigid waters in the winters. (Unfortunately, I have developed a considerably bad case of exostosis, more commonly known as surfer's ear, from years of winter surf sessions without adequate ear protection.) I have surfed all up and down the East Coast, some in California, and in Central America. I've experienced nearly all conditions imaginable: pre and post hurricanes, tropical storms and depressions, squalls, nor'easters, even snowstorms. In fact, one of my utmost favorite things is surfing during a rainstorm (sans lightning, of course). For me, and I suspect for most others, surfing is visceral. A pseudo-religious existence. Perhaps over-dramatically, many surfers will refer to it as a "way of life" rather than an activity. I can't say that surfing eclipses all of my life's responsibilities, but I will admit that I have canceled class to surf on more than one occasion. In the words of William Finnegan, a legendary surf explorer and even more accomplished author, "[M]y utter absorption in surfing had no rational content. It simply compelled me; there was a deep mine of beauty and wonder in it. Beyond that, I could not have explained why I did it."[21] Thankfully, my children have begun to find their own passion for surfing, and as they grow older, I look forward to watching them strengthen their bond with

[21] Finnegan, William. 2015. *Barbarian Days: A Surfing Life*. New York: Penguin Books.

the ocean and appreciate what Finnegan calls "the beautiful violence of breaking waves" (see Images 7.1 and 7.2).

When most people think of surfing, they picture a scantily-clad, bronzed man or woman carving the face of a blue giant, performing S-turns and tucking into pristine glass barrels. But this is only a fraction of the process. Actually, this is just the payoff. Most novice surfers are surprised to find that surfing consists mostly of paddling, which, for the untrained, can be extremely rigorous. Then, there is duck-diving, which occurs when a wave is about to break directly in front of the surfer. Grabbing the board by its rails, and burying the nose almost straight down, the surfer burrows deeper into the water under the impact zone (where the lip of the wave curls over and meets the surface of the water) and reemerges through the back of the wave. This ensures the surfer is not pushed backwards towards the shore, thereby rendering his or her efforts up to this point futile. Depending on the size of the waves, this process could occur multiple times as the surfer tries to paddle through the whitewash and out to the lineup. After all this, there is prolonged waiting for the right wave.

Image 7.1 Me with my oldest daughter, Stella, heading out for a surf session.
Source: Author

Image 7.2 My oldest son, Phoenix: a surfer in training. Source: Author

A knowledgeable surfer will know how to avoid rip currents, read breaks, identify peaks and shoulders, and interpret the set waves (a recurring series of 2–4 waves that are larger than the rest of the waves in the swell). In fact, judges use wave selection as a scoring criterion in professional surfing competitions.

Surfing demands an understanding of nature. Most expert surfers are self-taught meteorologists, reading variables such as wind direction and speed, swell periods and heights, tide cycles, even lunar phases to predict the best possible surf. Even with this knowledge, it is difficult to forecast much further than three or four days out. Professional surf competitions implement what are called *holding periods*, which are flexible times during which the contest can run, depending on the quality of surf. Because of the unpredictability of the ocean, scheduled competitions usually are tentative and often canceled and rescheduled in order to capitalize on the best conditions. To be a surfer requires more than boardshorts and a surfboard. In fact, surf culture even has terminology for the surf-poser: *kook* (which literally is adapted from the Hawaiian word *kukae*, meaning "shit").

Being called a kook is a devastating accusation and is usually reserved for the most egregious violations of unwritten surf etiquette. No, the most authentic surfers are more complex and deeper than their sexified avatars that canvas the walls of *Pacific Sunwear* stores in midwestern malls. They are more dimensional than vapid stoners like Jeff Spicoli in *Fast Times at Ridgemont High*, or existential nihilists like Bodhi in *Point Break*. Real surfers understand why surfing was known in Hawaii as the "sport of kings" nearly a millennium ago, and even before that, as man's 3000-year-old quest for symbiosis with nature.

In 2016, Samsung launched the Galaxy Surfboard: a bold attempt to breathe new technology into an ancient sport. The board is equipped with a waterproof smartphone-sized drawer that slides out and accepts the Samsung Galaxy S7, which then enables wireless Internet connectivity. Embedded on the topside of the board is an LED display, which relays information such as "wind direction, height, and frequency of the waves."[22] The rider also is notified of tweets and text messages. It seems we cannot disconnect even if we paddle out into the deep blue sea. The Galaxy Surfboard never went into full production, presumably because of the backlash it received online after posting its promotional commercial on YouTube. The tagline scrawled across the video reads: "Surfing can be a solitary sport. The surfer. Alone in the middle of the ocean… disconnected." Apparently, Samsung views disconnection as a problem in need of resolution. Perhaps the most poignant retort on the YouTube page came from a user named Russell O'Neill, who succinctly commented on the video: "I surf to avoid technology." In concurrence, I continued down this rabbit-hole of reading the YouTube comments section and came across an interesting reply to O'Neill's summation. A user named Abraão Caldas replied, "So just don't use it, you are being forced to use it?" This might seem like an unnecessary and combative response to the initial comment, possibly meant to troll the guy who is saying that he doesn't want a computer surfboard. But this is actually an updated (albeit less eloquent) version of Lynn White's argument that "a new device merely opens a door; it does not compel one to enter." Yet, the research I've presented in this book so far suggests that technology *does compel*, and that it is not neutral. Technology tempts and compels us towards good and bad.

[22] Boxall, Andy. 2016. Samsung Galaxy surfboard is every bit as absurd as you imagine. *Digital Trends*. May 11. https://www.digitaltrends.com/mobile/samsung-galaxy-surfboard-news/. Accessed 6 Mar 2018.

Consider the following two scenarios. Scenario #1: A surfer is floating on his Samsung Galaxy surfboard distractedly checking his Twitter feed that is embedded in the deck of his surfboard, failing to see a shark circling him. In this situation, this technology might have cost the surfer a limb or even his life. Scenario #2: The Galaxy Surfboard displays a text message sent from someone on the beach that reads, "SHARK!" This notifies the surfer that he is in danger, prompting him to swim safely to shore. Technology plays a role in both scenarios, in ways good and bad. Yet, the example of the Samsung Galaxy Surfboard is not meant to illustrate how technology is dependent on the context of the situation but also to show that when technology is present, our behavior is influenced and the overall experience altered. This is the non-neutrality of technology.

The Samsung commercial closes dramatically with these words on screen: "Progress knows no boundaries." While I agree with this generic statement, my inner surfer questions whether or not this product qualifies as progress. The digital readouts of a surfboard replace what I described earlier as the necessary characteristics that define true surfers. Much like the way an Internet search engine robs us of our generative processes, or a GPS system gradually degenerates our spatial abilities, the Samsung Galaxy surfboard dulls our senses, sacrificing analog connectedness for the digital. And this is not necessarily progressive. Companies like FlowRider® have found a way to bring surfing inland; their innovative sheetwave technology produces "an endless wave which pumps thousands of gallons of water over a composite membrane riding surface, creating a perfect perpetual wave."[23] These synthetic waves strip the surfer of everything but the payoff: riding the wave. There is no paddling, no duck-diving, no barrier to entry. There is only the gratification of riding a manufactured wave. FlowRiders have been installed in 180+ locations around the world, including hotels, water parks, cruise ships, and shopping malls. Just as the ancient Hawaiian kings intended.

This is not the first attempt at incorporating smart technology into surfing. The Search GPS Watch by Rip Curl is a smart-enabled watch that (in addition to displaying the time) conveys tidal data and GPS coordinates that "track wave count, speeds reached, and length of rides."[24] Each

[23] FlowRider. 2018. Our company. http://www.flowrider.com/about-flowrider-inc/. Accessed 8 Mar 2018.

[24] Rip Curl. 2018. Welcome to the search. http://searchgps.ripcurl.com/welcome/. Accessed 10 Mar 2018.

surf session can be synced to the Rip Curl smartphone app so that it can be shared with others on social media. Surfd.com ranked the Search GPS Watch runner-up for best surf watch of 2017, already making it far more successful than Samsung's failed attempt at surfing's first rideable iPad. The Smartphin is a surfboard fin that collects and analyzes oceanic data such as water temperature, pH levels, salinity, and acidity that is delivered to a smartphone app. The sensor also can track wave signatures in real time to help determine where to find the best surf. Pressure Profile Systems (PPS) has developed the pressure-sensing surf bootie, which map the amount of pressure the surfer exerts when performing maneuvers. And lastly, there is the puck-sized sensor device that, when mounted to the front of a surfboard, "reports ocean conditions and logs waves caught in real time, so a user's friends can check in on not only water conditions, but how the surfer is doing, helping them decide whether or not to head to that spot themselves."[25] To the surfing purist, these technologies violate the sanctity of surfing. But to tech-sympathizers, these various devices are the next step in the evolution of surfing.

The quantified self (QS) is a data-driven movement in which people collect self-tracking data to interpret and modify their behaviors. Self-tracking involves the quantification of some type of measurable activity, such as the number of steps you take each day, the number of calories you consume, and the number of hours of sleep you receive. We use self-tracking data to arrive at our own *self-quantification*, that is, the understanding of ourselves through data. And although self-quantification has always existed to some degree, technology, and even more specifically our smartphones, has helped to transcribe our daily minutiae into numerical data. One of the most obvious ways that we use data to gain self-knowledge is by tracking our health statistics. In 2014, Apple launched the Health app, which comes pre-installed on devices with iOS 8 and later. The app consolidates data that is entered manually, such as body measurements, vital signs, and reproductive health, as well as data that is collected via a motion sensor that runs continuously in the background, collecting activity data like the total number of steps taken, walking and running distance, elevation climbed, and standing hours. We use our devices to quantify ourselves in other ways, too. Ostensibly, we measure our general popular-

[25] Perry, Tekla. 2016. Flo Labs' IoT gadget is like Waze for surfers. *IEEE Spectrum*, November 17. https://spectrum.ieee.org/view-from-the-valley/at-work/start-ups/its-like-wazefor-surfers. Accessed 9 Mar 2018.

ity by the number of friends or followers we have on social media and by the number of likes and comments we receive on a post. In this sense, quantification becomes more of a validation of our social capital rather than a self-evaluation strategy, but we still are valuing ourselves as a function of data.

Our devices are perfect tools for data collection. They parse out our daily lives into quantifiable bits of information that keep us coming back for more. Visual notifications on our phones can pull us into distraction, indicating the number of unread news stories, unviewed shopping deals, unseen activity on social media, unlistened-to podcasts, and so on. Visual notifications also can quantify our lack of productivity, accentuating lingering to-dos such as unread texts, unread emails, missed calls, pending calendar events, and other tasks that are anxiety-inducing. In an era of constant connection, we have to develop methods for digital survival, such as Inbox Zero, a popular productivity lifehack proposed by Merlin Mann in 2007. The goal of the time-management program is to incorporate strategies for maintaining an inbox with zero unread messages so as to prevent you from "living in your inbox." But, as described by Silvia Killingsworth in her rebuttal article, "Zero Dark Inbox," this program is a disguised "coping mechanism for the anxiety created by a constant flux of email."[26] Visual notifications are constant reminders of to-do-ism, tethering us to our phones by compelling us to check them frequently. When we do extinguish all of our visual notifications, we feel a sense of gratification and accomplishment. But this feeling is short-lived, only clearing the queue of tasks so that we might field more. Sometimes quantifying our tasks leaves us feeling like we can only ever get back to zero and never ahead.

When I was in high school in the late 1990s, I ran cross-country. In that pre-smartphone era, we ran without the accompaniment of technology. Quite literally, our coach would drive us six to ten miles out into the country and tell us to run back to campus. No headphones, just the sound of feet beating the ground. In fact, I remember the only feedback I ever received from my coach was that I "ran heavy" when I got tired. Running heavy meant I had slipped out of form and was plodding my feet down, creating a loud thumping sound with each stride. Running sans technology created mental fortitude, leaving me alone with just my thoughts, and

[26] Killingsworth, Silvia. 2017. Zero Dark Inbox. *The New Yorker*, June 18. https://www.newyorker.com/culture/culture-desk/zero-dark-inbox. Accessed 9 Mar 2018.

forcing me to submit into a meditative state. Now, when I run, I'm too preoccupied by podcasts, music, and audiobooks to recognize when I am running heavy.

Every time I go for a run, the first thing I do is strap my smartphone to my arm and open an app called Runkeeper, which tracks the activity. To date, I have logged more than 350 runs on the app, totaling more than 1000 miles. In fact, the thought of running technology-free seems impossibly pointless now. There have been times when I got dressed, put my running shoes on, stretched, and then, because my phone battery was too low, aborted the run. Now, I run for the data; I must know the exact distance I ran, what my mile split times were, my overall time, and how it compared to my previous runs. But because the app always compares my workout to my personal bests, I often am disappointed with the output on my screen: "3.00 miles. 23:37 time. Your 68th fastest!" This run didn't even crack the top 50, and my partial letdown detracts from the main reason I run: to clear my mind and to feel better about myself. Self-quantification can be a valuable tool for reflection, but too much attention paid to our digital exhaust, and we can become data-obsessed, losing sight of the larger purpose.

The term *technoself* refers to the study of the adaptation of human identity to technological developments. Perhaps there is no greater time of adaptation than now. Consider the ways in which our devices, the Internet, and social media—all very recent developments—have reshaped how we look at the world, ourselves, and others. According to Rocci Luppicini, a leading authority in the emerging field of Technoself Studies:

> [D]igital technology is redefining key aspects of who we are online and offline, how we spend our time, how we create meaning, how we present ourselves, how we interact with and treat our technological creations, and how we interact with others online and offline.[27]

The idea of the technoself suggests that reality is viewed through technology. In the book, *The Accidental Universe*, Alan Lightman describes the technoself as a hybrid existence between the artificial and the natural, which ultimately leaves us disassociated from both. He says, "The twentieth-century digital technologies have certainly helped enable our techno-selves.

[27] Luppicini, Rocci. 2013. *Handbook of Research on Technoself: Identity in a Technological Society*. Hershey, PA: IGI Global.

But the more penetrating development has been the gradual psychological adaptation to a disembodied experience of the world."[28] The distinction is important; it is not that introducing technology ruins the activity—this is an anti-technology dogmatism. Rather, technology fundamentally alters our perception of the activity and of ourselves. We surfed for waves, and now we surf for wave counts. We ran for exercise, and now we run to log miles. And as technology encroaches into nearly every aspect of our lives, we leave a digital wake of data that defines who we are.

In Defense of Boredom

My daughter (age 9) and son (age 5) sit in the back of my car on the way to their school, which is a 15-minute drive from our house. Nearly every day, one of them asks the question, "Can we watch a movie?" They are referring to the dropdown DVD player that comes standard in most SUVs now. But they know the answer before they even ask. It's the same response they hear when they ask if they can bring their iPad in the car during this short commute. And each time, I feel like Clark Griswold in *National Lampoon's Vacation*, a well-meaning dolt of a father who forces his family to interact for the sake of memory-making. My wife and I do indulge the kids' requests to use their iPads and watch DVDs when we are taking long road trips, however, and there have been many times over the years that I have pointed out the views from above the Appalachian mountain roads, the setting sun over the sand dunes of the Carolinas, or the marshy lowlands of the south, only to look in my rear-view mirror to see everyone plugged into a headset, gazing down at a screen instead. I don't think this is what McLuhan had meant when he said, "We look at the present through a rear-view mirror." But my children don't care much for McLuhan yet; my daughter just wants to listen to Taylor Swift, and my son wants to play Minecraft. But during our morning commutes, we talk about things like school, friends, and plans for the weekend. Sometimes, the kids just look out the window. Their observations often lead to a discussion ("Dad, what does the blinking yellow arrow mean?"). Occasionally, we listen to NPR News, and I find myself attempting to translate foreign policy and economics into adolescent parlance. Other times, I try to indoctrinate them with a mini lesson on music history ("Here's a song by The Beatles—you

[28] Lightman, Alan. 2014. *The Accidental Universe: The World You Thought You Knew*. New York: Pantheon Books.

should know about John Lennon"). Adam Phillips wrote in his book, *On Kissing, Tickling, and Being Bored: Psychoanalytic Essays on the Unexamined Life* that "The capacity to be bored can be a developmental achievement for the child." I don't limit technology in the car because it is some sort of rite of passage that I had to endure as a kid, or because I dislike Taylor Swift, or because I don't see the cognitive value in Minecraft. I just believe in the usefulness of boredom and what it creates.

The concept of boredom has a fascinating history, though it only dates back to the mid-eighteenth century. There is little actual consensus on a definition for boredom. Scholars like Patricia Meyer Spacks argue that boredom, as we perceive it in modern terms, is a "social construction" instead of an objective condition of being. She furthers her argument, saying: "In the context of such understanding, the twentieth-century proliferation of the malaise—boredom at work, boredom in leisure, boredom while making love—signals not only an experiential but a conceptual problem."[29] Peter Toohey's book, *Boredom: A Lively History*, unpacks the complex and often misunderstood concept. There are, in fact, many different variations of boredom. There is *simple boredom*, a "primary emotion" that is derivative of disgust and "liable to vanish"; *existential boredom*, the restlessness with "a person's very existence"; and *hyperboredom*, "the loss of a sense of personal meaning," which also might be explained clinically as depression. Toohey offers up the following:

> A definition of boredom might go something like this: it is an emotion which produces feelings of being constrained or confined by some unavoidable and distastefully predictable circumstance and, as a result, a feeling of being distanced from one's surroundings and the normal flow of time. But that is very cumbersome. One of the tests for a good definition is that it's easy to remember. Let's try again: Boredom is a social emotion of mild disgust produced by a temporarily unavoidable and predictable circumstance.[30]

And so, the emotion of boredom becomes more pronounced when one feels "constrained or confined," such as when riding in the back seat of a car, knowing that boredom easily could be cured with an iPad. But boredom is inescapable. Even on those long road trips that I mentioned earlier, my kids

[29] Spacks, Patricia M. 1995. *Boredom: The Literary History of a State of Mind*. Chicago: University of Chicago Press.

[30] Toohey, Peter. 2011. *Boredom: A Lively History*. Yale University Press. ProQuest Ebook Central. http://ebookcentral.proquest.com/lib/coastal/detail.action?docID=3420713.

eventually become bored with technology. Boredom craves a change in circumstances, not technology. Indeed, boredom is relative to the situation. Philosopher Bertrand Russell writes in his book, *The Conquest of Happiness* (1930), that "We are less bored than our ancestors were, but we are more afraid of boredom." This is perhaps even truer today because we surround ourselves with devices, which give the illusion of meaningful engagement—the antithesis of boredom. When we reach for our smartphone out of boredom, we are not only seeking gratification from our device, but also, we are attempting to establish control over the situation. Boredom results from both a low level of control (limitation) and a high level of control (mastery) of a task[31]; for instance, a student might experience boredom in a classroom where he or she is either completely disinterested or already expert in the subject. But Russell states that boredom "is not to be regarded as wholly evil." Rather, he explicates two types of boredom: "The fructifying kind arises from the absence of drugs and the stultifying kind from the absence of vital activities." Let's first examine fructifying boredom.

The term "going dark" can refer to a willful decision to disconnect from technology in an attempt to regain more of our natural selves. Susan Maushart, a single mother of three teenagers (ages 14, 15, and 18), decided to perform an audacious experiment: unplug her family from all electronic devices for six months. Maushart fancied herself a modern-day Henry David Thoreau, who in 1844 abandoned his life in Concord, Massachusetts, and lived in a remote area, Walden Pond, for nearly two years. Maushart justified her decision to unplug by saying, "Thoreau hadn't run away from life. He'd run toward it." At the conclusion of her experiment, Maushart published *The Winter of Our Disconnect: How Three Totally Wired Teenagers (and a Mother Who Slept with Her iPhone) Pulled the Plug on Their Technology and Lived to Tell the Tale*. As the title implies, the experiment proved successful, and after six months technology-free, she and her three children found themselves more connected to each other, better rested, and generally happier than they had been prior. Importantly, each of them had to learn how to work through an initial phase of boredom; some pursued musical instruments, and others caught up on reading and having deep conversations with one another. The screen offers an easy out, a mindless preoccupation. But boredom urges creativity.

[31] Struk, Andriy. 2015. Exploring the relationship between self-regulation and boredom. https://uwspace.uwaterloo.ca/bitstream/handle/10012/9593/Struk_Andriy.pdf?sequence=3. Accessed 9 Mar 2018.

A 2014 study conducted by researchers at the University of Central Lancashire, United Kingdom placed individuals into two different, highly repetitive and boring scenarios, and then measured their level of divergent thinking. Participants engaged in either a highly boring reading or writing exercise, followed by a creative task. In the first scenario, participants wrote down telephone numbers directly from a phone book for 15 minutes, then were asked to list as many uses for two plastic cups in a three-minute time span. A second scenario had participants read from the same phone book for 15 minutes and then list as many creative uses for the plastic cups as possible in the allotted time. In short, participants who engaged in repetitive, boring tasks prior to the creative task produced more divergent thinking of a higher quality compared to those who had not experienced boredom. The authors concluded that "boredom can sometimes be a force for good" and that it "might be a worthwhile enterprise to allow or even embrace boredom in work, education, and leisure."[32]

Boredom is not something to avoid; it is to be embraced and harnessed. Indeed, we are all plagued (or privileged) by boredom. In a 1989 commencement address, Russian-American poet Joseph Brodsky encouraged the graduating students of Dartmouth College to "hail the boredom," for it puts our "existence into proper perspective." Boredom, according to Brodsky, is the opposite of inventiveness, which is a highly desirable but unsustainable phenomenon. We should all want to be inventive and original, but only some will succeed at this; rather, boredom will run throughout all of our lives, for it is "life's main medium." Prophetically speaking, Brodsky also warned the graduates of the coming of "self-gratifying gadgets":

> [O]ne can expect your being hit by boredom as soon as the first tools of self-gratification become available to you. Thanks to modern technology, those tools are as numerous as boredom's symptoms. In light of their function—to render you oblivious to the redundancy of time—their abundance is revealing.[33]

[32] Mann, Sandi and Rebekah Cadman. 2014. Does being bored make us more creative? *Creativity Research Journal* 26: 165–173. https://doi.org/10.1080/10400419.2014.901073.

[33] Brodsky, Joseph. 2015. Joseph Brodsky—Listening to boredom. https://lsoares.blogs.sapo.pt/joseph-brodsky-listening-to-boredom-1181316. Accessed 9 Mar 2018.

He concludes the commencement speech with sagely advice: "Try to embrace, or let yourself be embraced by, boredom and anguish, which are larger than you anyhow. No doubt you'll find that bosom smothering, yet try to endure it as long as you can, and then some more." Perhaps it is no coincidence that in South Korea, where smartphone ownership is among the highest globally, the ability to disconnect has become a competitive challenge. The International Space Out Competition is where participants are required to sit completely still, device-free, for two hours. The mental athlete with the lowest heart rate is crowned the champion. Although this event began as performance art that satirically commented on our inability to unplug, the challenge has grown in popularity and seriousness.

Most people lament boredom in the second way described by Russell, as stultifying. Boredom is considered by many to be a sense of purposelessness, a detriment to productivity and to personal health. And at least initially, boredom can increase impulsivity. Researchers have observed a direct correlation between impulsiveness and boredom, citing that the feeling to act impulsively, when stemming from boredom, functions as a self-correction tool to help mitigate a personal sense of meaninglessness.[34] In other words, when we are bored, we impulsively seek action to feel purposeful. Our smartphones are wonderful tools for this. Whenever we feel the slightest tinge of boredom, we can reach into our pockets for distraction-on-demand. Curing boredom with our smartphones is an instant gratification, but the avoidance of being bored can have even more consequential effects. A 2011 study of South African adolescents found that boredom is a relatively strong predictor of alcohol, cigarette, and marijuana use.[35] Our impulsivity to act out of boredom can lead to catastrophic decisions. In fact, researchers from the University of Virginia and Harvard University found that people would rather endure a negative experience than sit in a room alone with their thoughts. In one study, participants sat alone and device-free for 6–15 minutes at a time. At any point in the study, participants could voluntarily choose to self-administer an electrical shock to pass the time. Indeed, the majority of the male par-

[34] Moynihan, Andrew B., Eric Igou and Wijnand van Tilburg. 2017. Boredom increases impulsiveness: A meaning-regulation perspective. *Social Psychology* 48: 293–309. https://doi.org/10.1027/1864-9335/a000317.

[35] Sharp, Erin, Donna Coffman, Linda Caldwell, Edward Smith, Lisa Wegner, Tania Vergnani and Catherine Mathews. 2011. Predicting substance use behavior among South African adolescents: The role of leisure experiences across time. *International Journal of Behavioral Development* 35: 343–351.

ticipants gave themselves an electrical shock—choosing negative stimulation over no stimulation 67% of the time—and a quarter of female participants opted for the electrical shock. The researchers concluded that "Most people seem to prefer to be doing something rather than nothing, even if that something is negative."[36]

Other research has suggested that boredom, and how we choose to deal with it, is highly dependent on individual differences. Boredom is more present in men than in women,[37] and personality traits like inattentiveness and hyperactivity are more likely to trigger states of boredom.[38] In 1986, researchers developed a 28-item Boredom Proneness Scale (BPS) that measures and individual's susceptibility to being bored. More recently, the BPS has been shortened into 8-items and uses a 5-point Likert-type scale that ranges from *extremely uncharacteristic of me* (1) to *extremely characteristic of me* (5).[39] A higher score represents more proneness to boredom. The questions are as follows:

1. I often find myself at "loose ends" not knowing what to do.
2. I find it hard to entertain myself.
3. Many things I have to do are repetitive and monotonous.
4. It takes more stimulation to get me going than most people.
5. I don't feel motivated by most things that I do.
6. In most situations, it is hard for me to find something to do or see to keep me interested.
7. Much of the time, I just sit around doing nothing.
8. Unless I am doing something exciting, even dangerous, I feel half-dead and dull.

Boredom is something that each of us tolerates. Research consistently shows that boredom emerges out of a variety of situational contexts, is dependent on the individual type, and compels us to seek out both posi-

[36] Wilson, Timothy, David A. Reinhard, Erin C. Westgate, Daniel T. Gilbert, Nicole Ellerbeck, Cheryl Hahn, Casey Brown and Adi Shaked. 2014. Just think: The challenges of the disengaged mind. *Science* 345: 75–77.

[37] Chin, Alycia, Amanda Markey, Saurabh Bhargava, Karim Kassam and George Loewenstein. 2017. Bored in the USA: Experience sampling and boredom in everyday life. *Emotion* 17: 359–368. https://doi.org/10.1037/emo0000232.

[38] Gerritsen, Cory, Maggie E. Toplak, Jessica Sciaraffa and John Eastwood. 2014. I can't get no satisfaction: Potential causes of boredom. *Consciousness and Cognition* 27: 27–41.

[39] Struk, Andriy, Jonathan S.A. Carriere, Allan Cheyne and James Danckert. 2017. A short boredom proneness scale. *Assessment* 24: 346–359.

tive (fructifying) and negative (stultifying) experiences to escape it. The researchers from the study in which a large number of participants chose to self-administer electrical shocks in order to avoid boredom ultimately concluded that "The untutored mind does not like to be alone with itself." But when embraced, boredom can become a tool for tutoring our minds, helping us to see the world around us more vividly.

Boredom is on the brink of extinction, thanks to our ubiquitous devices. Smartphones offer to ameliorate any scenario where boredom might creep in: a classroom, at work, at home, in the car. Boredom is wrongly mistaken for being *mindless*. But what if boredom is repurposed to become *mindful*?

References

Apple. 2016. A message to our customers. Accessed March 4, 2018. https://www.apple.com/customer-letter/.

Astor, Maggie. 2017. Microchip implants for employees? One company says yes. *The New York Times*, July 25. Accessed March 4, 2018. https://www.nytimes.com/2017/07/25/technology/microchips-wisconsin-company-employees.html.

Boxall, Andy. 2016. Samsung Galaxy surfboard is every bit as absurd as you imagine. *Digital Trends*. May 11. Accessed March 6, 2018. https://www.digitaltrends.com/mobile/samsung-galaxy-surfboard-news/.

Brodsky, Joseph. 2015. Joseph Brodsky—Listening to boredom. Accessed March 9, 2018. https://lsoares.blogs.sapo.pt/joseph-brodsky-listening-to-boredom-1181316.

Carrascal, Juan Pablo, Christopher Riederer, Vijay Erramilli, Mauro Cherubini and Rodrigo de Oliveira. 2011. Your browsing behavior for a Big Mac: Economics of personal information online. In *Proceedings of the 22nd International Conference on World Wide Web*, 189–200.

Chin, Alycia, Amanda Markey, Saurabh Bhargava, Karim Kassam, and George Loewenstein. 2017. Bored in the USA: Experience sampling and boredom in everyday life. *Emotion* 17: 359–368 https://doi.org/10.1037/emo0000232.

Cisco. 2016. Internet of things. Accessed March 6, 2018. https://www.cisco.com/c/dam/en/us/products/collateral/se/internet-of-things/at-a-glance-c45-731471.pdf.

Digital Due Process. 2018. Accessed February 13, 2018. https://digitaldueprocess.org/.

Eveleth, Rose. 2015. How many photographs of you are out there in the world? *The Atlantic*, November 2. Accessed February 13, 2018. https://www.theatlantic.com/technology/archive/2015/11/how-many-photographs-of-you-are-out-there-in-the-world/413389/.

FBI. 2014. Going dark: Are technology, privacy, and public safety on a collision course? Accessed April 12, 2018. https://www.fbi.gov/news/speeches/going-dark-are-technology-privacy-and-public-safety-on-a-collision-course.

Finnegan, William. 2015. *Barbarian Days: A Surfing Life*. New York: Penguin Books.

FlowRider. 2018. Our company. Accessed March 8, 2018. http://www.flowrider.com/about-flowrider-inc/.

Gartner. 2017. Gartner says 8.4 billion connected 'things' will be in use in 2017, up 31 percent from 2016. February 7. Accessed March 5, 2018. https://www.gartner.com/newsroom/id/3598917.

Gerritsen, Cory, Maggie E. Toplak, Jessica Sciaraffa, and John Eastwood. 2014. I can't get no satisfaction: Potential causes of boredom. *Consciousness and Cognition* 27: 27–41.

ICS Haystack Panopticon. 2016. Accessed March 5, 2018. https://www.haystack.mobi/panopticon/.

Insecam. 2018. Accessed March 4, 2018. http://www.insecam.org/en/faq/.

Killingsworth, Silvia. 2017. Zero Dark Inbox. *The New Yorker*, June 18. Accessed March 9, 2018. https://www.newyorker.com/culture/culture-desk/zero-dark-inbox.

Legal Information Institute. 2018. 28 U.S. Code § 1651—Writs. Accessed March 20, 2018. https://www.law.cornell.edu/uscode/text/28/1651.

Lightman, Alan. 2014. *The Accidental Universe: The World You Thought You Knew*. New York: Pantheon Books.

Luppicini, Rocci. 2013. *Handbook of Research on Technoself: Identity in a Technological Society*. Hershey, PA: IGI Global.

Mann, Sandi, and Rebekah Cadman. 2014. Does being bored make us more creative? *Creativity Research Journal* 26: 165–173. https://doi.org/10.1080/10400419.2014.901073.

McLuhan, Marshall. 1964. *Understanding Media: Extensions of Man*. New York: McGraw-Hill.

Moynihan, Andrew B., Eric Igou, and Wijnand van Tilburg. 2017. Boredom increases impulsiveness: A meaning-regulation perspective. *Social Psychology* 48: 293–309. https://doi.org/10.1027/1864-9335/a000317.

Nakashima, Ellen. 2016. FBI paid professional hackers one-time fee to crack San Bernardino iPhone. *The Washington Post*, April 12. Accessed March 12, 2018. https://www.washingtonpost.com/world/national-security/fbi-paid-professional-hackers-one-time-fee-to-crack-san-bernardinoiphone/2016/04/12/5397814a-00de-11e6-9d36-33d198ea26c5_story.html?utm_term=.4e0beae065d7.

Perry, Tekla. 2016. Flo Labs' IoT gadget is like Waze for surfers. *IEEE Spectrum*, November 17. Accessed March 9, 2018. https://spectrum.ieee.org/view-from-the-valley/at-work/start-ups/its-like-wazefor-surfers.

Riley v. California. 2013. Accessed February 18, 2018. https://www.supremecourt.gov/opinions/13pdf/13-132_8l9c.pdf.

Rip Curl. 2018. Welcome to the search. Accessed March 10, 2018. http://search-gps.ripcurl.com/welcome/.

Sharp, Erin, Donna Coffman, Linda Caldwell, Edward Smith, Lisa Wegner, Tania Vergnani, and Catherine Mathews. 2011. Predicting substance use behavior among South African adolescents: The role of leisure experiences across time. *International Journal of Behavioral Development* 35: 343–351.

Spacks, Patricia M. 1995. *Boredom: The Literary History of a State of Mind*. Chicago: University of Chicago Press.

Struk, Andriy. 2015. Exploring the relationship between self-regulation and boredom. Accessed March 9, 2018. https://uwspace.uwaterloo.ca/bitstream/handle/10012/9593/Struk_Andriy.pdf?sequence=3.

Struk, Andriy, Jonathan S.A. Carriere, Allan Cheyne, and James Danckert. 2017. A short boredom proneness scale. *Assessment* 24: 346–359.

Tile. 2018. Accessed March 4, 2018. https://www.thetileapp.com/en-us/products/mate.

Toohey, Peter. 2011. *Boredom: A Lively History*. Yale University Press. ProQuest Ebook Central. http://ebookcentral.proquest.com/lib/coastal/detail.action?docID=3420713.

U.S. Department of Homeland Security. 2011. Accessed March 4, 2018. https://epic.org/foia/epic-v-dhs-media-monitoring/Analyst-Desktop-Binder-REDACTED.pdf.

U.S. Department of Justice. 2017. Deputy Attorney General Rod J. Rosenstein delivers remarks on encryption at the United States Naval Academy. Accessed March 21, 2018. https://www.justice.gov/opa/speech/deputy-attorney-general-rod-j-rosenstein-delivers-remarks-encryption-united-states-naval.

Warren, Samuel, and Louis Brandeis. 1890. The right to privacy. *Harvard Law Review* 4 (5): 193–220.

Weisman, Steve. 2017. Is identity theft protection worth it? *USA Today*, April 22. Accessed March 4, 2018. https://www.usatoday.com/story/money/columnist/2017/04/22/identity-theft-protection-worth/100554362/.

Wikileaks. 2017. Accessed April 5, 2018. https://wikileaks.org/ciav7p1/.

Wilson, Timothy, David A. Reinhard, Erin C. Westgate, Daniel T. Gilbert, Nicole Ellerbeck, Cheryl Hahn, Casey Brown, and Adi Shaked. 2014. Just think: The challenges of the disengaged mind. *Science* 345: 75–77.

CHAPTER 8

Conclusion

The final line of *The Great Gatsby* reads, "So we beat on, boats against the current, borne back ceaselessly into the past." Some interpret this to mean that the past is inescapable; it is galvanized history and unable to be repeated or modified. Another interpretation might translate this line as a commentary on the resiliency of those in pursuit of the American Dream, a fascination of Fitzgerald's. But I see it differently. I read this to mean that the human condition is singular and that it transcends time and place. Humankind always has shaped society through its technology, and for each conquest, there have been those who progressed ("boats") and those who resisted ("the current"). Even still, as we forge ahead into the next great technological development, we view our past nostalgically, as something we strive to "make great again" but that we are unable to restore. And this crystallization process is why technology should be approached with caution and thoughtfulness. Sherry Turkle implores that now "it is not a moment to reject technology but to find ourselves… to remember who we are—creatures of history, of deep psychology, of complex relationships." And so, we beat on—forever progressing with technology while longing for the natural past that once was. We must be careful about demonizing technology simply because it introduces change, for change is inevitable and necessary for evolution.

Henry David Thoreau often is invoked in conversations about technology. He symbolizes a natural romanticism in which his contempt for society and industrialization is overshadowed by his enthusiasm for environmentalism. His lived experience at Walden Pond, about which he

A. J. Reid, *The Smartphone Paradox*,
https://doi.org/10.1007/978-3-319-94319-0_8

wrote beautifully, might be considered the gold standard of disconnection. But Thoreau was highly critical of modernization and questioned whether or not technology actually improves our lives. Consider the following passage:

> [W]ithin the context of a given society, technological progress marches in only one direction; it can never be reversed. Once a technical innovation has been introduced, people usually become dependent on it, so that they can never again do without it, unless it is replaced by some still more advanced innovation. Not only do people become dependent as individuals on a new item of technology, but, even more, the system as a whole becomes dependent on it… Thus the system can move in only one direction, toward greater technologization. Technology repeatedly forces freedom to take a step back, but technology can never take a step back—short of the overthrow of the whole technological system.

This language reeks of technological determinism and parallels much of McLuhan's writing on technological progress and its inevitable consequences on society. But this passage was not written by McLuhan or Thoreau; it comes from the essay titled "Industrial Society and Its Future" written by Ted Kaczynski, also known as the Unabomber, whose mail bombings killed three people—the owner of a computer store, an advertising executive, and a lobbyist for the timber industry—and injured many more, including a computer science professor, a geneticist, the president of a commercial airline, and others at various American universities. The seeming randomness of his attacks becomes clearer when you read his views on technology.

It is an understatement to say that Kaczynski's terrorist actions were misguided and diabolical, but his extreme views are not entirely baseless. For instance, his concerns about the dependence on technology are more prescient than ever. According to Kaczynski, "as machines become more and more intelligent, people will let machines make more and more of their decisions for them, simply because machine-made decisions will bring better results than man-made ones." The brief historical trajectory of smartphones has shown us that technologies can quickly become demanding, instructive, and bullish, to a point of no return. Look no further than the sorority of digital assistants whom we have used to personify our devices; Siri, Alexa, Cortana all "know" more than we do, from a strictly informational standpoint, and we employ them regularly. Likewise, early polling indicates an increasing approval rate of autonomous cars, particularly among the younger and more educated populations.[1] By no means is this a defense of Kaczynski, or of technological determinism for that matter. Indeed, society ultimately shapes technology. But we might take a moment to look past the novelty of our technologies and consider whether they augment or replace our ability to think for ourselves.

I anticipate a humanistic renaissance in the coming years: an existential retreat into the qualities that make us human—interpersonal relationships, self-awareness, thoughtfulness, recursivity—and a pendulum swing away from the corporate-style technological determinism that compels us to buy the next iPhone. And I will welcome the hipster-inspired nontechnological revolution of stupid homes,[2] unplugged weddings,[3] and WiFi-blocking coffee shops.[4] Perhaps it is time that we re-envision boredom as a boon rather than a curse. A skill rather than a fault. Simplification in a world of overstimulation. Indeed, it was the advisement of Thoreau, the godfather of disconnection, to "Simplify, simplify, simplify!"

Mindfulness

The truth of the matter is that despite our smartphone habits, compulsions, and even addictions, we still need our phones. We have shaped a society that demands and expects immediacy, and our devices help to accelerate everything from information and communication, to personal transactions and gratification. We might reset ourselves by unplugging periodically and temporarily, but complete disconnection is not a wholly sustainable way of life for most. Therefore, we must learn how to self-regulate our smartphone habits. Food addiction experts often refer to

[1] Reinhart, R.J. 2018. Americans hit the brakes on self-driving cars. *Gallup*, February 21. http://news.gallup.com/poll/228032/americans-hit-brakes-self-driving-cars.aspx. Accessed 4 Mar 2018.

[2] Hague, Matthew. 2017. Stupid homes: Experts suggest people create space without technology. *The Globe and Mail*, April 18. https://beta.theglobeandmail.com/life/home-and-garden/stupid-homes-experts-suggest-people-create-space-without-technology/article34734653/?ref=http://www.theglobeandmail.com&. Accessed 4 Mar 2018.

[3] Bridal Guide. 2017. Why you might want to consider an unplugged wedding. https://www.huffingtonpost.com/bridal-guide/why-you-might-want-to-con_b_3331528.html. Accessed 3 Mar 2018.

[4] Mele, Christopher. 2017. Coffee shops skip wi-fi to encourage customers to actually talk. *The New York Times*, May 9. https://www.nytimes.com/2017/05/09/technology/coffee-shop-wifi-access.html. Accessed 5 Mar 2018.

overeaters having to "let the tiger out of the cage" three times per day. Behavioral addiction, arguably, is more difficult to manage than substance addiction; a recovering heroin addict abstains from heroin entirely, but behavioral addicts must learn to manage their destructive behaviors that are often unavoidable, such as eating food or using technology. Smartphone dependency is a particularly difficult condition to regulate because these devices have become ubiquitous and necessary in our daily lives, and there is little agreement on how to identify an unhealthy level of smartphone usage in the first place. We must not only learn how to let this tiger out of its cage but learn to cohabitate with it. So, before I offer my own take on how to rehabilitate smartphone dependency, I'd like to revisit why we would want to do so in the first place.

The smartphone is not a neutral delivery vehicle, as some have proposed. It does more than simply deliver us to information. The smartphone is designed inherently for connection; it connects us to information, to content, and to others. But our digital dalliances often compromise our analog ones. The mere presence of a smartphone draws from our mental and emotional capacity. Its overuse can atrophy our neurological processes and erode our cognitive abilities. Its primary use—socially integrative—directly influences our emotional states. It arrests our attention and encourages fragmentation of tasks. It fundamentally changes who we are and how we behave. The designers and developers of mobile technologies have weaponized the smartphone, capitalizing on our basic psychological responsiveness, turning each of us into binary data that can be bought and sold. The smartphone, for all it affords us, poses a threat indeed.

The first step in managing smartphone dependency is through mindfulness. Jon Kabat-Zinn, Professor Emeritus of Medicine at the University of Massachusetts, describes mindfulness as "The awareness that arises from paying attention, on purpose, in the present moment, and non-judgmentally."[5] Kabat-Zinn's Mindfulness-Based Stress Reduction (MBSR) program was founded in 1979 and offers online and in-person mindfulness training courses through the Center for Mindfulness at UMass Medical School. The MBSR program has treated more than 24,000 people for various illnesses and pain using a blend of Western medicine and Buddhist teachings and practices, or the Dharma. The practice of mindfulness incorporates meditation, of which the cognitive and physical benefits have been well-documented. Although, being mindful does not necessarily have to be distinct from technology.

[5] Kabat-Zinn, Jon. 1990. *Full Catastrophe Living: Using the Wisdom of Your Body and Mind to Face Stress, Pain, and Illness.* New York: Bantam.

A growing number of smartphone apps like Headspace, Calm, and Aura deliver meditative strategies in bite-sized chunks, effectively using technology to exploit the benefits of being technology-free. A survey of 200,000 iPhone users conducted by the Center for Humane Technology lists Calm as the highest ranked app for happiness. Headspace ranks third. These meditation-based programs are instructive and vary in length, but their common goal is to create awareness through calmness. In the book, *The Art of Stillness*, Pico Iyer argues that we need this now more than ever:

> In an age of speed, I began to think, nothing could be more invigorating than going slow. In an age of distraction, nothing can feel more luxurious than paying attention. And in an age of constant movement, nothing is more urgent than sitting still.

Since you have gotten this far into this book, I suspect that you might be contemplating your own smartphone habits. Perhaps you have a nasty habit of squandering time on social media, or maybe you are like me and check email incessantly. You are not alone. A 2015 study[6] analyzed the email habits of two million users who swapped over 16 billion email messages over two months. Results indicated that 90% of users reply to emails within one day, but the most frequently occurring reply time was under two minutes. The constant stream of emails and the compulsion to respond quickly only further reinforces checking habits. The allure of a variable interval rewards system like email is that sometimes it can be gratifying and other times anxiety-inducing. Either way, when we are anticipating or dreading incoming messages, there is a small draw of cognitive resources that deprives us of complete focus and attention. We can combat this by raising our self-awareness.

Apps like Moment, QualityTime, App Usage, BreakFree, and Flipd all monitor smartphone usage by recording screen time, counting screen unlocks, and enabling time limits and restrictions for usage. There are social media hashtag campaigns like #ShutOffSundays, #GetBored, and #DeviceFreeDinner; online challenges like the Bored and Brilliant project, developed by Manoush Zomorodi, a podcast series that assigns six

[6] Neporent, Liz. 2015. Most emails answered in just two minutes, study finds. *ABC News*, April 13. http://abcnews.go.com/Health/emails-answered-minutes-study-finds/story?id=30280230. Accessed 9 Mar 2018.

daily challenges aimed at "anyone trying to preserve their humanity in the digital age"[7]; and social movements like the Sabbath Manifesto, which recommends a day of disconnect every week, or the National Day of Unplugging, which, in its ninth year, encourages people to unplug for a 24-hour period in order to "relax, reflect, get outdoors, and connect with loved ones."[8] The National Day of Unplugging took place on March 9–10, 2018, and included more than 65,000 registered participants. These apps, campaigns, programs, and movements certainly are capable of increasing our self-awareness, but sometimes we need more; we need direction.

If you have a desire to change your smartphone habits, then you have already taken the first step in doing so. Recognizing that you need to modify your behavior is a prerequisite for technological mindfulness. But in addition to the self-quantification of our device usage, we also must search for a deeper understanding of how we are using our smartphones, for what reasons, and what we are obtaining as a result. Below is a short 5-minute mindfulness exercise that I have developed out of a mosaic of mindfulness training programs, cognitive behavioral therapy techniques, and meditative practices.

As I stated in Chap. 1, this is not a self-help book, and I am not a trained clinician, psychiatrist, or therapist. However, in my pursuit of writing this text, I read what probably amounts to a small library worth of books on this subject. I spoke with gaggles of students, experts, parents, students, teenagers, and children. I collected research on users' habits. I tracked and examined my own smartphone usage to an excruciating degree. As far as I can tell, the vast majority of us are not *addicted* to our smartphones, but many of us are not satisfied with our behaviors, either. There is not a universal solution to curing smartphone dependency, but there are many ways to mask its symptoms. A profusion of websites, news articles, television segments, and books offer explicit strategies for curbing smartphone usage. And some of it is really good advice, though it has become clear that regulating smartphone usage is more nuanced than that. The one central truth that I have uncovered is that there is no short-

[7] Note to Self. 2015. The case for boredom. http://www.wnyc.org/story/bored-brilliant-project-part-1. Accessed 2 Apr 2018.

[8] National Day of Unplugging. 2018. National day of unplugging wrap-up 2018. https://www.nationaldayofunplugging.com/unplugged-blog/2018/4/16/national-day-of-unplugging-wrap-up-2018. Accessed 9 Apr 2018.

1. Find a quiet++, calming space and sit upright comfortably on the floor.
2. Inhale a deep breath and exhale. Repeat this five times.
3. With your phone in your hand, close your eyes.
4. Contemplate the following:

    - Be aware of your fingers. Where do they intersect with the device? Do they move involuntarily?
    - How does your phone make you feel? Anxious? Stressed? Happy?
    - Do you feel a need to check, unlock, or look at the phone?
    - What do you get from this device? A sense of belonging? Accomplishment?

5. Return to the deep breathing. Inhale and exhale slowly, five times.
6. Imagine the role you want your smartphone to play in your life.
7. Open your eyes.

cut to a healthy relationship with technology. It is something we must actively pursue. The first step in doing so is to establish a digital mindfulness. Second, we must surround ourselves in an environment conducive to device regulation in order to break free of our usage patterns. We must learn to control our technology rather than be victimized by it. In addition to self-awareness and mindfulness, consider implementing the following heuristics:

- *Designate technology-free areas.* Whether it is an entire room, or just a piece of furniture, declare this defined space to be technology-free. The dinner table is often used as an example of a sacred space, and rightfully so. But how about your bed? The couch?
- *Block times for deliberate activities on your smartphone.* This strategy might require a reformation of others' expectations of your response time or accessibility. Set aside specific times for activities such as responding to emails and scrolling news or social media feeds rather than engaging in these activities sporadically throughout the day.

- *Track your smartphone usage, and set goals.* A 2017 study[9] on smartphone habits found that users consistently underestimate their usage in terms of time spent on the device as well as the number of times the device is checked. There are numerous free apps that monitor your smartphone usage. The first step to device management is to create an awareness of your typical usage.
- *Turn off device notifications.* Device notifications are the gateway to device usage. Turn off your email, news, social media notifications. Check your smartphone on your own terms, and do not let notifications dictate guide your behavior.
- *Clear your attention cache.* Attention residue, argues Cal Newport,[10] follows us when we task-switch, which makes it more difficult to focus deeply on the task at hand. Clear your attention cache by breaking up tasks with a short walk.

Device Legislation

Sometimes, when self-regulation fails, we legislate change from a user design perspective. Don Norman is the co-founder of the User Experience/Usability consulting firm, Nielsen Norman Group, and the Director of the Design Lab at the University of California San Diego. Norman is a self-described "cognitive designer." Or, in his own words: "I take what we understand about the human being, about human cognition, and I apply that to making technology, services, systems better for the people who are involved." Norman is most commonly associated with what are known as *Norman doors*, or doors that are poorly designed and/or constructed and which lead to confusion and user error. Norman's main contention with all design is that misuse of a product is due to the design itself rather than the user. To Norman, there is no such thing as user error, only bad design.

One of Norman's signature contributions to the field of design is his articulation of forcing functions. A design that utilizes a forcing function does so to prevent the user from taking an unwanted action; the product deters the user from making an error. Take, for instance, shopping carts.

[9] Reid, Alan J. and Chelsea N. Thomas. 2017. A case study in smartphone usage and gratification in the age of narcissism. *International Journal of Technology and Human Interaction* 13: 40–56.

[10] Newport, Cal. 2016. *Deep Work: Rules for Focused Success in a Distracted World*. Grand Central Publishing.

In urban areas where homelessness is common, shopping carts often double as mobile storage units for those who are displaced. But shopping cart theft has been purported to cost an estimated $800 million worldwide.[11] To prevent their carts from being stolen and repurposed, many retail stores have implemented forcing functions such as the Cart Anti-theft Protection System (CAPS), which is an electronic device that locks the cart's wheels if it leaves the store premises. Forcing functions intentionally make products more difficult to use; such is the case with prescription drug bottles and baby safety gates. Indeed, we encounter forcing functions routinely in our daily lives in order to minimize human error. In his seminal book, *The Design of Everyday Things*, Norman explains:

> Forcing functions are a form of physical constraint: situations in which the actions are constrained so that failure at one stage prevents the next step from happening. Starting a car has a forcing function associated with it—you must put the ignition key into the ignition switch. Some time ago, the button that activated the starter motor was separate from the ignition key, so that it was possible to attempt to start the car without keys; the error was made frequently. In most modern automobiles, the starter switch is activated by turning the key—an effective forcing function that makes you use the key to do the operation.[12]

Essentially, a forcing function replaces the need for thoughtfulness; it excuses a product from having to communicate its design to the user, and the user does not need to be considerate of its use. It shifts us into autopilot mode (this is quite literally true for pilots). Through intentional design, a forcing function ensures there is no room for human error because it removes the human factor entirely. In doing so, a forcing function undermines the skills needed for decision-making, and we are finding more and more ways to apply forcing functions to help regulate smartphone behaviors.

Some municipalities have taken legislative action to stymie device distraction. In Washington state, being caught using your smartphone while driving could earn you a DUI-E, Driving Under the Influences of

[11] Schwartz, Karen. 2011. Shopping carts need reliable security too. *BizTech Magazine*, May 27. https://biztechmagazine.com/article/2011/05/shopping-carts-need-reliable-security-too. Accessed 9 Mar 2018.

[12] Norman, Don. 2013. *The Design of Everyday Things: Revised and Expanded Edition*. New York: Basic Books.

Electronics,[13] which carries penalties similar to that of drunk-driving. In 2017, Honolulu became the first major city to ban pedestrians from viewing their smartphones while crossing the street, fining them $35 for each offense.[14] The city of Boston is considering a bill that proposes a $200 fine for "jay-texters," which includes pedestrians using a mobile device or wearing headphones/earbuds while crossing the street.[15] It is likely, though, that even the threat of jail time and fines is not strong enough to force us to disengage from our smartphones, but a lucrative way of generating revenue instead.

City planners and engineers also have begun to design public infrastructure with our device obsession in mind. Authorities in Chongqing, China actually demarcated separate lanes on its city sidewalks: a lane for those who are walking, and a lane for those who are walking while on their smartphones.[16] The gesture was satirical in nature, though this did not stop Utah Valley University in Orem, Utah from adopting similar walking lanes for its students.[17] The city of Bodegraven in the western Netherlands is piloting a program that has installed strip lighting embedded in the ground of busy intersection corners. The lights are synced with the traffic signal and illuminate in red or green, depending on the traffic pattern. Similarly, in Augsburg, a city in southern Germany, subway train platforms feature ground-implanted flashing red and green lights, notifying travelers who might be preoccupied by their devices not to wander into dangerous, and perhaps fatal, areas.

[13] Lindblom, Mike. 2017. Put down that cellphone; distracted-driving law is here. *The Seattle Times*, July 21. https://www.seattletimes.com/seattle-news/transportation/here-comes-washingtons-new-ban-on-driving-under-the-influence-of-electronics/. Accessed 9 Mar 2018.

[14] Mohn, Tanya. 2017. Reading this while walking? In Honolulu, it could cost you. *The New York Times*, October 23. https://www.nytimes.com/2017/10/23/business/honolulu-walking-and-texting-fine.html. Accessed 15 Mar 2018.

[15] Teitell, Beth. 2017. In Honolulu, walking and texting can cost you $99. But in Boston, phone zombies roam free. *Boston Globe*, November 12. http://www.bostonglobe.com/arts/2017/11/12/honolulu-walking-and-texting-can-cost-you-but-boston-phone-zombies-roam-free/0Xux8FnjNhS9wGDDUMXOdM/story.html. Accessed 12 Mar 2018.

[16] Benedictus, Leo. 2014. Chinese city opens 'phone lane' for texting pedestrians. *The Guardian*, September 15. https://www.theguardian.com/world/shortcuts/2014/sep/15/china-mobile-phone-lane-distracted-walking-pedestrians. Accessed 2 May 2018.

[17] Kaplan, Sarah. 2015. Texting while walking? There's a lane for that. *The Washington Post*, June 17. https://www.washingtonpost.com/news/morning-mix/wp/2015/06/17/texting-while-walking-theres-a-lane-for-that/?utm_term=.ae6e4c774efe. Accessed 27 Apr 2018.

We even legislate devices in academia to varying degrees. In France, before he was elected president, then-candidate Emmanuel Macron campaigned on a total ban of smartphones in schools. His education minister, Jean-Michel Blanquer, supported the decision, calling it a matter of "public health."[18] In 2006, New York City's then-mayor, Michael Bloomberg, introduced a citywide cell phone ban in all public schools. Bloomberg justified this unpopular stance, saying, "We are not going to allow iPods and BlackBerrys and cellphones and things that are disruptive in the classroom. Classrooms are for learning."[19] However, in 2015, Mayor Bill de Blasio reversed the decision, announcing that the ban on devices would be lifted, citing that "Parents should be able to call or text their kids."[20] Some schools, including the one my children attend, have espoused more drastic measures of device containment, such as requiring students to physically decommission their phones during the school day using the Yondr case: a smartphone-sized pouch that remains locked while in a designated phone-free area. To unlock the pouch and retrieve their device, the student must touch the case onto a centralized hub called an unlocking base.

Yondr has become a popular tool in music and comedy venues, too. Performers such as Dave Chappelle, Jack White, Alicia Keys, Donald Glover (aka Childish Gambino), and Guns N' Roses now insist that their audiences put away their smartphones by providing them with a Yondr at the ticket entrance.[21] Artists and musicians are not confiscating their audience's phones for fear of bootlegging; Jack White told *Rolling Stone*, "The way they react tells me what to do next. And if they're not really *there*, I don't know what to do next."[22] But forcefully disabling devices prevents

[18] Samuel, Henry. 2017. France to impose total ban on mobile phones in schools. *The Telegraph*, December 11. http://www.telegraph.co.uk/news/2017/12/11/france-impose-total-ban-mobile-phones-schools/?WT.mc_id=tmg_share_tw. Accessed 3 Mar 2018.

[19] Herszenhorn, David. 2006. Mayor repeats policy: No cellphones in school. *The New York Times*, May 6. http://www.nytimes.com/2006/05/06/nyregion/06klein.html. Accessed 15 Mar 2018.

[20] Reuters. 2015. New York City ends ban on cellphones in public schools. https://www.reuters.com/article/us-usa-new-york-cell-phones/new-york-city-ends-ban-on-cellphones-in-public-schools-idUSKBN0KG1IS20150107. Accessed 9 Mar 2018.

[21] Morrissey, Janet. 2016. Your phone's on lockdown. Enjoy the show. *The New York Times*, October 15. https://www.nytimes.com/2016/10/16/technology/your-phones-on-lockdown-enjoy-the-show.html. Accessed 15 Mar 2018.

[22] Knopper, Steve. 2018. Artists to fans: Put your phones away. *Rolling Stone*, February 28. https://www.rollingstone.com/music/features/how-yondr-is-creating-phone-free-concerts-w517177. Accessed 9 Mar 2018.

students and concert goers from using their phones only temporarily, and it likely will only intensify anxiety and further problematize the detachment issue.

Instead, Dr. Judson Brewer, Director of Research at the Center for Mindfulness at UMass Medical School argues that we should use a scaffolding approach to build digital mindfulness. We can begin by creating device-free environments (this is the forcing function), but then we must supplement this with a cognizant reflection (this is mindfulness). Eventually, we might begin to remove the scaffolding of forcing functions and rely solely on our learned mindfulness to forge new pathways for appropriate device usage. In my lengthy conversation with Dr. Brewer, he stressed that prescriptive steps for digital use by themselves are futile gestures:

> This isn't something where you can say "Here's tip one, two, three, and you're done." We are developing full programs for this sort of thing, and I think technology addiction is probably going to be one of the hardest ones to work with. In general, just knowing the underlying principles is a good place to start. [The user] has to understand what the dependency is, so that they can map out their habit loops and see the relative rewards that they are getting from the smartphone use. Then, they have to be able to tap into the greater rewards of being aware. If they are mistaking excitement for happiness, then their brains are never going to learn something different.

Imposing sanctions on our devices is not the solution; and left alone, it is ineffective in the long term. When it comes to our children, we understand that in order to teach them how to live healthily, we must introduce a balanced diet at an early age and then continue to preach nutrition and exercise. Force-feeding them broccoli or confiscating sugary drinks will work in the short term, but this does not promote healthy living, as it undermines self-regulatory development. For musicians, politicians, and city planners, short-term smartphone regulation is acceptable; it is not their responsibility to edify their audiences on healthy smartphone habits, but this responsibility most certainly falls within the moral and ethical responsibility of schools to educate—not just regulate—their students on modern digital citizenship just as they do with nutrition.

We also might begin to demand that device makers assume more responsibility in the design of their products. The congressional testimonies from Mark Zuckerberg in April 2018 did more than clarify Facebook's involvement with the data firm Cambridge Analytica and its attempt to deliberately influence the 2016 presidential election; it brought to the forefront what we all know and fear: we have ceded too much control to technology companies. Perhaps device legislation should fall on the companies that openly admit to hooking its users on an app or a product (such as the aforementioned Dopamine Labs), or that embrace the mindset that technology operates within an attention economy. Perhaps the burden should lie with the purveyors of technology as well as its users. In what seems like a contrived public relations move, Facebook has been running an ad campaign on television, movie theaters, and online, which aptly sums up how we got to this point. The spot is a heartwarming montage of Facebook posts and videos overlaid with a narrator's voice:

> We came here for the friends… But then something happened. We had to deal with spam, clickbait, fake news, and data misuse. That's going to change. From now on, Facebook will do more to keep you safe and protect your privacy, so we can all get back to what made Facebook good in the first place: friends. Because when this place does what it was built for, then we all get a little closer.[23]

Admittedly, the commercial is moving. But while the social media giant is attempting to clean up its public image, it also is sidestepping the newly revised Internet regulations established by the European Union's General Data Protection Regulation (GDPR), by rerouting 1.9 billion Facebook user accounts through Ireland, which is impervious to the strict reform laws.[24] What Facebook is doing, and what is saying it is doing, are polar opposites. The commercial reminds me of similar efforts by BP in the wake of the largest oil spill in US history, the Deepwater Horizon. In the four months following the catastrophe, BP spent $100 million on advertisements to reassure the public that it had their best interest in mind.[25]

[23] Facebook. 2018. https://www.youtube.com/watch?v=Q4zd7X98eOs. Accessed 19 Apr 2018.

[24] Ingram, David. 2018. Exclusive: Facebook to put 1.5 billion users out of reach of new EU privacy law. *Reuters*, April 18. https://www.reuters.com/article/us-facebook-privacy-eu-exclusive/exclusive-facebook-to-put-1-5-billion-users-out-of-reach-of-new-eu-privacy-law-idUSKBN1HQ00P. Accessed 21 Apr 2018.

[25] Dubois, Shelley. 2010. Update: BP's advertising budget during the spill neared $100 million. *Fortune*, September 1. http://archive.fortune.com/2010/09/01/news/companies/BP_spill_advertising_costs.fortune/index.htm?section=magazines_fortune&utm_source=twitterfeed&utm_medium=twitter&utm_campaign=Feed%3A+rss%2Fmagazines_fortune+%28Fortune+Magazine%29. Accessed 2 May 2018.

Just as we should not allow companies like BP to self-police their environmental impacts, we should hold technology companies and developers accountable for personal and social impacts. And there is a movement in younger generations to expect more from technology companies. One such group making waves is SSAAD: Stanford Students Against Addictive Devices. This student-run collective is led by four computer science majors at Stanford University, who regularly host protests to raise awareness about device addiction and to insist that companies like Apple and Google acknowledge and help mitigate addictive behaviors associated with their products. I spoke directly with two of the leaders of SSAAD, Sanjay Kannan and Cameron Ramos, with regard to the ethical responsibility that tech companies bear. The following conversation unfolded:

Me: To what degree do you feel technology companies that design and develop smartphones and mobile apps have a moral/ethical responsibility to the way consumers use their product?

SSAAD: Any consumer buying any product should be entitled to the implications of using that product. In this sense, the bare minimum from device makers is (1) acknowledging that phone dependence is a legitimate issue and (2) making device usage patterns far more transparent than they are right now. If users *knowingly* maintain unhealthy relationships with their devices, it is not necessarily a device maker's ethical responsibility at that point—but we are nowhere near that yet.

But do device makers have an ethical responsibility to go a step further, and actually introduce anti-addictive features (like the ones we propose)? We say yes.

Given how necessary smartphones have become (beyond frivolous reasons), it is not tenable if the choice given to users is either (a) keeping your addictive device as it is or (b) turning it off altogether. There has to be a middle ground where users still derive value from their devices, but with the option to cut out the frivolous stuff. Since companies still make their profits off selling you the phone in the first place, there isn't even much of a financial argument against this.

Me: How much do you feel the user is responsible for regulating his/her own use of the smartphone? (Some critics say if Apple products are addictive, then just don't buy them...).

SSAAD: For users, avoiding devices altogether is unrealistic. The ultimate decision to assess and curtail an individual's usage is made by that individual, and that individual alone. So the user bears significant responsibility for self-regulation. That being said, we can't really talk about this personal responsibility until users have the tools to monitor and act on their usage patterns. This is why the device makers need to take action.

Me: Is the smartphone a neutral technology? Or, is it positively charged for user engagement?

SSAAD: I can't speak to this authoritatively, but my understanding is this: No one went into the process of creating the smartphone with the intention of manufacturing dependence. Rather, this dependence is a product of a technical and societal ecosystem that has grown up around smartphones. For instance, checking your e-mail on-the-go was once a welcome convenience, and now it is practically an expectation. In any event, it doesn't matter so much whether or not the smartphone is fundamentally neutral, but rather that we live in a world where the smartphone is de facto charged for user engagement.

Me: You are the next generation of designers. Where do you see our smartphone (or related) technology in 5 years? 10 years?

SSAAD: I speak mostly for myself (and not our entire group) in answering this question. I hope that just as our electronics transitioned into the foreground of our lives over the last two decades, so too will they fade into the background as they advance. That is to say: Many devices are addictive in part because of how much value and efficiency they add to our lives, and ideally, we will move into a future where they deliver this value in a less intrusive, more passive way.

A New Generation

We are perhaps a generation with more technological capability than we know what to do with or than what is ultimately good for us. Nevertheless, here we are. Many have expressed their acceptance of our new digital existence, arguing that we are simply evolving alongside technology, just as we always have. An article on Medium.com titled "Your Brain is Your

Phone"[26] echoes Marshall McLuhan, the father of media studies, stating "smartphones have become an externalized part of our brains." But this article fails to articulate what McLuhan would have been quick to point out—that extensions are accompanied by amputations. Just as the smartphone extends our access to information and to others, it amputates so much more: our cognitive processes, our memories, our relationships, our culture. As technology continues to march forward, we owe it to future generations to invest in ourselves and to coexist with technology, rather than be dominated by it, so that they might know us. Kranzberg cautions us that "Many of our technology-related problems arise because of the unforeseen consequences when apparently benign technologies are employed on a massive scale."[27] Arguably, the largest and most important "unforeseen consequence" is how our children are affected by the smartphone.

Catherine Steiner-Adair is a clinical psychologist who specializes in social and emotional resiliency in children. Her book, *The Big Disconnect*, weaves a tapestry of parent and child narratives throughout research on the consequential effects of tech-dependency. It's no surprise that technology usage during the formative years of a child's life heavily impacts his or her character, concretizing the beliefs, attitudes, emotional intelligences, and neurological development of the child. Naturally, technology influences children differently depending on their age and amount and type of media consumption. But starting from a very early age, even before language skills are acquired, children are adept at observing the digital habits of those surrounding them, and at interpreting what these behaviors signal. This potentially can be just as impactful as the child's own technology usage. Adair warns:

> The message we communicate with our preoccupation and responsiveness to calls and email is: *Everybody else matters more than you. Everything else matters more than you. Whatever the caller may say is more important than what you are telling me now*. Meanwhile, a child is waiting to connect.[28]

[26] Yates, Kiera. 2017. Your brain is your phone. *Medium*, August 28. Retrieved from https://howwegettonext.com/your-brain-is-your-phone-ab850d67fe3f. Accessed 26 Apr 2018.

[27] Kranzberg, Melvin. 1986. Technology and history: Kranzberg's laws. *Technology and Culture* 27: 544–560.

[28] Steiner-Adair, Catherine and Teresa Barker. 2013. *The Big Disconnect: Protecting Childhood and Family Relationships in the Digital Age*. New York: HarperCollins Publishers.

The intangible effects of our smartphone habits on our children might not be enough evidence for us to reconsider our behavior. After all, technology is a cheap babysitter.

Some argue that our smartphone habits can have a direct effect on the physical well-being of children. A 2017 study found that there was an increase in emergency department visits for children aged 0–5 from 2005 to 2012, during which time AT&T expanded its 3G network.[29] The implication, according to the study, is that as mobile Internet access increased, so did parent distractibility and inattentiveness to their children. This conclusion is somewhat speculative and does not account for all variables, but it does raise an important point: the temptation of smartphones is great enough to pull us away from our loved ones, even when they need us most. The study considers what this short-term distractedness means for longer-term investments in children. Two researchers from the University of North Texas conducted a literature review of studies that examined the effects of parents' smartphone use on child safety. Of the 27 articles considered, the eclecticism of findings showed that while parents were in the presence of their smartphones, they were less responsive to their children, engaged with their phones while driving with children in the vehicle, and left children unattended while bathing. The review also included findings from studies that showed children exhibited riskier and attention-seeking behaviors when their parents were digitally preoccupied and that children's technology use increased with their parents'.[30] The evidence of distracted smartphone use is especially damning from a parent-child interaction perspective, as smartphones undermine safety in younger children. We arm our houses with security systems, we require our children to wear seatbelts in the car, and we expect safety in schools, but we give them a device that can expose them to the raw and unfiltered world unsuitable for children's eyes.

There is a lot of hand-wringing over kids and technology. The American Academy of Pediatrics (AAP) strongly recommends no more than one hour per day of screen time for children ages 2–5 years, limited and supervised "high-quality programming" for children ages 18–24 months, and

[29] Palsson, Craig. 2017. Smartphones and child injuries. *Journal of Public Economics* 156: 200–213.

[30] Kildare, Cory and Wendy Middlemiss. 2017. Impact of parents mobile device on parent-child interaction: A literature review. *Computers in Human Behavior* 75: 579–593.

no screen time whatsoever for children under 18 months.[31] However, in 2016, the AAP made one technology exception for children of all ages, following a study that found that video chat on a smartphone already was being used by families, despite screen time recommendations.[32] In other words, FaceTime doesn't count as screen time. Further, a 2017 study observed that using video chat with infants might loosely promote socio-cognitive learning.[33] But if we are to take a cue from the procurers of technology, they are sending a very different message.

Despite their friction in many other areas, tech entrepreneurs Bill Gates and the late Steve Jobs had similar views on the role that technology should play in children's lives. Both men shielded their kids from technology at an early age; Gates forbade his children from having a smartphone until the age of 14, and Jobs's children were not permitted to use an iPad. And these are not the only examples of tech hypocrisy. Naomi Baron writes in her book, *Words Onscreen*, about the trend among technology experts in Silicon Valley to send their children to low-tech schools such as the Brightworks School in San Francisco and the Waldorf School of the Peninsula, located in Los Altos, California. She writes:

> Silicon Valley parents [send] their children to the Waldorf School of the Peninsula, where digital technologies are out and paper, pen, and knitting needles are in. Parents included the chief technology officer of eBay, along with employees of Google, Apple, and Yahoo. These folks were hardly technophobes. But they believed there is a time and place for using digital tools, and early schooling isn't one of them.

Admittedly, after reading this, I began to panic slightly. Particularly, I wondered if my kids are being overexposed to technology. The answer to this question will vary for each parent and child, but my wife and I have agreed that our kids will have regulated access to technology while at

[31] American Academy of Pediatrics. 2016. American Academy of Pediatrics announces new recommendations for children's media use. https://www.aap.org/en-us/about-the-aap/aap-press-room/pages/american-academy-of-pediatrics-announces-new-recommendations-for-childrens-media-use.aspx. Accessed 27 Apr 2018.

[32] McClure, Elizabeth, Yulia Chentsova-Dutton, Rachel Barr, Steven Holochwost and W. Gerrod Parrott. 2015. Facetime doesn't count: Video chat as an exception to media restrictions for infants and toddlers. *International Journal of Child-Computer Interaction* 6: 1–6.

[33] Myers, Lauren, Rachel B. LeWitt, Renee Gallo and Nicole Maselli. 2017. Baby FaceTime: Can toddlers learn from online video chat? *Developmental Science* 20.

home, and that smartphones will be off-limits until age 16 (for the reasons I have laid out in this book). And if you are wondering how we will communicate with our children without a smartphone, I will refer your question to any member of every generation that has come before you and me. Plus, there are many sensible products available now that facilitate communication without the drawbacks of a fully enabled smartphone; for instance, the GizmoPal by LG is a wristwatch that affords two-way communication and location tracking.

Even though you might philosophically disagree with this view, chances are that you are likely a self-evaluative person when it comes to smartphone and other technology usage (you are reading a book on smartphone dependency, after all). And as a recent study points out, "[I]f the parents showed awareness of the dangers of smartphone usage and showed controlling abilities, the negative effects of children's smartphone usage could be decreased."[34] The solution to our infatuation with technology is not to completely disconnect from it. Rather, we should develop self-awareness of our technological habits, moderate them if necessary, and explicitly model them for future generations to see. We should, however, approach all technology with skepticism and with caution—aware that with every new technology comes a new set of problems, often unforeseen.

During a phone conversation with Dr. Baron, I asked her about her personal thoughts on children and technology. Specifically, I inquire about how she perceived the difference between a parent being distracted by a screen in front of her children and a parent distracted by a good book. I inquired: Aren't both media guilty of disconnecting us from the present and leaving children seeking our attention? Her response was both illuminating and satisfying:

> So what is the difference between having your nose in a book and having your nose in a phone? Your kids know, I'm sure, that your phone is an interactive device that can get you to someone away from you and [them]. They know that same instrument can be used for phone calls. They know that buzzes come. And that you stop in the middle of a conversation and you go read something. But you interrupt what the social flow was because this device said, 'I'm more important.' When you have a print book, or a news-

[34] Cho, Kyung-Seu and Jae-Moo Lee. 2017. Influence of smartphone addiction proneness of young children on problematic behaviors and emotional intelligence: Mediating self-assessment effects of parents using smartphones. *Computers in Human Behavior* 66: 303–311.

> paper, or a magazine, what you're doing in essence, is saying somebody wrote something that's really interesting and engaging. You're modeling a behavior that you want your kids to engage in. And it's a static platform. There's nobody interrupting. The book doesn't buzz at you. If you're doing something with your children, the question becomes, is that a behavior you'd like them to have?

Admittedly, I asked this question because in the days leading up to my phone conversation with Dr. Baron, I had found myself in this very position. I was standing at the kitchen island reading Carl Bode's *The Portable Thoreau* while my two older children were eating a snack and conversing about the usual topics of the day: friends, school, weekend plans. Physically, I was standing there, but my mind was in *Walden*. I was completely tuned out. After a while, however, my daughter noticed and began questioning me:

Stella: Who is (*mispronounces*) Thoreau?
Me: (*Without looking up*) He was an author in the 1800s.
Stella: What did he write?
Me: (*Now, looking up*) Most people know him for his book about a place called Walden Pond. He wrote a lot about nature and simplicity. I'm reading him again because I am writing about him in my book.
Stella: Oh. What is your book about again?

My literary distraction at the kitchen island had actually facilitated a meaningful, semi-educational conversation that might not have occurred otherwise. In fact, after finishing the snack, we went to the computer, searched for images of Walden Pond, and conspired to take a road trip there one day. Could this have happened if the book had been replaced with a digital copy of *Walden* that I had been reading on my iPhone? Sure, I suppose, but it is unlikely. Afterwards, I thought about the interaction. I had modeled an important behavior for my children; Thoreau said himself: "To read well, that is, to read true books in a true spirit, is a noble exercise, and one that will task the reader more than any exercise which the customs of the day esteem."[35] When I have finished writing this book, Stella tells me, she'll be the first to read it.

[35] Bode, Carl. 1974. *The Portable Thoreau*. The Viking Press, Inc.

There is a new generation quietly watching us and taking note of our technology habits, and they are eagerly awaiting their turn. As my children grow older (they are 9, 5, 1, and 1 at the time of this writing), they become more astutely aware of how adults interact with their phones, and this will inform the ways in which they perceive and interact with their own technologies as young adults and beyond. There have been times where I was holding my phone while simultaneously telling them to put down their iPads and do something productive instead. I realize that, to them, it doesn't matter *how* I am using my smartphone, whether I am proofreading a draft, responding to emails, or playing Words with Friends™. They simply notice that when I am engaged with my smartphone, I am only half-present with them. But, many working adults reside in a world that values immediacy and connectedness. We are held accountable to unwritten digital expectations and demands that are not articulated in job descriptions, and this places us into a technology captivity, where disconnection is not a luxury; it makes our lives harder. We must find a way to reconcile our digital and our analog lives, where the former is necessary, but the latter is more important.

I am sounding an alarm, and I'm not the only one; the voices calling for digital mindfulness are growing louder. Perhaps a complete withdrawal from industrialized society, as Thoreau did, is not feasible in the twenty-first century. But we can begin our personal reclamation by liberating ourselves from our devices, even if only incrementally. This process begins with an awareness of the problem and a willingness to change. As for me, I'm making a concerted effort to be more mindful of my technology habits. My children have inspired me to reevaluate my relationship with technology and to prioritize people and moments over devices. I only hope that after reading this book, I have convinced you to do the same.

It's a funny thing about smartphones. They can connect us to everything *and* they can divorce us from everything. They deliver us to information *and* strip us of knowledge. They boost productivity *and* make us less productive. They're good. They're bad. They're neutral, but they're not. And we're still figuring it all out.

References

American Academy of Pediatrics. 2016. American Academy of Pediatrics announces new recommendations for children's media use. Accessed April 27, 2018. https://www.aap.org/en-us/about-the-aap/aap-press-room/pages/american-academy-of-pediatrics-announces-new-recommendations-for-childrens-media-use.aspx.

Benedictus, Leo. 2014. Chinese city opens 'phone lane' for texting pedestrians. *The Guardian*, September 15. Accessed May 2, 2018. https://www.theguardian.com/world/shortcuts/2014/sep/15/china-mobile-phone-lane-distracted-walking-pedestrians.

Bode, Carl. 1974. *The Portable Thoreau*. The Viking Press, Inc.

Bridal Guide. 2017. Why you might want to consider an unplugged wedding. Accessed March 3, 2018. https://www.huffingtonpost.com/bridal-guide/why-you-might-want-to-con_b_3331528.html.

Cho, Kyung-Seu, and Jae-Moo Lee. 2017. Influence of smartphone addiction proneness of young children on problematic behaviors and emotional intelligence: Mediating self-assessment effects of parents using smartphones. *Computers in Human Behavior* 66: 303–311.

Dubois, Shelley. 2010. Update: BP's advertising budget during the spill neared $100 million. *Fortune*, September 1. Accessed May 2, 2018. http://archive.fortune.com/2010/09/01/news/companies/BP_spill_advertising_costs.fortune/index.htm?section=magazines_fortune&utm_source=twitterfeed&utm_medium=twitter&utm_campaign=Feed%3A+rss%2Fmagazines_fortune+%28Fortune+Magazine%29.

Facebook. 2018. Accessed April 19, 2018. https://www.youtube.com/watch?v=Q4zd7X98eOs.

Hague, Matthew. 2017. Stupid homes: Experts suggest people create space without technology. *The Globe and Mail*, April 18. Accessed March 4, 2018. https://beta.theglobeandmail.com/life/home-and-garden/stupid-homes-experts-suggest-people-create-space-without-technology/article34734653/?ref=http://www.theglobeandmail.com&.

Herszenhorn, David. 2006. Mayor repeats policy: No cellphones in school. *The New York Times*, May 6. Accessed March 15, 2018. http://www.nytimes.com/2006/05/06/nyregion/06klein.html.

Ingram, David. 2018. Exclusive: Facebook to put 1.5 billion users out of reach of new EU privacy law. *Reuters*, April 18. Accessed April 21, 2018. https://www.reuters.com/article/us-facebook-privacy-eu-exclusive/exclusive-facebook-to-put-1-5-billion-users-out-of-reach-of-new-eu-privacy-law-idUSKBN1HQ00P.

Kabat-Zinn, Jon. 1990. *Full Catastrophe Living: Using the Wisdom of Your Body and Mind to Face Stress, Pain, and Illness*. New York: Bantam.

Kaplan, Sarah. 2015. Texting while walking? There's a lane for that. *The Washington Post*, June 17. Accessed April 27, 2018. https://www.washingtonpost.com/news/morning-mix/wp/2015/06/17/texting-while-walking-theres-a-lane-for-that/?utm_term=.ae6e4c774efe.

Kildare, Cory, and Wendy Middlemiss. 2017. Impact of parents mobile device on parent-child interaction: A literature review. *Computers in Human Behavior* 75: 579–593.

Knopper, Steve. 2018. Artists to fans: Put your phones away. *Rolling Stone*, February 28. Accessed March 9, 2018. https://www.rollingstone.com/music/features/how-yondr-is-creating-phone-free-concerts-w517177.

Kranzberg, Melvin. 1986. Technology and history: Kranzberg's laws. *Technology and Culture* 27: 544–560.

Lindblom, Mike. 2017. Put down that cellphone; distracted-driving law is here. *The Seattle Times*, July 21. Accessed March 9, 2018. https://www.seattletimes.com/seattle-news/transportation/here-comes-washingtons-new-ban-on-driving-under-the-influence-of-electronics/.

McClure, Elizabeth, Yulia Chentsova-Dutton, Rachel Barr, Steven Holochwost, and W. Gerrod Parrott. 2015. Facetime doesn't count: Video chat as an exception to media restrictions for infants and toddlers. *International Journal of Child-Computer Interaction* 6: 1–6.

Mele, Christopher. 2017. Coffee shops skip wi-fi to encourage customers to actually talk. *The New York Times*, May 9. Accessed March 5, 2018. https://www.nytimes.com/2017/05/09/technology/coffee-shop-wifi-access.html.

Mohn, Tanya. 2017. Reading this while walking? In Honolulu, it could cost you. *The New York Times*, October 23. Accessed March 15, 2018. https://www.nytimes.com/2017/10/23/business/honolulu-walking-and-texting-fine.html.

Morrissey, Janet. 2016. Your phone's on lockdown. Enjoy the show. *The New York Times*, October 15. Accessed March 15, 2018. https://www.nytimes.com/2016/10/16/technology/your-phones-on-lockdown-enjoy-the-show.html.

Myers, Lauren, Rachel B. LeWitt, Renee Gallo, and Nicole Maselli. 2017. Baby FaceTime: Can toddlers learn from online video chat? *Developmental Science* 20: e12430.

National Day of Unplugging. 2018. National day of unplugging wrap-up 2018. Accessed April 9, 2018. https://www.nationaldayofunplugging.com/unplugged-blog/2018/4/16/national-day-of-unplugging-wrap-up-2018.

Neporent, Liz. 2015. Most emails answered in just two minutes, study finds. *ABC News*, April 13. Accessed March 9, 2018. http://abcnews.go.com/Health/emails-answered-minutes-study-finds/story?id=30280230.

Newport, Cal. 2016. *Deep Work: Rules for Focused Success in a Distracted World*. Grand Central Publishing.

Norman, Don. 2013. *The Design of Everyday Things: Revised and Expanded Edition*. New York: Basic Books.

Note to Self. 2015. The case for boredom. Accessed April 2, 2018. http://www.wnyc.org/story/bored-brilliant-project-part-1.

Palsson, Craig. 2017. Smartphones and child injuries. *Journal of Public Economics* 156: 200–213.

Reid, Alan J., and Chelsea N. Thomas. 2017. A case study in smartphone usage and gratification in the age of narcissism. *International Journal of Technology and Human Interaction* 13: 40–56.

Reinhart, R.J. 2018. Americans hit the brakes on self-driving cars. *Gallup*, February 21. Accessed March 4, 2018. http://news.gallup.com/poll/228032/americans-hit-brakes-self-driving-cars.aspx.

Reuters. 2015. New York City ends ban on cellphones in public schools. Accessed March 9, 2018. https://www.reuters.com/article/us-usa-new-york-cell-phones/new-york-city-ends-ban-on-cellphones-in-public-schools-idUSKBN0KG1IS20150107.

Samuel, Henry. 2017. France to impose total ban on mobile phones in schools. *The Telegraph*, December 11. Accessed March 3, 2018. http://www.telegraph.co.uk/news/2017/12/11/france-impose-total-ban-mobile-phones-schools/?WT.mc_id=tmg_share_tw.

Schwartz, Karen. 2011. Shopping carts need reliable security too. *BizTech Magazine*, May 27. Accessed March 9, 2018. https://biztechmagazine.com/article/2011/05/shopping-carts-need-reliable-security-too.

Steiner-Adair, Catherine, and Teresa Barker. 2013. *The Big Disconnect: Protecting Childhood and Family Relationships in the Digital Age*. New York: HarperCollins Publishers.

Teitell, Beth. 2017. In Honolulu, walking and texting can cost you $99. But in Boston, phone zombies roam free. *Boston Globe*, November 12. Accessed March 12, 2018. http://www.bostonglobe.com/arts/2017/11/12/honolulu-walking-and-texting-can-cost-you-but-boston-phone-zombies-roam-free/0Xux8FnjNhS9wGDDUMXOdM/story.html.

Yates, Kiera. 2017. Your brain is your phone. *Medium*, August 28. Accessed April 26, 2018. Retrieved from https://howwegettonext.com/your-brain-is-your-phone-ab850d67fe3f.

Index[1]

[1] Note: Page numbers followed by 'n' refer to notes.

A. J. Reid, *The Smartphone Paradox*,
https://doi.org/10.1007/978-3-319-94319-0

Printed in the United States
By Bookmasters